EXAMINING THE CATHOLIC INTELLECTUAL TRADITION

Volume 2:

ISSUES AND PERSPECTIVES

EXAMINING THE CATHOLIC INTELLECTUAL TRADITION

Volume 2

Issues and Perspectives

Edited by
Anthony J. Cernera
and
Oliver J. Morgan

SACRED HEART UNIVERSITY PRESS
FAIRFIELD, CONNECTICUT

Library of Congress Cataloging-in-Publication Data

Examining the Catholic intellectual tradition / edited by
    Anthony J. Cernera and Oliver J. Morgan
        p. cm.
    Includes bibliographical references and index.
    ISBN 1-888112-04-2 (hardcover)
        1. Catholics—Intellectual life. 2. Catholic learning and
scholarship. 3. Catholic universities and colleges—Philosophy.
I. Cernera, Anthony J., 1950- II. Morgan, Oliver J.

BX1795.I57 E83 2000
282—dc21   99-087071

Examining the Catholic intellectual tradition. Volume 2:
    Issues and perspectives / edited by Anthony J. Cernera
    and Oliver J. Morgan
    ISBN 1-888112-09-3 (hardcover)

CONTENTS

PREFACE

The origins of this volume lie in a conversation that the two of us had four or five years ago while taking a walk after Vespers at Mt. Saviour Monastery, a Benedictine community in Elmira, New York. It was a beautiful summer evening and we started talking about what was going on at both of our institutions. We both mentioned being formed as students in the Catholic intellectual tradition. We also agreed that this tradition was supposed to be an important part of what our institutions were about, that it should inform our life together, and that we had the responsibility of transmitting and developing that tradition. Then, we scratched our balding heads and asked, "What does it mean?"

We decided that perhaps we would embark on a project together. We have been doing this kind of idea-sharing for about thirty years now. Some of the projects have been successful, some have not been so successful. But we decided that it might be a good idea to undertake a project that would be of service not only to the University of Scranton and Sacred Heart University but could also be of use to other Catholic colleges and universities in the United States. We decided to bring together a collections of essays that would grapple with what we called the Catholic intellectual tradition. We discussed further, that if a first volume had some value, perhaps we would then bring together a gathering of people from Catholic colleges and universities to think through more carefully what it means to engage that tradition in the day-to-day life of our colleagues and universities.

Examining the Catholic Intellectual Tradition (Fairfield, CT: Sacred Heart University Press, 2000) brought together a collection of essays by noted Catholic intellectuals and scholars on the tradition. It was well received as a valuable preliminary resource to begin an informed conversation about the heritage as well as the lived experiences behind the term "Catholic intellectual tradition." Soon after, we set about organizing a conference entitled "Examining the Catholic Intellectual Tradition." This meeting was held at Sacred Heart University from November 10-12, 2000. Contained in this volume are the papers and presentations that served the 160 people gathered at this conference as reference points for our common reflection and discussion as well as several additional essays that we believe will be of interest and use to the readers.

So, this book is the second step along the way. We hope that we will continue this conversation and investigate in even more detail the relationship of the Catholic intellectual tradition to a number of different intellectual pursuits and disciplines in the curriculum and our academic life. As stewards of this tradition, we dare to think creatively and boldly, and we humbly carry this tradition into this new century and well beyond.

A special word of thanks is due to David L. Coppola, executive assistant to the president of Sacred Heart University, and Sidney Gottlieb, professor of English at Sacred Heart University, for their efforts in bringing this work to completion.

Anthony J. Cernera and Oliver J. Morgan

STEWARDS OF THE TRADITION

CHAPTER ONE

Stewards of the Tradition: Christ the Center

ROBERT P. IMBELLI

T he rubric under which this evening's presentation is placed is "Stewards of the Tradition." My own contribution will be to focus our attention upon what I consider to be the very heart and center of the Catholic intellectual (or, as I prefer, "wisdom") tradition: the Lord Jesus Christ himself. My presentation will be in three parts. First, I will consider the notion of tradition and defend the claim that Jesus Christ is indeed the living center of the tradition. Second, I will suggest that the "crisis" of the Catholic intellectual tradition is, at its most profound, a Christological crisis. Third, I will hazard some suggestions regarding the context of the Catholic college and university and the challenge of reaffirming the Christic center. Because of limitations of time, all this will be done briefly, but, I hope, in a way suggestive of further development.

The Christic Center of Tradition

In considering "tradition," I find it helpful to distinguish three interconnected senses of the word. Prior to Vatican II when Catholics spoke of "tradition" they most commonly intended the *tradita*: those things that had been handed down, whether Scripture, creeds, or catechetical formulations. These *tradita*, often referred to as "the deposit of faith," were presumed to be handed down unchanged through the centuries, often enshrined in the venerable Latin of the Tridentine Mass and the texts of Denzinger.

A second sense of "tradition," come newly to the fore since Vatican II, is that of *traditio*. Here tradition indicates less what has been handed down, than the very process of handing down, of "traditioning" (as is sometimes said): the ongoing interpretation and reinterpretation of the past into the present. Here the center of concern is the present and the future; and one often encounters the language of "accommodation" and "inculturation."

But I would suggest a third sense of tradition, less frequently invoked, yet foundational to the previous legitimate uses. I refer to this by the Latin designation, *Traditus*. Here tradition is the One who is handed down, Jesus Christ himself as the living heart and center of Christian tradition. Thus when we speak of "Stewards of the Tradition," at its theologically most profound level we are speaking of our institutions and ourselves as bearers of the multiple riches of the mystery of Christ.

Now this Catholic wisdom tradition, in all three senses, but especially the third, comes to privileged expression in the Eucharistic liturgy. Here the Real Presence of Christ is proclaimed and enacted. I concur, then, with authors like Aidan Kavanaugh and Catherine LaCugna who speak of liturgy as *theologia prima*, the living theology which nourishes and sustains our second order reflection. Liturgy is the primary bearer of tradition, because here, in sacramental fulness, Jesus "hands himself over" for the life of the world.

Let me highlight three historical moments in the Catholic intellectual tradition; three "snapshots" of its Christic center. The first is the liturgical feast we celebrate today (November 10th), the feast of St. Leo the Great. Leo, as you know, was the bishop of Rome, a great preacher and defender of the mystery of the Incarnation. His exposition of the Church's teaching concerning Christ was acclaimed by the Council of Chalcedon (451 A.D.) as the voice of orthodoxy.

Father Gerald McCool presents a second salient moment in the expression of the Catholic intellectual tradition's living center.

He evokes the passionate sermon preached at the University of Paris by the young Franciscan theologian, St. Bonaventure. At a time of crisis and confusion, of factionalism and intellectual disarray, Bonaventure proclaimed Christ as the flaming center of devotion and thought. For Bonaventure, Christ alone was the teacher of truth: "Christ, the Word, Pre-existent and Incarnate, the universal master of every student—*Christus omnium magister.*"[1]

Having invoked a patristic and a medieval witness, let me, lastly, quote from two contemporaries. Anthony Cernera and Oliver Morgan, in the article they authored for their jointly edited volume on the Catholic intellectual tradition, well articulated what I have been calling the Christic center of that tradition. They wrote: "For Catholicism . . . the center-point of human history is that the Son of God became incarnated in Jesus of Nazareth. The eternal Word of God is made visible in the flesh. This has consequences for all of human history, both before the historical event of Jesus and into the future."[2]

The Crisis of Tradition

With such testimony by distinguished witnesses, it would seem that the tradition's center is secure. Yet, if as Father McCool contends sorrowfully, the Catholic mind or intellectual tradition is in a state of acute crisis today, I would suggest that a key dimension of that crisis is the loss of a robust Christic center.[3] Obviously, here too I can only signal some signs of the times pointing to what I discern to be a Christological amnesia and neglect in some quarters of contemporary Catholicism.

For a number of years now, I have noted in theological writings, both scholarly and popular, what I call a "unitarianism of the Spirit." As the term implies, these authors tend to speak almost uniquely of God in terms of "Holy Spirit," neglecting the traditional language of "Father" and "Son." Sometimes this development is fueled by a misguided ecumenism that seeks not to cause offense. But its outcome is the invocation of a "generic brands" deity that only exists in an abstract realm, uninhabited by any living tradition. Have we not unfortunately heard such anodyne invocations in faculty convocations and commencements even in Catholic colleges?[4]

Moreover, do not such vague and nondescript generalizations seep all too readily into our attempts to articulate the vision and mission of our institutions of higher education? So, to choose an example with which I am most familiar, one hears repeated, in almost mantra-like fashion, that the aim of education in the Jesuit tradition is "to educate men and women for others." Undoubtedly, an admirable sentiment; but one not at all distinctive to Jesuit colleges and universities. Indeed, its incantation risks carrying an undertone of smugness regarding other institutions' purposes.

Now the phrase "men and women for others" is culled from an address by the then-Father General of the Society of Jesus, Pedro Arrupe. What I find intriguing is that even in official digests of his talk one rarely finds the full expression of Arrupe's thought on the matter. Here is the key sentence: "Today our prime educational objective must be to form men and women for others; men and women who will not live for themselves but for God and his Christ—for the God man who lived and died for all the world . . ."[5] There is a striking Christocentrism to Arrupe's vision that is faithful to the Ignatian tradition and that one sorely misses in the reductionist and abbreviated versions too often transmitted.

Finally, when pressed to characterize what is distinctive about the Catholic vision and the Catholic intellectual tradition, one frequently encounters appeals to terms such as "sacramental consciousness" and "incarnational sensibility" (more often than not, accompanied by a well-known line from the Jesuit poet, Gerard Manley Hopkins, "The world is charged with the grandeur of God"). Now, I do not dispute the validity of these claims, nor the beauty of the verse. But I maintain that unless this widespread appeal is explicitly founded upon the confession of the unique Incarnation in Jesus Christ, who is thereby *the* Sacrament of encounter with God, we will lack the one sure foundation for renewal and transformation, both personal and institutional.

In sum, reading and listening to statements of vision and mission, I often feel as St. Augustine did in his *Confessions*. Augustine gratefully benefitted from the writings of the Platonists he had read, but failed to find there the one salvific name he longed for: that of Jesus Christ.[6] What Ignatius and Hopkins and Arrupe took for granted, we must learn to appropriate and articulate anew.

Renewing the Christic Center

Having reviewed some signs of Christological forgetfulness, let me pass on to signs of promise, hopeful indications of Christological renewal.

I would first point to the theological work of Frans Jozef van Beeck, S.J., who is a participant in our conference. Father van Beeck is the author of a multi-volume work on Catholic systematic theology entitled *God Encountered*, that, when complete, will be a milestone in American Catholic theology. In a preliminary programmatic essay towards his *magnum opus*, van Beeck summed up its guiding vision of renewal in theology and pastoral practice in these words: "This renewal, if it is to be authentically Christian, must go back to the original and abiding realization that Christ is alive and present in the Spirit, a realization found everywhere in the New Testament and one that remains the original source of all Christian faith and identity experience."[7]

With regard to the distinctive vocation of Catholic colleges and universities, this "abiding realization," that the living Christ is the heart of the Catholic wisdom tradition, must inspire and direct more than our theological offerings and ministerial programs, important as these undoubtedly are. It also holds implications for mission statements and curriculum decisions; for environment and art; for class size, administrative policies, and, yes, for hiring.[8] Passing from a merely notional apprehension to a real apprehension of these matters (to use Cardinal Newman's categories), will require imaginative and discerning leadership and commitment. But so has every authentic renewal in the Church.

For Newman, the mind's passage from the notional to the real is mediated by the imagination that allows the mind to engage and energize the heart. And poetry is a prime vehicle for this heart-felt enfleshment of the word. Another sign of hope, then, arises from the recent study by Peggy Rosenthal, *The Poets' Jesus*. Reminiscent of my earlier cautions regarding "incarnationalism without Incarnation," Rosenthal writes, "Even for many practicing Christians, the late-twentieth century's strong spirituality of incarnational presence was linked only weakly to the name and person of Jesus."[9] But in the last chapter of her work, entitled "Jesus Present," she discusses a number of contemporary American poets, like Andrew Hudgins, Scott Cairns, Denise Levertov, and Vassar Miller. Her analysis of their common ground is noteworthy: "They seem, at the end of two millennia in which this central figure of Christianity [Jesus Christ] has been reshaped and reconfigured, very comfortable with the orthodox configurations yet energized by what they mean for human life at this moment."[10] Indeed, Denise Levertov's persuasion is particularly radical: "The miracle of God assuming flesh in the Incarnation, and continuing to become the 'bread of life' in the Eucharist informs her faith in the very possibility and meaning of metaphor."[11] Only Real Presence is able to ground and guarantee real presences.

One final sign of Christological hope bears mentioning. Over the past ten years a number of graduate students in theology seem to be moving beyond the shop-worn labels of "liberal" or "conservative" to a new engagement with the tradition. Often they sense that they were deprived, through faulty religious education, of life-giving roots. Hence they undertake an in-depth study of the patristic or scholastic traditions for their doctoral dissertations. This is *ressourcement*, return to the sources, not for the sake of nostalgia, but for the sake of authentic *aggiornamento* that is more than mere cultural accommodation. They are captivated by Christ, the *Traditus*; and hence they diligently search the *tradita* for signs of the Beloved to whom we must bear witness in the present, the "today" of faith.

I quote one young Catholic theologian who speaks for many:

> Let us leave liberal/conservative behind us. And let us leave behind us, too, that Catholicism which had allowed its distinctive colors to bleed into beige. Let us embrace the spicy, troublesome, fascinating, and culture-transforming person of Jesus Christ and let *him* shape our experience and our world.[12]

Then, I am convinced, we shall discover anew that *ex corde ecclesiae* is ever *ex corde Christi.*[13]

Notes

1. Gerald A. McCool, "Spirituality and Philosophy: The Ideal of the Catholic Mind," in Anthony J. Cernera and Oliver J. Morgan, ed., *Examining the Catholic Intellectual Tradition* (Fairfield, CT: Sacred Heart University Press, 2000), 35.

2. Anthony J. Cernera and Oliver J. Morgan, "The Catholic Intellectual Tradition: Some Characteristics, Implications, and Future Directions," in Cernera and Morgan, *Examining the Catholic Intellectual Tradition*, 209, 210.

3. McCool sets forth a number of factors contributing to the crisis in "Spirituality and Philosophy," 45-49.

4. At a rather more elevated theological level, I suggest that concern about the spread of this "unitarianism of the Spirit" underlies the controversial Declaration of the Congregation for the Doctrine of the Faith, *Dominus Iesus*.

5. Pedro Arrupe, S.J., *Justice with Faith Today* (St. Louis: Institute of Jesuit Sources, 1980), 124.

6. St. Augustine, *Confessions*, Book 7, Chapter 9.

7. Frans Jozef van Beeck, *Catholic Identity after Vatican II* (Chicago: Loyola University Press, 1984), 55.

8. See Brian Daley, S.J., "Christ and the Catholic University," *America*, 169, no. 5 (September 11, 1993). Monika Hellwig also offers helpful reflections in her article, "The Catholic Intellectual Tradition and the Catholic University," in Cernera and Morgan, *Examining the Catholic Intellectual Tradition*, especially 10-18.

9. Peggy Rosenthal, *The Poets' Jesus: Representations at the End of a Millennium* (Oxford: Oxford University Press, 2000), 153.

10. Rosenthal, *The Poets' Jesus*, 166.

11. Rosenthal, *The Poets' Jesus*, 165.

12. Robert Barron, "Beyond Beige Catholicism," *Church*, 16, no. 2 (Summer 2000), 10.

13. See the profound pastoral-theological reflection of Pope John Paul II, "*Novo Millennio Ineunte*" (Boston: Pauline Books, 2001), especially Part 3, "Starting Afresh from Christ."

CHAPTER TWO

Revitalizing Religion in the Academy

KATHLEEN A. MAHONEY

The invitation to speak about "Stewards of the Catholic Intellectual Tradition" affords an opportunity to present findings from a recently completed evaluation for the Lilly Endowment reviewing its funding in the area of religion and higher education over the past ten years. My comments present a slice of that study which I co-authored with James Youniss of the Catholic University of America and John Schmalzbauer of the College of the Holy Cross. Our findings are available in a public report entitled "Revitalizing Religion in the Academy."[1]

The panel convened this evening is called "Stewards of the Catholic Intellectual Tradition" and I took as my task an examination of the stewards themselves. With that in mind, I first turned the *Oxford English Dictionary*, which was, as always, a rewarding venture. The venerable dictionary offered fifteen full definitions of the word "steward," with an additional thirteen variants, leaving us twenty-eight different ways to use the word steward as a noun. A few examples of the definitions offered for the word "steward" are in order. A steward can signify "an official who controls the domestic affairs of a household, supervising the service of his master's table." There is a variant of this: the steward as a servant of the college, who is charged with the duty of catering. On a more exalted note, a steward can be used as a title for an officer of the royal household, such as the "lord high steward" or the "great steward." Devoid of royalty *per se*, we in this country are probably more familiar with the notion of a steward as one who manages the affairs of the estate on behalf of the employer. For those who move in ecclesiastical circles, the word steward often signifies "an administrator and dispenser of wealth and favors, an individual who is regarded as a servant of God and God's people." The threads tying these twenty-eight definitions for the word steward together are threefold. First, it involves an individual; second, this individual is charged with responsibility for a valuable resource; and third, a steward does his or her work on behalf of someone else.

Given these characteristics of a steward, a host of questions comes to mind when considering the Catholic intellectual tradition. Who are the stewards? On whose behalf are the stewards acting? What valuable resources are these stewards charged with? And how does an individual become a steward? Here I would like to focus on a few questions relative to Catholic intellectual life. Who are the stewards? What do we know about them? Are they willing and able to steward?

There has been a great deal of rather lively discussion over the past ten years about religious identity and mission in Catholic higher education. (As an aside, I mention that this conversation is also going on in Protestant higher education, and much of what I say tonight applies to it as well.) In reading the literature on religion and higher education published over the past ten years, and in our interviews conducted as part of our evaluation for the Lilly Endowment, we found that those interested in religion and the intellectual life and sympathetic to the project of the Catholic intellectual tradition have three broad concerns: pluralism, literacy, and loyalty.

Pluralism has created a number of serious challenges in American higher education, although at the beginning of the twenty-first century, we would be hard-pressed to find a college that did not hold up pluralism, diversity, toleration and multi-culturalism as valued social and intellectual resources. Nonetheless, these very laudable phenomena create significant challenges for colleges wishing to express their religious identity in denomina-tionally specific and normative ways. In Catholic higher education, the question becomes one of how an institution committed to true pluralism and diversity can marshal its corporate intellectual and academic resources in the service of a particular religious tradition—in this case, Catholicism.

Second, there is significant concern about the issue of literacy, or more precisely, theological and religious illiteracy among faculty and staff. Though many faculty and staff, Catholic and non-Catholic, are supportive of and committed to the religious mission of the institutions in which they work, few are possessed of a deep understanding of and appreciation for the Catholic intellectual tradition.

Third, there is concern over the issue of loyalty. The research university model, wherein moral values and religious beliefs were separated from teaching and scholarship, has eroded a sense of Christian vocation among scholars during the twentieth century. Loyalty to disciplinary guilds, memberships in professional associations, and a long record of scholarly publications are the chief criteria for tenure and hallmarks of an academic life honorably lived. That acknowledged, what resources and motivation do faculty members have to contribute to and engage the Catholic intellectual tradition?

These concerns are not exclusive to Catholic higher education; similar issues surface in Protestant circles. They resonate in discussions in American higher education at large, which seeks greater coherence and a deeper sense of meaning and mission in light of increasingly complex social and technological realities. But I do think that such concerns are more acute in Catholic higher education. In Catholic circles, when individuals talk or write about the challenges raised by pluralism, literacy, and loyalty, they often frame them as part of an intergenerational crisis. Simply, and I am oversimplifying here, there is a perceived crisis wherein the torch is being passed from a generation of religious "haves" to a generation of religious "have-nots."

Many of you are familiar with Thomas Landy and the good work of the *Collegium* program for faculty and graduates students. In 1990, he wrote, "In the next five to seven years as many as half of our religious faculty and their traditional Catholic lay colleagues who were hired in the postwar boom will retire." Peggy Steinfels made a similar claim in 1995: "We have a decade, in which this question of identity must be honestly addressed and definitely taken on as a commitment and core project of institutions that hope to remain Catholic." In a similar vein, in 1999, Charles L. Currie, S.J., the president of the Association of Jesuit Colleges and Universities, pondered in print whether he was presiding over the demise of Jesuit education. In a recent issue of the *Chronicle of Higher Education*, Currie responded to an article about the declining number of women and men religious in higher education: "It is going to take a lot of hard work and imagination to keep these traditions alive."[2] There is, of course, very good reason to be concerned about the declining number of women and men religious who are working in higher education. For generations, they embodied in many significant ways the religious mission of the institutions in which they worked. They made immense contributions in Catholic higher education, and thus concerns about the religious identity and mission of Catholic higher education are well-founded.

But let us shed some light on those who are occasionally depicted, implicitly and explicitly, as the religious have-nots. To whom is the torch is being passed? Our research for the Lilly Endowment included a survey of faculty and staff who participated in Lilly-funded programs. (There are, of course, many faculty interested in the Catholic intellectual life who have not participated in a Lilly-funded program.) On average, about 2.5 percent of faculty members in Catholic institutions have participated in Lilly-funded programs such as Collegium, giving evidence by their involvement of an interest in the Catholic intellectual tradition; they are looking for ways to integrate their religious beliefs with their work in the academy. The average participant is about forty-five years old. Men and women have participated at roughly comparable rates, yet at the level of leadership in discussions about religion and higher education, women are underrepresented. Members of minority groups are underrepresented across the board. As a cohort, those who have participated in Lilly-funded programs score high on traditional markers of religiosity, e.g., 40 percent attend religious services at least once a week and 19 percent attend more than once a week.

Relative to this conversation on the Catholic intellectual life, our data temper criticism to the effect that faculty in Catholic colleges are wholly secular or disinterested in religion. Ninety-three percent of those responding to our survey say they are committed to the religious mission of the institutions in which they work. Eighty-four percent try to connect their personal religious beliefs with their teachings and research. When asked whether they agreed or disagreed with the statement, "One should attempt to insulate one's academic work from one's personal values," 95 percent disagreed. Seventy-six percent claimed that their religious beliefs were relevant to the content of their disciplines. Moreover, these individuals are heavily involved in what might be called identity and mission activities. Eighty percent have been involved in on-campus discussions about religion, while 84 percent have been involved in discussions about mission statements. Fifty-nine percent have been in discussions about or involved with Catholic studies programs, 45 percent have conducted service learning courses, and 32 percent have participated in campus Bible study or prayer groups.

Let me conclude with a few reflections about these findings and one recommendation. In the first instance, I hope to temper laments over this new generation of stewards. Like Father Currie, Peggy Steinfels, and Tom Landy, I recognize and am deeply concerned about the religious identity of Catholic institutions, particularly in light of the declining number of religious. On the whole, lay faculty do not take up their work in higher education with the same social, cultural, intellectual, and theological resources as their religious colleagues. Yet at the same time, it is somewhat encouraging to know that there is a cadre of faculty working in Catholic higher education who are interested in the Catholic intellectual tradition and integrating their religious beliefs with their scholarly endeavors.

Charles Currie was right: it will indeed take hard work and imagination to keep religious traditions alive in the light of the declining numbers of sisters, brothers, and priests working in higher education. I wish to elaborate on his claim. It is going to take hard work to reconceptualize, reimagine, and recast our lay faculties in our collective imagination as full players in terms of religious identity and mission.

How can we identify potential stewards and provide them

with the resources that would turn them into good stewards? How can we turn the have-nots into the haves? A number of individuals are convinced that Catholic colleges should "hire for mission." But it is not enough nor is it easy to do so, for setting out to "hire for mission" presumes that there are young Ph.D.'s and faculty who are well-versed in the Catholic intellectual tradition. Many faculty are committed to mission, but often lack the theological and religious resources necessary to engage and advance the Catholic intellectual tradition. Therein a recommendation: Catholic colleges and universities, either individually or corporately, would be well served by development of substantive seminars and colloquia that would orient and introduce faculty, junior and senior, to the history, theology, and traditions of their institutions, making conversations about religion normative throughout faculty members' careers.

This is, I believe, an opportune moment. In conducting our study for the Lilly Endowment, we found growing interest in religion and spirituality rippling across the academy—through Catholic colleges, Protestant institutions, and even secular universities. There are faculty members in Catholic colleges and universities who are interested in advancing the Catholic intellectual tradition. It is a fertile time to capitalize upon their interest in religion, to encourage and invest in these current and future stewards of the Catholic intellectual tradition.

Notes

1. Kathleen A. Mahoney, *et al.*, "Revitalizing Religion in the Academy" is available at http://www.resourcingchristianity.org/downloads/Essays/PublicReport.pdf.

2. Thomas Landy, "Lay Leadership in Catholic Higher Education: Where Will It Come From?" *America* (March 17, 1990): 264-68; Margaret O'Brien Steinfels, "The Catholic Intellectual Tradition," *Occasional Papers of the ACCU* (1995); Charles L. Currie, "Where Are We and Where Are We Going in Jesuit Higher Education: Sunset or Sunrise?," *America* 182 (May 20, 2000): 7-11; "Catholic Colleges Lack Plan to Deal with Decline in Number of Priests and Nuns, Report Says," *Chronicle of Higher Education* (November 10, 2001): A34.

CHAPTER THREE

Catholic Intellectual Life

DAVID J. O'BRIEN

I would like to set before you three distinct and related headings while thinking about this question—Catholic intellectuals, Catholic intellectual life, and Catholic colleges and universities. I will leave it to others better educated than I to carry the heavy water on Catholic intellectuals, and it is heavy. Here, we encounter all the great issues of faith and reason—Athens and Jerusalem—that are deep in the fabric of Christian history. I would simply offer a few propositions.

First, Catholics have made well-documented progress in achieving positions of leadership and accomplishment in American culture in and out of the academy. While I know of no major studies of the matter, there is plenty of anecdotal evidence to suggest that Catholics who are intellectuals, writers, and artists experience the segmentation of religion and professional work similar to that of other Americans. As one report said, and perhaps in exaggerated terms, of many Notre Dame faculty, "Their faith is for them and other Christians on the faculty a private matter. Their beliefs and commitments bear the same relationship to Notre Dame as they would to any corporation that was their employer. The Christian life informs their personal relationships and conduct but it is unconnected with their professional life as teachers, scholars, and researchers."

It is interesting that Kathleen Mahoney mentioned data from her study there, that people do not really accept that kind of separation, but it is one that has been regularly noted by people on Catholic colleges and elsewhere. One suspects the same would be said of Catholics of an intellectual bent working outside the Catholic sub-culture as well. Maybe Pope John XXIII got it right some forty years ago now. Indeed, it happens too often, he wrote, that there is no proportion between scientific training and religious instruction. The former continues and is extended until it reaches higher degrees while the latter remains at an elementary level. Numerous Ph.D.'s settle for pablum and platitudes in church, and I might add, even politics.

Pastoral care for Catholic intellectuals is a worry, especially now that shrinking religious orders are already overburdened with campus ministry on non-Catholic, private and public campuses. We seem to have few resources even when there is interest for reaching out to intellectual and artists. Moreover, intellectual networks that once connected people with one another, and with Catholic thinking, seem beset by lack of support due to ideological divisions and generational discount annuities. My generation's multiple Catholic disappointments are a poor basis for attracting younger people with religious interest. Post-sub-cultural Catholicism has perhaps to look in different places to find ways to reconnect faith, Church, and the lives of serious thinking Catholics. I have in mind Thomas Merton's combination of the deepest moments of the tradition and the farthest reaches of humanity's quest for meaning, or put another way, the fullest points of God's presence and God's absence. The action, in short, is probably a long way from the ecclesiastical bog. Therefore, one imperative seems to be to identify, nourish, and support Catholics who are intellectuals. We have the opportunity to provide them with resources to build a vital relationship between their faith and their work, and between their work and the life and work of the Church. Who will do that and how to do that are the initial and crucial questions of the present and future.

Second, Catholic intellectual life. Here the problem is fairly clear but even harder to address. The problem is the decreasing intellectual tone of much of the popular Catholic faith and life noted by many observers. We refer to it sometimes as illiteracy and we have all of our favorite groups to blame, with religious educators, youth ministers, and even social justice advocates taking their share of the hits. I think it has something to do with the impact of democracy on religion. Once Christianity is extracted from a formative cultural role among a distinct people, it takes on an evangelical spirit in which religious experience regularly trumps religious learning. And Scripture with a popular hermeneutic shapes Christian imagination. Sustaining a vital Christian intellectual life, in any American community of faith, is a real challenge.

Here I draw on Bernard Lee and his associates on the school's ministry rather than the schools of theology. They call for a practical theology that is most intimately connected with pastoral ministry. In short, how do we learn to read our experience of life in terms of our faith, and how do we learn to read our faith in terms of our experience of life? All those projects which involve theological reflection get trivialized not simply because participants don't understand the tradition, but just as often because the theological reflectors or ministers neither understand nor appreciate the culture. Excellent pastoral ministry led by people who respect the people they work with, is deeply formed in the Christian tradition's spirituality, and at the same time is alert to deep religious currents in American culture, is the best way to a revitalization of Catholic intellectual life in the Church as a whole. But like all other areas of contemporary Catholic life, achievement of a high level of Catholic intelligence would require acknowledgement of shared responsibility and an effective mechanism for pastoral planning. Obvious enough, perhaps, but also rare. So, once again, whose responsibility is it and how would one fill that responsibility if one wishes to?

Third is the related question of higher education—if we can still stand discussion of Catholic higher education ten years after the publication of *Ex Corde Ecclesiae* and fifteen years since the conversation about *Ex Corde* began. Catholic colleges and universities need to provide trained teachers and research opportunities that draw on the Catholic intellectual tradition and on the life of the contemporary Church—not only in theology where the claim is acknowledged, but in all disciplines and programs. Thus, seek growing interest in Catholic studies, which is nothing more than self-conscious attention to Catholic life and thought with adequate human and financial resources essential to Catholic education and obviously a matter of simply integrity. I would argue that fulfillment of that responsibility would require, though, an uncharacteristic cooperation among the many Catholic institutions of higher education in dozens of projects, most of which have already been proposed. In seeking a positive and constructive orientation towards the Church as we find it, Catholic colleges could do worse than try to focus on the two problems outlined earlier. That is, pastoral care for Catholic intellectuals, and strategic planning for Catholic intelligence. The former is mostly a question of will, the latter could perhaps get started here and there with simple, but sincere invitations.

Everything I have suggested turns on the pastoral life of the American Catholic Church. We need pastoral care for Catholic intellectuals, artists, and writers, and we need to help people probe the religious dimensions of everyday experience. Helping people find God, I think, is the definition of pastoral care. In the United States, we would also say that pastoral care is helping one another to find God, often in unexpected places through community found in parishes in the numerous small groups and apostolic movements. Most of our arguments should be made on pastoral grounds, which may be also our best potential common ground.

In my judgment, American colleges and universities could make no better contribution to the life and work of the Church, and then to the eventual renewal of Catholic intellectual life worthy of our labors than by launching intellect and inter-disciplinary projects focusing on American pastoral Catholic practice. After all, the best solution to the problem of Catholic intellectual life is an intelligent, engaged, and enthusiastic Church. That would stir some interest in the matter of shared responsibility. Too often, we consider the whole question of Catholic intellectual life, like the question of Catholic social teaching, as if it were in some other realm than the world of pastoral care, the world of parishes, dioceses, movements, and pastoral programs.

I want to end by suggesting that we cannot have an intelligent and engaged Catholicism without a spiritually and liturgically rich community of faith.

CHAPTER FOUR

The Work of Catholic Intellectuals

MARGARET O'BRIEN STEINFELS

I have been asked to talk about "Catholic" and "intellectual,"
about the condition they are in now, and the challenges we
face in the future. The brevity of my presentation puts me in
mind of a sermon and so if you will indulge me, I would like to
read the text for my "sermon":

> In the daily exercise of our pastoral office, we sometimes
> have to listen, much to our regret, to voices of persons
> who though burning with zeal are not endowed with too
> much sense of discretion or measure. They say that our
> era in comparison with the past eras is getting worse. And
> they behave as though they have learned nothing from
> history, which is nonetheless the teacher of life. They
> behave as though, at the time of formal councils, every-
> thing was a full triumph for the Christian idea. We feel
> we must disagree with these prophets of doom who are
> always forecasting disaster as though the end of the world
> were at hand.

Some of you will recognize the words of Pope John XXIII in his
opening address to the first session of the Second Vatican Council
on October 11, 1962. Having, in that opening, addressed his critics,
the pope went on to highlight the purpose of the Council, as he
said, was not "the discussion of one particular article or another

of a document on the Church. For this," he said, "a Council is not necessary." Rather as he went on to say, "The substance of the ancient doctrine of the deposit of faith is one thing, and the way in which it is presented is another. And it is the latter that we must take into great consideration, with patience if necessary—everything being measured in the forms and propositions of the *magisterium*, which is predominately pastoral in character."

The pope was no liberal, but he was not a conservative either. In any case, I do not mean to quote him to either effect, but to remind us of the spirit in which he called the Council, the spirit with which the Council was conducted by the bishops and eventually received by the faithful. That spirit was one of confidence and expansiveness, enthusiasm and even ebullience. Confidence in a sense that the Catholic tradition was strong enough and smart enough to teach the world, as well as to learn from the world. If I had to describe my own work at *Commonweal* in reference to the Catholic tradition and to the Council, it would certainly be in that spirit.

The Catholic intellectual tradition is strong enough and smart enough to provide us with the tools, the conceptual frameworks, rhetorical systems, systems of political and moral thought, and sometimes even language to help us to look at our culture, our politics, our own somewhat confused nation and our shrinking world with its ever greater need for conscientious care and conservation. This tradition of ours can genuinely inform and guide our understanding of how to see issues, how to analyze them, and how, if need be, to change the world around us.

John XXIII, the bishops at the Council, and a receptive faithful were filled with a spirit: they were members of a confident and expansive Church that saw its intellectual heritage available for tackling the great issues of the time and the great issues of our cultures. This confidence, it seems to me, made a place for the Catholic intellectual to be a public intellectual. I will not say a great deal about that tonight. But obviously, those of us who are not in the academy are in some other world. I will call them public intellectuals: politicians, writers, editors, poets, artists, and policy makers. There is a wide range of such people. There are Catholics, public intellectuals, who make use of and know how to make use of this tradition as it applies to their work and their civic life. I think many of us felt we were given a mandate from the Council to engage the world with that tradition.

Of course, as we all recognize, in a culture such as our own that has never fancied Catholics or intellectuals in particular, this in itself is a somewhat counter-cultural activity. On the other hand, the Church, besides teaching, had much to learn from the world, even from the Catholic faithful who had more often been regarded as aliens than as allies in doing the work of the God. This gives and gave a certain positive, sometimes exuberant and even aggressive character to one's work and one's view of the world. Catholics in the United States certainly took that spirit of confidence and expansiveness and ran with it.

As we look to the future, we cannot help but stop for one moment in the present because there are few of us, I think, who would find in today's Church the same spirit operating at the same level of energy. It is there, of course, but it is muted. I do not claim, as some might, that two popes, John XXIII and John Paul II, really have a different Church in mind or a different set of doctrines. It is certainly the same message and the same Church, but not, I think, operating in the same spirit. Oddly enough, the current pope, who began his pontificate as a young man, relatively speaking, does not seem to provide the Church with the same sense of confidence or expansiveness that John XXIII, who was quite old when elected, brought in like a breath of fresh air.

Or perhaps, as many say, it is not the pope, it is the Vatican itself. Yet by his episcopal appointments in particular, and by the documents coming from various curial offices, we now seem to have become a church full of fear and anxiety, a faith community more restrictive than expansive, more anxious than confident. Inevitably this has an effect on the intellectual life of the Church and of Catholics generally. Indeed, the current pope has given us the phrase, "the culture of death," which seems to embody not simply a critical stance toward our culture—indeed a stance that is warranted in some ways—but an indictment that seems a death warrant to the kind of dialogue that was one of the sterling outcomes of Vatican II. When you expect the worst and anticipate the darkest motives in others, it does not help one to engage the world or carry on a dialogue with it. Such a spirit shrinks our intellectual horizons, offers automatic answers to complicated questions, and shrouds itself in the mantle of truth rather than embracing the joys and sorrows of this world.

Well, that is the bad news, at least as I see it, at the current time. But there is a future. In these circumstances, what is to be done? The first thing, obviously, is to keep the faith. The attitude and behavior of others does not exonerate any of us from the beliefs and practices that are ours as Catholics. We are all obliged to teach and to learn, in season and out.

Second, we must maintain the health and solidity of our institutions. As we live into the future, Catholics in the United States have a powerful set of institutions to preserve, to foster, to transmit the Catholic intellectual tradition, which is a faith tradition as well as a tradition that helps us to engage our world. The preservation and growth of these institutions is in many ways in our hands as lay people. They are not in the hands of the Vatican, except in some theological sense which I do not yet understand. Their faithfulness to the Christian tradition and their intellectual and financial solidity rest with all of us. These are largely self-governing institutions and, relatively speaking, independent ones. Most of them are certainly as independent as any secular school in the United States. These are not, however, and should not be little centers of defiance or rebellion, but serious and sober places that are able to think when everything else seems to be running amok. When I mention these places, obviously I am thinking of a place like Sacred Heart University, and other Catholic colleges and universities and the serious efforts they are all making in different ways to devise a means to maintain Catholic identity and to foster a rich intellectual life. It takes time, it takes money, it takes brains, it takes effort.

I am also thinking of things like think tanks. There is the Cushwa Center for the Study of American Catholicism. There is the Erasmus Institute, the Jesuit Institute at Boston College, and the Woodstock Center at Georgetown. Many schools are devising mechanisms like think tanks to tackle these issues and I think they should be encouraged. There are also plans afoot for a free-standing Institute for Advanced Catholic Studies, which needs to be nourished and encouraged and given money. I am also thinking of journals and magazines, obviously like *Commonweal*, and our friendly colleagues downtown, *America Magazine,* and other independent associations that Catholics have founded and fostered, sometimes with a very narrow agenda, but nonetheless an agenda that can help link these questions of our world and our faith.

Third, lay people must be committed to this as intellectuals, as citizens, as faith-filled collaborators in the work that Jesus sent out to this Church of ours. A good deal could be said about this, but I think we have to face the real question of who is going to do the work. It will have to be us. We need to think seriously about how we are going to do it.

So let me close as I began, with the words of John XXIII, this time as he addressed the closing and exciting and "revolutionary" first session of the Council, which he did on December 8, 1962:

> The vision of this grand prospect which reveals the whole course of the coming year, so rich in promise, stirs up in the heart a more ardent hope for the realization of the great goals for which we have convoked a Council. Namely, that the Church founded on faith, strengthened on hope and where ardent charity may flourish with a new and useful vigor and fortified by holy ordinances, may be more energetic and swift to spread the kingdom of Christ.[1]

Notes

1. Xavier Rynne, *Letters from Vatican City* (New York: Farrar, Straus, and Co., 1963), Appendix II.

CHAPTER FIVE

"Catholic" and "Intellectual": The Way I See It

BRIAN STILTNER

I am a member of a transitional generation. Born in 1966, I am the child of the last generation of American Catholics who saw Catholic schooling as a religious obligation and a way to maintain a distinctive subculture. Already by the time I was being sent to grade school in the 1970s, suburban Catholics such as my family were enculturated in a pluralistic society, not sure why it was so necessary to send their children to a Catholic school and whether it was worth the increasing costs, except that they were starting to have qualms about the quality of public schools. So I, who went to Catholic schools from third grade onward, was sent there secondarily for religious reasons and primarily for the order and higher quality education. (I was a hyper-curious child who needed some order, frankly.) Yet this schooling was immensely influential to my developing understanding of faith and appreciation of the world around me. Catholic schooling reached its fruition, for me, at St. Charles Borromeo High School in Columbus, Ohio, one of the few remaining all-boys schools these days. There I learned Latin and Greek, took AP English and AP Chemistry, and had four years of religion, including courses in Social Justice and Moral Decision-Making that were the earliest roots of my eventual career. These four years, which were crucial to making me who I am today, had their power on me because

they built on a base of parochial education and were complemented by a Jesuit college education and finally—what I think was
appropriate after all this Catholic schooling—by graduate
education at a multi-denominational divinity school and graduate
school.

My Catholic schooling is the context for my remarks tonight
for two reasons. First, this education inculcated in me an attitude
about being Catholic and intellectual that has greatly shaped my
work as a Catholic scholar. Second, the social and chronological
location of my education calls attention to a generational shift
with major implications—potentially negative implications—for the
future of the Catholic intellectual tradition. (Much has been
written about the way of thinking of Generation X, its approach
to media, knowledge, and institutional religion. But I am the very
earliest of Generation X, and there is a significant difference
between my attitudes and those of the youngest members of this
generation and the next one, sometimes called Generation Y. This
shift involves very different attitudes about the authority
structures of the Church, the university, and institutions in
general, and about acquiring and using information.) I will talk
first about what being Catholic and intellectual means to me, and
then indicate some challenges facing Catholic scholars in the
postmodern era.

Probably the most important attitude I took away from my
Catholic schooling was an appreciation of the beauty and value of
all academic disciplines. As students, we were expected to take all
our courses seriously and were given no reason to believe that we
couldn't excel in all of them. There were no awkward attempts to
force Catholic lessons into difference parts of the curriculum;
there was a simple confidence that all truth coheres. It is a notion
that I have found beautifully expressed in the poems of Gerard
Manley Hopkins, one of which I will quote in full:

As kingfishers catch fire, dragonflies draw flame;
As tumbled over rim in roundy wells
Stones ring; like each tucked string tells, each hung bell's
Bow swung finds tongue to fling out broad its name;
Each mortal thing does one thing and the same:

Deals out that being indoors each one dwells;
Selves—goes itself; *myself* it speaks and spells,
Crying *What I do is me: for that I came.*

I say more: the just man justices;
Keeps grace: that keeps all his goings graces;
Acts in God's eye what in God's eye he is —
Christ. For Christ plays in ten thousand places,
Lovely in limbs, and lovely in eyes not his
To the Father through the features of men's faces.[1]

 This poem expresses three characteristics of the Catholic
intellectual tradition that are significant to me, that I hope inform
my intellectual endeavors, and that are an important gift to the
cultures and traditions with which Catholicism interacts. The first
is the sacramental imagination.

 The underlying theological conviction is that every created
thing and creature reflects the glory of God's handiwork. "Each
mortal thing does one thing and the same: / Deals out that being
indoors each one dwells." It is a commonplace how sacramentality
is central to Catholicism—to its liturgical practice, theology,
cultural expressions, and scholarship. This conviction has under-
girded the Catholic intellectual tradition's serious engagement with
various sectors of human knowledge: early on, philosophy, then
later on adding the natural sciences, the social sciences, and most
recently, cross-cultural studies. A fuller treatment, following David
Tracy and others, would incorporate the sacramental imagination
under the analogical imagination—"a specific intellectual practice
. . . [that] seeks to discern the similarities or the unities that exist
among events, entities, or state of affairs that seem different."[2] In
short, the analogical imagination refers to Catholicism's distinctive
emphasis on *both/and* instead of *either/or.* In the case of sacramentality, the analogical imagination affirms *both* supernatural *and*
natural realities, *both* God *and* the world; it coordinates these
through creation-oriented theology, natural law theory, liturgy,
and art.

 A second characteristic of the Catholic intellectual tradition is
entailed by sacramentality: attentiveness to the distinctive nature

of things. Appropriate to the sacramental imagination is to start each quest for truth with observation, with paying attention. The approach is bottom-up rather than top-down. The method is to let things reveal themselves, speak on their own terms. Hopkins did this wonderfully in his poetry: "As kingfishers catch fire, dragonflies draw flame"; "rose-moles all in stipple upon trout that swim"; "Nothing is so beautiful as Spring — / When weeds, in whiles, shoot long and lovely and lush"; "Towery city and branchy between towers; / Cuckoo-echoing, bell-swarmèd, lark-charmèd, rook-racked, river-rounded." One pays attention to see and know what is, as well as to be impressed by its beauty. There is an interesting tension between the sacramental confidence that God is disclosed in the natural world and the method of starting with observation and attention. If the former is stressed too much, then the academic disciplines become mere tools for trying to prove theological convictions. If the latter is stressed too much, the disciplines forget why theology is important and set themselves up as better, rather than as complementary, ways of knowing. This is an analogical tension, the best approach to which is to affirm *both/and.* The Catholic intellectual tradition strives to get the delicate interplay right and, on the whole, I think it succeeds.

At the same time, the Catholic sacramental imagination is not starry-eyed. As Terrence Tilley puts it, the tradition is better described as "hopeful" rather than "optimistic." Discussing the Catholic notion of redemption, he writes, "An important factor that differentiates this form of hope for redemption from an optimistic attitude is that the latter need not recognize the 'darkness' in and of the world."[3] Catholic writers, artists, dramatists, and musicians have a knack for expressing the beauty and goodness of the world without neglecting the dark undertones of human experience and culture that cry out for reform. To take just one example, the Irish rock group U2's last two albums contain numerous expressions of the highs and lows of human life. U2 offers, for instance, a celebration of nature and the workaday world reminiscent of Hopkins:

> See the world in green and blue
> See China right in front of you

See the canyons broken by clouds
See the tuna fleets clearing the sea out
See the Bedouin fires at night
See the oil fields at first light
See the bird with a leaf in her mouth
After the flood all the colours came out
It was a beautiful day.[4]

Just as frequently, the group presents moral outrage or plaintive queries at the injustices that, it appears, God fails to stop:

God has got his phone off the hook, babe.
Would he even pick up if he could?
It's been a while since we saw that child
hangin' 'round this neighbourhood
See His mother dealing in a doorway,
see Father Christmas with a begging bowl.
Jesus' sister's eyes are a blister,
the high street never looked so low.[5]

Note that in this lyric, U2's outrage is generated in part by a confidence that God, Jesus, and Mary are joined incarnationally to human experience. It is an analogical, sacramental imagination that allows these affirmations of beauty and gloom; it is an imagination informed by Christian hope that leads to the coordination of good and bad in the final words of their most recent album:

What once was hurt
What once was friction
What left a mark
No longer stings
Because Grace makes beauty
Out of ugly things.[6]

Hopkins' poems and U2's songs are representative of the Catholic intellectual tradition's conviction that the act of knowing has an aesthetic dimension. The tradition also claims that the act of knowing has a moral dimension; this is my third characteristic.

The description of a grace-filled world leads ineluctably to a commitment to the dignity of each person as created in the image of God. "Christ plays in ten thousand places, / Lovely in limbs and lovely in eyes not his / To the Father through the feature of men's faces." Much could be said here about moving from this apprehension of God in fellow persons to the affirmation of human rights and the common good. For now, I'd like simply to note that, as before, there are tensions that arise from this analogical claim. One concerns theology and theological anthropology. Human beings are good because they are God's creatures and are so loved by God that God fully took on human flesh—its joy, pain, limitations, and expectations—in the Incarnation. But something is missed if that is all we assert about human worth, for it could suggest that we value other persons, and ourselves, merely as channels to valuing God. But humans are real, eternally connected to God but not the same as God, and we have been called by God "very good."

So the Catholic-Christian moral vision not only imputes infinite worth to persons, but appraises a value that resides there that a supremely just God himself recognizes. Another tension concerns political thought. The Catholic social tradition has arrived at an unequivocal embrace of pluralist democracy. The sacral age, when the Church demanded a privileged place in the polity, has fallen to the wayside in the forward progress of civilization. And yet a genuine democracy should never leave behind its Christian inspiration. To a dialectic imagination, the following argument of Jacques Maritain is likely to be confusing, but it makes sense within the analogical, sacramental imagination that animates Catholic social theory:

> The more the body politic—that is, the people—were imbued with Christian convictions and aware of the religious faith which inspires it, the more deeply it would adhere to the secular faith in the democratic charter; for, as a matter of fact, the latter has taken shape in human history as the result of the Gospel inspiration awakening the "naturally Christian" potentialities of common secular consciousness, even among the diversity of spiritual

lineages and schools of thought opposed to each other, and sometimes warped by a vitiated ideology.[7]

These are among the reasons I embrace the Catholic intellectual tradition. It affirms faith and reason, aesthetic appreciation and moral development. With these characteristics of the Catholic intellectual tradition in mind, I'd like to name very briefly what I personally have found to be some of the joys and difficulties of working within this intellectual tradition. One joy is the interdisciplinary engagement. Working in the Catholic intellectual tradition disposes me to be interested in a lot of things! Why? Because, in various ways, truth, beauty, and moral challenges are to be found in political science, sociology, computer science, literature, and so on. A corresponding difficulty is intellectual fragmentation and the need to justify one's ideas in many courts. For example, like many Christian ethicists and theologians, I pay a lot of attention to the work of contemporary philosophers, yet the interest is usually not mutual.

A second joy is to pursue learning that is valued for its own sake, for the pure satisfaction of intellectual growth and the aesthetic appreciation of the world. At the same time, it is no easy task to excite contemporary university students to such appreciation. It is not impossible, certainly, but economic and cultural trends push increasingly for instrumental education: preparation for a career. I don't want to state this too broadly or stereotypically. Students need training for a career, and no humanist like myself would stay in this business if he or she did not encounter on a regular basis students who get excited over the ideas we present. The challenge here is directed to cultures and institutions. What is the best way for Catholic universities to make theology, philosophy, and the humanities both compelling and viable to the students of the twenty-first century?

A third joy for me has been engaging the prophetic tradition of Catholic-Christian thought. A recent example was hearing Sister Helen Prejean speak at Sacred Heart University on October 31, 2000. Her passionate witness against capital punishment, thoroughly interwoven with concrete compassion for victims' families, stirred in me and many others a desire to reinvigorate our moral, political, and spiritual commitments. What particularly struck me was her metaphor of Christ's cross that has two arms, one reaching out to embrace death-row inmates and their families, the other reaching out to enfold victims' families.[8] I can think of other symbols besides the cross that can seize our imagination for stopping capital punishment; I cannot think of another that captures as profoundly the reality of emotional loss and justified rage when a loved one is murdered *and* the possibility, indeed the necessity, of healing forgiveness. Again, the analogical imagination reconciles—perhaps tenuously and painfully—what our culture would force us to choose between.

Helen Prejean's ministry to death-row inmates and to victims' families stands at the near end of a long line reaching back to Jesus, who said, "Father forgive them; for they know not what they do," and to the prophets who held out to the Jewish people the opportunity for healing and restoration through moral and spiritual reform. A related difficulty is the difficulty of being prophetic, failing to live up to the awesome responsibility of resisting the awful ways human beings can treat each other. This obstacle is rooted in the human heart and faces both individuals and institutions. As Reinhold Niebuhr conveyed with the dichotomy "moral man/immoral society," and John Paul II with the category "structures of sin," it is all too easy for relatively benign intentions to become morally corrupted, especially in collectivities.[9]

My fourth joy in working in the Catholic intellectual tradition is being able to contribute to the ongoing implementation of the Second Vatican Council in the life of the Church and the Catholic academy. I am a post-Vatican II baby whose understanding of the Church and of his role as a layperson has been thoroughly shaped by the Council's articulation of the Church as the People of God. I internalized this understanding both in a number of informal ways (for example, as I saw laypersons have roles in the liturgy, as lay teachers had as much influence on my faith as clerical teachers, as I was inspired by movements like the Catholic Worker) and in formal ways (namely, as I learned about the Vatican II understanding of the Church in high school and college). When I first got involved in social service projects at college, wrote articles for the student newspaper on topics ranging from arming the Contras in Nicaragua to rethinking birth control, I always had the nascent sense that I was speaking for the Church, my Church, playing a small role in shaping its thought and practice, particularly the practice of Catholic lay people in the modern world. That is an exciting, if daunting and occasionally burdensome, vision. It is a vision I carry into being a moral theologian.

Yet difficulties for me as a teacher and scholar arise here as well. (Some are occasioned by *Ex Corde Ecclesiae*, a topic I will leave aside here.) A major challenge is making Vatican II relevant to the newest generation of Catholics, today's college-aged and younger students. Do they care, can they care, about what they take for granted and have already moved quite beyond? More broadly, how can today's Catholic young adults—raised in a digital, hyperlinked, media-saturated culture—come to appreciate the Catholic intellectual tradition, this ancient tradition stretching back through 2000 years of systematic theology, philosophical speculation, and largely European history? I like to think that if it matters to me, a member of Generation X, then it can matter to Generation Y and beyond, but I know it is a daunting task for us teachers. When it comes to teaching the Catholic intellectual tradition to today's students, I often feel more like a contemporary of Maritain than of Madonna.[10]

Vatican II opened as many questions about the role of the lay theologian as it did opportunities. Vatican II greatly legitimized the role of the lay theologian. At the same time, it tended to accelerate the lay person's movement into the crosscutting conversations and engagements of a pluralistic world. So as moral and systematic theologians inhabit the overlapping worlds of the Catholic scholarly community and the secular academy, a number of tensions arise—from justifying the place of theological studies in a public university to justifying to the Church's hierarchy our critical reflection upon the *magisterium*. *Ex Corde Ecclesiae* offers a model of being a theologian that tries to respond to the conflict between these worlds, but at the expense, most Catholic professors feel, of Vatican II's understanding of the competency of laypersons and the Church as the People of God. The way forward will undoubtedly be difficult.

Taking off from this point, I will conclude with a few directions for the future, each of which is quite challenging and requires coordinated efforts among many Catholic institutions. One is the need for better primary, secondary, and family/parish education of young people into the Catholic intellectual tradition. If we want students at the collegiate level to explore and appropriate the Catholic intellectual tradition, they need to have a good foundational education in the tradition, just as we cannot expect them to learn the college-level math they need for the technical twenty-first century without studying algebra, geometry, and trigonometry in high school. Can Catholic universities fill a role that is not remedial, but perhaps that assists Catholic high schools, grade schools, and parishes in their roles? (At Sacred Heart, REAPS is an institution that plays such a role by training parochial school teachers in the Hartford archdiocese.) Of course, such initiatives do not address the facts that many Catholic students have not attended parochial schools, and that many students at a Catholic university are not Catholic.

A second direction involves coming to grips with how to teach the Catholic intellectual tradition in the postmodern era. Some commentators on education have claimed that the only way to make teaching viable to Generation X and beyond is to replace the model of the teacher as a disseminator of knowledge to the model with the teacher as a facilitator of learning that students accomplish largely on their own and access through the web and other multimedia. Classrooms should be transformed from lecture halls to project rooms where students learn by creating and applying information to real-life problems.[11] I imagine the Catholic intellectual tradition can be taught, and perhaps more effectively, with the assistance of new technology. Parts of it, such as the ethical and social teachings, may even be well suited to a problem-based and project-based approach. But an embrace of the postmodern, technological era entails a fundamental shift in how we think about tradition, its authority, and its content. I am unsure how much justice will be done to the Catholic intellectual tradition by these new educational models. At any rate, it is an open question that cannot be avoided and must be explored creatively.

A third direction is to put renewed effort into "doing" the Catholic intellectual tradition, as opposed to studying it and talking about it. We must certainly study and examine, but then how can we nurture, promote, renew, and expand the Catholic intellectual tradition in all its cultural manifestations? The question must be directed more broadly than to Catholic theology and philosophy. Fortunately, that is the purpose of tomorrow's working groups. It was the question raised by David O'Brien when he convoked people to Holy Cross last November to talk about the future of Catholic intellectual and cultural life. Some basic ideas are taking shape at a number of institutions. I would like to see Catholic universities exposing their students to novelists, poets, musicians and filmmakers who express Catholic themes in their work, and even sponsoring such work. I would like to see initiatives for engaging the Catholic intellectual tradition in courses and research projects in the natural and social sciences. These initiatives often take place through Catholic Studies programs and core curricula, which are two means among others for "doing" the Catholic intellectual tradition. Whatever form the initiatives take, they should be cognizant of and responsive to the technological and multicultural global environment that is taking shape. As the Catholic Church is ever more a worldwide church, the study and practice of the Catholic intellectual tradition must be attuned to the multiple enculturations of Catholicism. In addition, "doing" the Catholic intellectual tradition should not be limited to universities, so we need to explore the creation or rejuvenation of institutions that support Catholic-themed arts and letters.

A final point for consideration would be for educators to make a renewed appropriation of our prophetic traditions. This would open so many avenues that for now it is best to close with another open question: What will it mean for Catholic education in the next century to claim its prophetic roots?

Notes

1. Gerard Manley Hopkins, "As Kingfishers Catch Fire," in *Hopkins: Poems and Prose* (New York: Knopf, 1995), 18.

2. Terrence W. Tilley, *Inventing Catholic Tradition* (Maryknoll, NY: Orbis Books, 2000), 126.

3. Tilley, *Inventing Catholic Tradition*, 134.

4. U2, "Beautiful Day," *All That You Can't Leave Behind* (Interscope Records, 2000).

5. U2, "If God Will Send His Angels," *Pop* (Island Records, 1997).

6. U2, "Grace," *All That You Can't Leave Behind*.

7. Jacques Maritain, *Man and the State* (Chicago: University of Chicago Press, 1951), 113.

8. Sister Helen Prejean, "The Journey of *Dead Man Walking*," *Sacred Heart University Review* 20 (Fall 1999/Spring 2000), 1-30.

9. See Reinhold Niebuhr, *Moral Man and Immoral Society* (New York: Scribner's, 1932); and John Paul II, "Sollicitudo Rei Socialis: On Social Concern" (1987), in *Catholic Social Thought: The Documentary Heritage*, ed. David J. O'Brien and Thomas A. Shannon (Maryknoll, N.Y.: Orbis Books, 1992), paragraph 36.

10. For a positive account of the distinctive faith of Generation X, see Tom Beaudoin, *Virtual Faith: The Irreverent Spiritual Quest of Generation X* (San Francisco: Jossey-Bass, 1998).

11. See Peter Sacks, *Generation X Goes to College: An Eye-Opening Account of Teaching in Postmodern America* (Chicago: Open Court, 1996), ch. 14.

CHAPTER SIX

College Educators and
the Maintenance of Catholic Identity

MICHELE DILLON

The publication of the Vatican's apostolic constitution on higher education, *Ex Corde Ecclesiae* (1990), and the U.S. Bishops' agreement that external oversight is necessary to ensure the maintenance of Catholic identity at Catholic colleges and universities, reignited public discussion of the role of Catholic higher education in America. The ensuing dialogue has sharpened attention to the ways in which Catholic institutes of higher education maintain their dual commitment to be centers of Catholicism and of intellectual inquiry. Although *Ex Corde Ecclesiae* hastened an evaluation of the contemporary mission of Catholic colleges and universities, the purpose of Catholic higher education has for many years being in need of clarification and explication.

The socio-demographic and economic changes of the latter decades of the twentieth century presented new challenges to the institutional task of Catholic higher education. The new institutional environment must adjust to: 1) the significant advance in the educational achievements and social status of American Catholics and the de-ghettoization of Catholics as a minority subculture; 2) the changing expectations of an information economy in which qualifications in science and technology rather than immersion in the liberal arts are increasingly valued; and 3) the cultural changes attendant on the greater visibility of Asian and Hispanic immigrant groups in American society.

Catholics, therefore, are rethinking the means by which Catholic higher educational institutions can best serve the intergenerational transmission of Catholic identity. Thus far, discussion of the issue has tended to rely primarily on the viewpoints advanced by theologians, bishops, and Catholic intellectuals whose voices are frequently heard in the Catholic public sphere.[1] Although faculty and administrators at Catholic colleges and universities directly encounter the routines, dilemmas, and challenges of Catholic higher education, their voices have been relatively scant in the public conversation about Catholic identity.[2] Yet, in accord with the Second Vatican Council's affirmation of the fact that people are the "authors and artisans" of culture, faculty and administrators have a privileged position in the ongoing construction and maintenance of Catholic identity. In recognition of the critical role played by faculty and administrators at Catholic colleges and universities, this research essay presents an overview of their disposition toward the Catholic tradition and their opinions with respect to its integration with academic inquiry.

The empirical findings reported in this essay are based on a survey of Catholic identity conducted among faculty and senior administrators at Catholic colleges and universities in the United States. The survey was initiated and sponsored by the Office for Mission and Planning at Sacred Heart University, Fairfield, Connecticut in the Spring of 2000, under the leadership of University President, Anthony Cernera, Ph.D., and Donna Dodge, Ph.D., Vice President, Office for Mission and Planning. The study is an extension of Sacred Heart University's commitment to encouraging dialogue about the Catholic intellectual tradition and ways in which colleges and universities might approach the challenges confronted in articulating its relevance in contemporary times.

Sample

In the Spring of 2000, a sample of 40 Catholic colleges and universities was randomly chosen from a comprehensive listing of all Catholic colleges and universities in the U.S. Each college/university had an equal probability of being selected. From the list of 40 colleges/universities, a random sample of 42 faculty was systematically selected from each of the colleges/universities. Each person who was listed as teaching in an undergraduate department/academic program had an equal probability of being chosen for the sample. This method yielded a target sample population of 1,680 faculty members. The sample population of administrators comprised all of the presidents and two other senior administrators (deans/provosts) from each of the 224 Catholic colleges and universities listed in the directory issued by the Association of Catholic Colleges and Universities (ACCU).

A self-administered questionnaire was mailed to each of the faculty members in the faculty sample population, and to the administrators in the administrator sample. The questionnaire was seven pages long and included closed-response and open-ended questions. Faculty and administrator questionnaires followed a similar structure and format with the exception that the wording of some of the questions was tailored depending on whether the questionnaire was directed to a faculty member or to an administrator. An accompanying letter explained the origins of the study and my research interest in the issue of Catholic education and cultural pluralism. In the letter and on the questionnaire respondents were assured of the anonymity and confidentiality of the survey process, and were advised of the fact that the survey results would be presented at a public conference on the Catholic intellectual tradition being organized by Sacred Heart University for November, 2000. The respondents were asked to return their completed questionnaires in a stamped envelope addressed to me. Of the 1,680 questionnaires sent to faculty, 472 completed questionnaires were returned, yielding a response rate of 28%. Of the 672 questionnaires sent to administrators, 183 completed questionnaires were returned, yielding a response rate of 27%. These response rates compare favorably with the rate of response for self-administered mail questionnaire surveys of similar length and format sent to general populations.

The issue of non-response inevitably raises questions about the extent to which the sample respondents are representative of the population of Catholic college faculty and administrators which comprised the original sample. There is no direct way of ascertaining whether the respondents are different than the non-respondents, unless one were to re-contact and interview the non-respondents about their reasons for choosing not to participate in the initial survey. The probability is high, however, that the sample of non-respondents would still choose not to respond to the follow-up survey.

On the one hand, it could be argued that those who returned a completed questionnaire are more interested in and committed to Catholicism than those who did not respond and that, therefore, the survey results are biased in favor of the affirmation of Catholic identity. By the same token, however, it could be argued that those who responded are more negatively disposed toward the issues surrounding Catholic institutional identity and thus saw the survey as an opportunity to communicate their antipathy. Ultimately, what is important is that the initial sample was randomly drawn thus giving each person an equal chance of being selected irrespective of their religion or of their views on Catholic identity and independent of any other arbitrary characteristics. Confidence in the survey results is also strengthened by the fact that the respondents appear to be proportionally divided in terms of expected socio-demographic and institutional characteristics, thus suggesting that the opinions of any sub-group of the sample population are not under-represented to a significant degree.

Survey Results

Socio-demographic and Institutional Profiles of the Respondents

In the sample of administrators (N=181), 53% were presidents and a further 26% were vice-presidents. Eight percent were deans, 7% provosts, and 6% held other administrative posts. Almost half of the administrators had a graduate degree in the humanities (49%), one-fifth in the social sciences (22%), and another one-fifth in religious studies/philosophy (21%). Few administrators held graduate degrees in business (5%) or in science/engineering disciplines (4%). The majority of the administrators, 59%, were men and 41% were women. The modal age category was 45-54 years (55%), and one-third (32%) were in the 35-44 age bracket.

The sample was almost evenly divided between administrators from general universities (41%) and liberal arts colleges (38%), with a further 7% from research universities. Fourteen percent were at Associate of Arts or other colleges. Well over half of the administrators (63%) worked at institutions with enrollments of between one thousand and five thousand students, 24% worked at colleges with fewer than one thousand students, and 13% at schools with over five thousand students. The institutions were located primarily in urban (54%) and suburban areas (32%) with 14% in rural settings. Regionally, 40% were in the Midwest, 30% in the Northeast, 11% each in the West and Mid-Atlantic, and 8% in Southern states.

Almost all of the administrators were raised Catholic (88%) and the same percentage reported their current religious affiliation as Catholic. Currently, 84% of administrators attend church at least weekly, with a substantial 39% of these reporting daily church attendance. Sixty-five percent said that religion was very important in their families while growing up, an additional 31% said it was important, and only 4% said it was not important.

In the faculty sample (N=472), 68% were men and 32% were women. Over one-third of the faculty were full professors (37%), another 39% were associate, and 22% were assistant professors. Just 2% of the respondents were instructors. Thirty percent were faculty in Humanities departments, 26% in the Social Sciences, 25% in Sciences/Engineering, and 19% in Religious Studies/ Philosophy departments. The faculty respondents were relatively evenly divided in age: 34% were between 45 and 54 years, 28% were aged 55-64, and 24% were in the 35-44 age category.

Sixty-six percent of the faculty were employed at general (43%) or research universities (23%), one-third were at liberal arts colleges (32%), and just 3% at other colleges. The majority of faculty respondents (56%) came from institutions with an enrollment of between one thousand and five thousand students, and 28% came from schools that had between five thousand and ten thousand students. Less than one in ten faculty worked at schools that had either fewer than one thousand (7%), or more than ten thousand (8%) students. Similar to the sample of administrators, the majority of faculty were at schools in urban (61%) or suburban areas (35%) and only 4% were in rural locations. Regionally, most faculty were employed at institutions in the Midwest (39%) or the Northeast (34%). Fifteen percent were in the West, 9% in Mid-Atlantic states, and only 2% in the South.

Almost two-thirds of the faculty respondents were raised as Catholic (60%), 27% were raised Protestant, 5% were raised Jewish, and less than one in ten (8%) had no religious upbringing. The vast majority (84%) said that religion was very important (47%) or important (37%) in their families while growing up and 16% said it was not important. Just over half of the faculty (53%) reported their current religious affiliation as Catholic, 17% as Protestant, 4% as Jewish, and 11% as other. Fifteen percent said they were atheist or agnostic. Over half (54%) of the faculty went to church at least once a week with 14% of these reporting daily church attendance. A further 6% went to church once or twice a month, 13% went several times a year, 18% went on special occasions only, and 9% said they never attend church.

Just less than half of the faculty reported attending Catholic elementary (46%), high school (42%), and college (42%), and 26% went to Catholic graduate schools. Over one-third of the faculty majored in the humanities as undergraduates, 28% in science/ engineering, and 23% in the social sciences. Fourteen percent majored in religious studies/philosophy. The vast majority of faculty (86%) said that as students they had enrolled in one or more classes in religion, philosophy, church history, or theology.

Three-quarters of the administrators went to Catholic elementary (71%), high school (75%) and college (76%), and almost half (45%) went to Catholic graduate schools. Administrators were most likely to have majored in the humanities (49%). Among the remainder, relatively similar proportions majored in the social sciences (17%), science/engineering (14%), or religious studies/ philosophy (16%). Nevertheless, almost all of the administrators (96%) reported that they had enrolled in at least one religious-oriented class while in college.

Personal Involvement in the Catholic Doctrinal Tradition

Faculty and administrators were given a closed-response question asking them to indicate how much importance (a lot, some, or none) they personally attach to specific aspects of the Catholic tradition. The vast majority of administrators said that they attach "a lot" of importance to social justice teaching (89%), communal ethics (78%), and the coupling of faith and reason (74%). Just under half said they personally attach a lot of importance to the Church's liturgical rituals (49%), and to the fact that the Church is publicly engaged (47%), while a further 44% said they attached "some" importance to each of these aspects. On the other hand, it is noteworthy that only 12% of the administrators said that they personally attach a lot of importance to the papacy. An additional 55% attach some importance and a substantial 33% said they attach no importance to the papacy.

Faculty respondents were significantly more likely than the administrators to say that they attach "some" rather than "a lot" of importance to aspects of the tradition.[3] Overall, however, the vast majority said that they personally attach either a lot or some importance to the Church's social justice tradition (92%), the Church's communal ethics (88%), the Church as publicly engaged (74%), and the coupling of faith and reason (71%). Over half of the faculty respondents said they attach a lot or some importance to the Church's liturgical rituals (58%). Strikingly similar to the administrators, only 12% of faculty said they personally attach a lot of importance to the papacy. An additional 31% said they attach some importance to it, but a substantial 57% (compared to 33% of administrators) reported attaching no importance to the papacy. In sum, while there were some significant differences between administrators and faculty in the amount of personal importance they attached to aspects of the Catholic tradition, both groups were positively disposed toward the same aspects, and both were negatively disposed toward the papacy.

There were also some significant differences within the faculty sample. Faculty who themselves were undergraduates at Catholic colleges/universities were significantly more likely than graduates of non-Catholic schools to say that they attach importance to all aspects of the Catholic tradition. Somewhat similar substantial majorities of Catholics (96%), Protestants (90%), and respondents who were either agnostic or atheist (87%) said they attach importance to Catholic social teaching, and to the Church's emphasis on communal ethics (Catholics: 94%; Protestants: 88%; Agnostic/Atheists: 75%). Protestants, however, were significantly less likely than Catholic faculty to attach importance to the Church's public engagement and to the coupling of faith and reason; and atheistic/agnostic faculty were significant less likely than both their Catholic and Protestant colleagues to attach importance to these two latter dimensions of the tradition. Irrespective of particular religious affiliation, frequency of church attendance was also positively associated with personal attachment to all aspects of the tradition. Finally, women were significantly less likely than men to say that they attach importance to the papacy.

Regression Analyses

A statistical procedure called regression analysis was used to identify which of the significant independent variables (e.g., gender, frequency of church attendance, whether or not the respondent was Catholic, and whether or not the respondent had graduated from a Catholic college), when examined in relation to one another, remained significant predictors of the variation observed in the dependent variable (e.g., the personal importance attached to the coupling of faith and reason). Regression statistical models control for overlap between independent variables and identify the additional amount each variable contributes, independent of the other variables, to explaining the variation in the dependent variable. Regression is thus a parsimonious way of sorting out the comparative explanatory power of discrete independent variables.[4]

The results from the regression analyses pointed to a nuanced rather than monolithic effect of the independent variables. Church attendance independent of religious affiliation was by far the strongest predictor (beta = .41) of importance attached to the coupling of faith and reason.[5] Being Catholic (beta = .21) and graduating from a Catholic college (beta = .14) remained significant predictors but they contributed far less to the overall amount of variance explained. Church attendance (beta=.28), and being Catholic (beta=.24) were the best predictors of importance attached to the Church's public engagement, each contributing approximately one-quarter of the variation in faculty attitudes. On the other hand, being Catholic was the best predictor of the valuing of the Church's liturgical rituals and of the papacy, although in both cases church attendance was also a significant predictor. All three religious variables (being Catholic, attending church, being a Catholic college graduate) were virtually equal in their accounting for faculty respondents' valuing of the Church's emphasis on communal ethics, whereas being Catholic (beta=.17), and a woman (beta=.14) were the best predictors of importance given to the Catholic social justice tradition.

In sum, the regression models confirmed that being Catholic, attending church, and graduating from a Catholic college combine as significant predictors of attachment to different aspects of the tradition. In addition, gender contributes to the amount of overall variance explained in each model, but is a significant predictor only in regard to attachment to the Church's social justice tradition and to its liturgical rituals. These variables' hierarchical importance in accounting for attachment varies, however, depending on which aspect of the tradition is specified. In some instances the most important piece of information is knowing whether the respondent attends church frequently, whereas in other instances, knowing whether the faculty member is a Catholic or is a Catholic college graduate is more salient to predicting the attitudes in question.

When combined, the independent variables accounted for a greater proportion of overall variance in some dimensions (e.g., coupling of faith and reason) than in others (e.g., communal ethics). This indicates that the independent variables included in the analyses (e.g., frequency of church attendance) are stronger predictors of faculty dispositions toward select aspects of the Catholic tradition than are others. To explain more of the variance in faculty attitudes toward, for example, the Church's emphasis on communal ethics, we would have to experiment with including additional and/or different variables in the model.[6]

Perceived Relevance of the Catholic Tradition

In an open-ended question, faculty and administrators were asked to state which aspects of the Catholic tradition they considered to have the most relevance for contemporary times. The written responses to this question paralleled the respondents' assessment of the personal importance of different aspects of Catholicism. Over half of the administrators mentioned Catholic social teaching (53%), one-third mentioned the Church's emphasis on morality (31%), and one-fifth mentioned Catholic spirituality (21%), theology (20%), and the coupling of faith and reason (19%). Somewhat smaller minorities highlighted the Church's valuing of community (17%), the sanctity of the individual (16%), the Church's global presence (12%), its openness to other faiths/ traditions (10%), and the affirmation of such values as hope, love, and trust (10%). Only 8 percent mentioned Catholic education.

Similarly, 45% of the faculty respondents mentioned Catholic social teaching, and 31% mentioned the Church's moral absolutes. Smaller minorities highlighted the Catholic valuing of community (18%), the sanctity of the individual (16%), faith and reason (14%), the Church's global presence (14%), Catholic spirituality (13%), and theology (11%). Twelve percent of the faculty mentioned Catholic education. Fewer than one in ten mentioned Catholic symbols (9%), openness to other traditions (9%), the valuing of hope, love, and trust (7%), and the Church's public presence (7%). Five percent of both faculty and administrators mentioned the papacy.

Theological/Doctrinal Reading

The questionnaire included a closed-response question asking administrators and faculty whether they had read some portions or the complete text of specific encyclicals issued during John Paul II's papacy. As might be expected, a significantly greater proportion of administrators than faculty said that they had read the papal encyclicals. One noteworthy exception was *We Remember: A Reflection on the Shoah* which was read by a similar minority of both administrators (40%) and faculty (39%). *Ex Corde*

Ecclesiae was read by 97% of administrators and by a substantial 72% of faculty. The majority of faculty also reported having read *Fides et Ratio* (61%), *Veritatis Splendor* (56%), and 44% said that they had read some or all of *The Gospel of Life* (44%). In contrast, over a half to three-quarters of administrators reported reading the latter three encyclicals.

Once again, there were intra-faculty differences. Faculty who were Catholic college graduates were significantly more likely than graduates from other colleges, and Catholics were more likely than non-Catholic faculty to have read all of the specified papal encyclicals. It is noteworthy that Protestant faculty were significantly more likely than agnostic/atheistic faculty to have read *Veritatis Splendor* and *Fides et Ratio*. On the other hand, relatively similar proportions of Protestant and agnostic/atheistic faculty reported having read *Ex Corde Ecclesiae* (59%, 53%), and *The Gospel of Life* (22%, 19%). Male faculty respondents were significantly more likely than women to have read *Fides et Ratio* and *Veritatis Splendor*. There was also a positive association between frequency of church attendance and the tendency to report having read the encyclicals.

Regression analyses were performed to identify the independent effects of these discrete variables on the likelihood of faculty to have read the papal encyclicals. The resulting models indicated that being Catholic and having attended a Catholic college were the best predictors of having read *Fides et Ratio* and *Ex Corde Ecclesiae*. Church attendance and graduating from a Catholic college were the strongest predictors of the likelihood to have read *Veritatis Splendor* and the *Gospel of Life*. None of the variables in the regression model for the likelihood of faculty having read *We Remember* were significant due to the relatively small amount of variation that existed in the faculty sample with respect to this encyclical.

A substantial minority of the faculty respondents also reported reading one or more religious magazines on a regular or occasional basis (46%). Specifically, 30% said that they read *America*, 22% read *Commonweal*, and 40% read other magazines such as *Crisis*, *First Things*, *National Catholic Reporter*, *Christian Century*, or their local diocesan paper. Almost all of the administrators (92%)

reported reading one or more religious magazine either regularly or occasionally. Seventy percent of administrators read *America*, 55% read *Commonweal*, and 85% reported reading other religious magazines.

In addition, 80% of administrators and 58% of faculty said that they had read some books in theology, religion, or spirituality in the year preceding the survey. Moreover, a substantial proportion of both groups (48% of administrators and 39% of faculty) said they had enrolled in a lecture course, seminar, or workshop on some aspect of theology, religion, or spirituality since finishing their graduate training. Among the recently read books were Karen Miller, *Searching for Darwin's God*; Garry Wills, *Saint Augustine*; George Marsden, *The Soul of the University*; Mary Gordon, *Joan of Arc*; Parker Palmer, The *Courage to Teach*; George Weigel, *Witness to Hope*; Sallie MacFague, *The Body of God*; Andrew Greeley, *The Catholic Imagination*; Donald Cozzens, *The Changing Face of the Priesthood*; John Haught, *Science and Religion*; John Polkinghorne, *Faith of a Physicist*; John Quinn, *Reforming the Papacy*. Other authors cited include Simone Weil, C.S. Lewis, Patricia Hampl, and Charles Curran.

The Promotion of Catholic Identity in Campus Practices

Two-thirds (67%) of the faculty respondents and 87% of administrators stated that they had talked about the issue of Catholic identity in a formally organized forum at their respective college campuses. The size (based on student enrollment) and type of educational institution (whether research university, comprehensive university, or liberal arts college) did not affect whether faculty or administrators had talked about the issue.

Faculty and administrators differed significantly in their attitudes toward the priority that Catholic colleges should give to discussion of identity. Seventy-five percent of administrators but only 32% of the faculty said that *high* priority should be given to discussing it. The majority of faculty (62%), nonetheless, agreed that *some* priority should be given to the issue. Similarly, 71% of administrators compared to 38% of faculty said that Catholic colleges should make a greater effort to highlight their Catholic identity. Faculty (37%) were more likely than administrators (22%) to say that "things are fine as they are."

Among the faculty, Catholic college graduates were significantly more likely than other graduates, currently affiliated Catholics were significantly more likely than non-Catholics, frequent church attendees were more likely than those who attended occasionally or never, and men were significantly more likely than women to favor both the high prioritization and a greater effort towards the highlighting of Catholic identity on campus. Regression analyses indicated that church attendance and being Catholic were the strongest predictors of faculty attitudes favoring the high prioritization and greater effort being made toward the highlighting of the institution's Catholic identity, although being a Catholic college graduate also remained a significant independent predictor in both instances. In addition, gender remained independently significant in contributing to the amount of variance explained with respect to attitudes toward the institutional highlighting of identity.

There were also some significant differences among administrators on these questions. In a regression model, the size of institution emerged as a significant predictor of administrators' attitudes toward the prioritization of campus discussion of Catholic identity. Administrators from larger colleges/universities were less disposed to this than were their counterparts from smaller institutions. On the other hand, the single best predictor of agreement with the view that colleges and universities should make a greater effort to highlight their identity was whether the administrators were themselves graduates of Catholic colleges.

In a closed-response question, respondents were asked whether in their opinion it was appropriate for Catholic colleges and universities to specifically highlight the Catholic tradition in various public and classroom settings. The vast majority of both faculty and administrators tended to agree with such practices. In each case, however, administrators were significantly more likely than faculty to endorse the highlighting of Catholic identity whether in public advertisements for faculty positions (91%, 76%), in letters to prospective students (91%, 84%), in theology classes (94%, 84%), with a core curriculum that includes readings in

Catholic philosophy, theology, and social teaching (86%, 73%), and in campus public discussions of controversial topics such as global population policies, or capital punishment (90%, 75%). A substantial deviation from this overall consensus, however, emerged in regard to non-theological classes. Here, only 41% of faculty compared to 76% of administrators agreed that it was appropriate for the Catholic tradition to be highlighted. It is indicative of the tensions surrounding the integration of Catholicism within the standard curriculum that comparatively fewer of both administrators and faculty agreed with this item relative to the highlighting of Catholicism in other forums.

As with the intra-faculty patterns observed thus far, a significantly greater proportion of respondents who were Catholic college graduates than those who graduated from other institutions favored the highlighting of the Catholic tradition in all of the specified forums. Frequency of church attendance was also positively associated with a favorable disposition toward the highlighting of Catholic identity in the various contexts. Agnostic/atheistic faculty were significantly less likely than Protestants, who, in turn were significantly less likely than Catholic faculty to agree with the highlighting of the Catholic tradition in theology classes, a core curriculum, and in non-theological classes. The only significant gender difference observed was that women were less likely than men to agree with the idea of highlighting Catholicism in a core curriculum.

Regression analyses showed that the independent effect of gender remained significant, but it was a weaker predictor than either being Catholic or church attendance in accounting for variation in attitudes toward a core curriculum in Catholic thought. Being Catholic and church attendance were similarly strong predictors of attitudes toward highlighting Catholicism in the other forums specified, although in the case of both theological and non-theological classes, church attendance was the slightly stronger predictor.

Catholic Institutional Identity and Academic Freedom

Faculty and administrators were asked a closed-response question about their perception of the difficulty involved in maintaining academic freedom and encouraging awareness of Catholic institutional identity. In response, almost three-quarters of the faculty (72%) compared to less than half of the administrators (45%) saw the task as "difficult" or "somewhat difficult." Administrators were more likely to see the balance as being not difficult (55%) to maintain. Faculty who were at research or general universities rather than at liberal arts colleges were more negative in their assessments of the difficulty of maintaining both academic freedom and Catholicism.

A follow-up, open-ended question gave the survey respondents an opportunity to elaborate on their views of the issues involved in maintaining the institution's dual identity as Catholic and academic. One administrator who saw no difficulty in maintaining both tasks stated:

> The Catholic traditions themselves invite thought, reflection, dialogue, and communal sharing. What better setting can one find for this than a college?

Others similarly argued:

> Catholic colleges must remain true to their founding identity and mission. Otherwise academic freedom as a basic tenet exists in a vacuum.

> Truth in disciplines (academic) cannot contradict the Ultimate Truth. True liberty can only be found in the truth.

> Both are values which must be maintained. I see no conflict because I believe God's truth will always shine faith. However, public perception is often the problem.

Some of the administrators, as the following two quotes indicate, simply acknowledged the tension inherent in the balance:

> A specific religious heritage, whatever it may be, implies certain boundaries and, thus, limitations.

Faculty, as they take advantage of the academic freedom which is theirs, must be cognizant of the mission of the institution with which they have contracted.

Other administrators who saw some difficulty in balancing academic freedom with the institutions' Catholic identity tended to point to the importance of maintaining awareness of the diversity of faculty backgrounds and interests:

Maintaining an ecumenical outreach to faculty (not excluding them and their faith) makes for sensitive discussions.

It matters when curricular offerings are skewed in such a way as to accommodate religious beliefs as opposed to a broader liberal approach.

The stipulations of *Ex Corde* raise a number of serious concerns among faculty that are hard to respond to. Although I am confident that we will be able to maintain academic freedom, I find it difficult to convince faculty of this.

Some administrators, on the other hand, were critical of faculty and questioned their willingness to engage openly with the issues surrounding Catholic institutional identity:

The awareness of religious identity, in a non-judgmental frame, is more difficult than maintaining academic freedom.

The difficulties are primarily within the institution—reluctance on the part of the faculty to discuss openly—to remove the political correctness mentality that prevents many from speaking on religion.

There is a pervasive misunderstanding about the purpose and scope of *Ex Corde* which leads some faculty to think that academic freedom will be seriously threatened.

Notwithstanding the concerns voiced by administrators, many of the faculty, while seeing the task of balancing freedom and Catholicism as difficult, were nonetheless quite moderate in their evaluation of the tensions at issue. The following quotations from faculty respondents provide a good sense of faculty perceptions of the difficulties involved:

Awareness of religious identity is not the same as adherence to Catholic identity.

Every university is based on some set of principles that might at some time conflict with free discussion of issues: e.g., the commitment to democracy and equality, in some cases, might conflict with a commitment to excellence. What matters is how open the intellectual climate in the classroom is.

If religious identity is used to frame questions and issues that might be confronted I think it can foster excellence. If it prescribes answers, it would be a problem.

The institution needs to be what it claims to be and those hired ought to respect its identity. If faculty comport themselves with objectivity—treating all sides of an issue with fairness and not impugn the religious identity of the institution—I see no problem with the fact that the faculty member may not hold a position held by the institution.

The two are in tension. As long as the tension exists, there can be a Roman Catholic university. When the tension is resolved one way or the other, the institution becomes either a secular university or an ecclesiastical institution.

Faculty and administrators were also given a closed-response question asking them to evaluate whether the goal of affirming a college or university's Catholic identity was different to affirming the identity of particular sub-groups (e.g., ethnic groups) on campus. Sixty percent of administrators compared to just under half of the faculty respondents (48%) said that maintaining Catholic identity was "very different" from affirming the identity of various racial or ethnic sub-groups on campus. Faculty (36%) were more likely than administrators (27%) to see these goals as somewhat different, and similar proportions of both faculty (16%) and administrators (13%) saw the goals as being not different.

Some administrators saw the maintenance of Catholic identity as counter-cultural and thus more challenging, as indicated by one respondent who stated:

> It is much easier to affirm identity for groups whose identity is *championed* by society; being "Catholic" is being counter-cultural—always a tough issue!

For the most part, however, administrators were likely to stress that Catholicism is an overarching identity for Catholic institutions, part of their defining essence, rather than an affirmation of sub-cultural diversity. The following three quotations illustrate this view:

> Catholic speaks to the global mission more than any other single issue.

> It goes to the very nature of the institution.

> Because identity is the basis upon which such institutions were founded. Yet it is much more than heritage.

Other administrators pointed to the multi-layered nature of their institution's identity, as in the following quotation:

> We are a Catholic university, one perspective from which we look outward and inward. We are a Hispanic university (some would say Hispanic-serving), another perspective from which we look outward and inward. Religion is an aspect of culture, so too ethnicity. Much of our religious expression, the paradigm of our institutional spirituality, the content of our religious celebration and the intellectual discourse is Hispanic.

We are at greater pains to affirm the Franciscan part of our identity rather than the "Catholic."

Faculty respondents also emphasized the overarching nature of Catholic institutional identity, as in the following three quotations:

A college's identity as a Catholic college defines what it essentially is. It is not a matter of affirming something; it is explaining its essence and reason for being.

A search for, and maintenance of, diversity is not the same as an affirmation of an identity.

In a Catholic institution, the whole institution is committed to and guided by its goals and identification. Sub-groups are legitimate sub-units.

Many faculty respondents, however, drew attention to the challenge of translating identity into mission, and the need for recognition of the multiple strands contained within Catholicism and within an academic community:

To affirm the identity of the whole is obviously different from affirming the identity of a part. The problem is not identity, but the mission associated with the identity.

There are different flavors of Catholic identity. It is tough to accept this sometimes.

Because it affects everyone in "some way." The "some way" is what needs to be worked out so as to include as many as possible.

A choice precludes other choices. Someone whose cultural identity includes religion (e.g., Islam) will not feel "affirmed" by discussion of Catholic identity.

Work Routines

The faculty questionnaire included several closed-response questions that aimed to establish the extent to which faculty respondents' presence at a Catholic college/university impacted on their work routines. One set of questions asked faculty whether being at a Catholic college/university has had any influence on the content of their teaching, research, and student advising. In response, 61% said it had an impact on their teaching, whereas 32% said it influenced their research. Just less than half (45%) said it influenced the advice they give to students. There were no significant gender differences among faculty in their responses to these questions. Catholic college graduates, currently affiliated Catholics, and frequent church attendees followed the trend for the sample as whole by their tendency to say that their teaching rather than research was influenced by being at a Catholic school. At the same time, however, faculty in each of these groups were significantly more likely than their respective counterparts to say that being in a Catholic environment influenced the content of their teaching, research, and advising. In the regression model, church attendance was the best predictor of teaching content being influenced by the faculty member's presence at a Catholic school although being a graduate of a Catholic college was also significant.

Faculty and administrators were also asked whether they have given much thought to incorporating Catholicism in their daily academic activities. In response, 68% of faculty reported having given either a lot (31%) or some (37%) thought to how they might draw on aspects of the Catholic tradition in their classroom teaching, whereas 94% of administrators reported having given a lot (62%) or some (32%) thought to introducing new initiatives on campus that would affirm their institution's Catholic identity. More noteworthy perhaps is the fact that 32% of faculty said that they had not given any thought to the idea. At the same time, of course, it is somewhat surprising that even 6% of administrators reported having given no thought to introducing new Catholic identity initiatives on campus in view of the impetus provided by the discussion of *Ex Corde Ecclesiae* in Catholic circles.

Nevertheless, 38% of faculty said that they envisage incorporating aspects of the Catholic tradition in future courses, research, or other academic activities in which they are engaged, and a further 14% said that there was a possibility that they might do this.

Among the faculty, Catholic college graduates (85%, compared to 56% of other graduates), currently affiliated Catholics (82%), and frequent church attendees (79%) were significantly more likely than their respective counterparts to say that they had given either some or a lot of thought to ways in which to incorporate Catholicism in their teaching. Equal proportions of Protestant (52%) and agnostic/atheistic (48%) faculty reported not having given any thought to including Catholic themes in their teaching. The regression model showed that being Catholic independently contributed 17% of the variance, being a Catholic college graduate independently contributed 21%, and church attendance contributed 22%.

Talking About the Catholic Intellectual Tradition

Faculty and administrators were asked a closed-response question ascertaining how comfortable they feel (or would feel) in talking about the Catholic intellectual tradition to students, students' parents, departmental/campus colleagues, and colleagues at a secular college/university. Just over half of the faculty respondents said that they would feel "very comfortable" in talking about the tradition to students in their class (53%), to parents (50%), and to a departmental colleague (55%), and just under half would feel very comfortable in talking to a colleague at a secular university or college (47%). A substantial minority in each case said that they feel or would feel "somewhat" comfortable in these circumstances, and smaller, but still relatively substantial, minorities said they would not be comfortable in talking about the Catholic intellectual tradition in any of these various contexts (ranging from 17% for departmental colleagues to 25% for students' parents). As we might anticipate, a greater proportion of administrators (ranging from two-thirds to three-quarters) reported feeling "very comfortable" in talking about the Catholic intellectual tradition to students (75%), students' parents

(74%), and colleagues at their own institution (66%). It is noteworthy that somewhat fewer administrators (62%) said that they would be very comfortable in talking about the tradition to colleagues at a secular institution.

Not surprisingly, Catholic faculty were significantly more likely than non-Catholics, and frequent church attendees were significantly more likely than others, to indicate feeling comfortable in these situations. Similar proportions of Protestant and agnostic/atheistic faculty stated that they would not feel comfortable in talking about the Catholic tradition to students (37%, 38%), students' parents (43%, 44%), departmental colleagues (27%, 25%), or colleagues at a secular college or university (27%, 29%). Male faculty were significantly more likely than female faculty to say they would feel very comfortable in talking to students and parents about the tradition, but there were no apparent gender differences with respect to talking to colleagues.

The regression models investigating the independent effects of these variables showed that being a Catholic was the single best predictor of comfort in talking both to students and to students' parents, although being a Catholic college graduate and church attendance remained significant. By contrast, in the case of comfort in talking to colleagues (either at one's own or at a secular school), being a Catholic college graduate was the best predictor in the models, followed by being Catholic. It is noteworthy, however, that across the four models, there is a greater amount of explained variance in regard to talking to students and parents than in talking to colleagues.

In response to an open-ended question, faculty and administrators listed the themes they would emphasize in talking about the Catholic intellectual tradition to colleagues at a secular university. Many of the respondents highlighted Catholic social thought, the compatibility of faith and reason, Catholic thought as the core of philosophy and theology, the valuing of human dignity, the perception of everything as sacred or sacramental, and ethics as important questions. The space for religious tolerance in the tradition and, as one faculty respondent stated, "the ability to accept difference" were also noted. Similarly, others variously mentioned the "plurality of traditions" and freedom within the

COLLEGE EDUCATORS AND CATHOLIC IDENTITY / 61

tradition, and the openness of the tradition to "the deepest questions." One administrator, a member of a Protestant denomination, spoke about what he identified as the Catholic tradition's recognition of the importance of balancing individual and community imperatives. He phrased this as:

> Its position as one of the great wisdom traditions that invites one to balance commitment to the individual with the needs of the common good and equally the struggle to develop conscience and freedom in some kind of healthy balance.

Perceptions of Working at a Catholic College or University

The questionnaire used open-ended questions to ask faculty and administrators what they particularly like about being at a Catholic college/university, and what, if anything, they particularly dislike about being at a Catholic college/university and that they think might be different if they were employed at a secular college/university. Fourteen percent of faculty did not complete the question asking what they like about being at a Catholic college/university. Among those who provided written responses (N = 405), a relatively broad range of characteristics were mentioned. It was possible, however, to categorize the discrete points into a smaller number of general themes.

The most frequently cited characteristic was that of freedom of discourse and the related freedom of being able to integrate religious beliefs as part of their faculty routine (29%). Other frequently cited themes revolved around the respondents' appreciation of the school's emphasis on social, ethical, and spiritual values (22%), and the sense of community (22%). Smaller proportions of faculty said they liked the school's emphasis on a philosophical core (9%), and the well-behaved and respectful students (4%). A further 4% offered miscellaneous reasons, ranging from the school's discouragement of sexual harassment to the physical environment of the campus. One in ten of the faculty respondents (10%) said they did not like anything about being at a Catholic institution.

The following quotations reflect the various ways in which faculty expressed their valuing of the freedom to talk openly and seriously about religious issues:

> There is no question, no area of thought that cannot be engaged in class, in faculty seminars, etc.

> The open public discussion of religious and ethical concerns.

> One is free to speak on all issues and express one's views—if the Church bishops become stricter on Church positions it might raise some problems, i.e., I do not accept the current position on women in the Church, or birth control, for example, and state both.

> I like the public affirmation/support for interrelating faith and reason, the presumed compatibility of rigorous scholarship/intellectual activity and a faith. I also appreciate the sense that values do/should undergird our behavior/beliefs as individuals and as a community.

> I can speak about God any time I want without fear of reprisal.

> I am not Catholic but am an active Lutheran. I like being able to be open about being a person of faith. I also like being in an environment where my beliefs and traditions are constantly juxtaposed to a different tradition.

> The intellectual life is not purely speculative but rather also practical in orientation. The "True" and the "Good" go together.

> Validates my Catholic identity. Can explore Catholic social teaching and its application without negative sanctions. Can more comfortably explore ethical/moral issues in a social scientific context.

The awareness of one's services through teaching as living the mission.

I am critically committed to this tradition and appreciate the freedom to teach within this context.

As indicated at the beginning of this section, other faculty respondents (22%) pointed explicitly to ethical, social, and spiritual values in the Catholic tradition and the personal and communal realization of these values on campus. As exemplified by the following, the values highlighted included an emphasis on service, social justice, and a focus on the person as a synthesized whole.

The shared commitment to respect the human person as made in the image and likeness of God.

The profound insight that there are ethical and spiritual dimensions intrinsic to academia; in secular institutions their presence is unevenly obscured, or worse, denied.

There really are lots of students who are committed (and comfortable in their commitment) to careers involving service/help to others even if not well paid.

I am not a Catholic but I find the emphasis on spiritual values refreshing.

My own spiritual development has taken off since I've been here. I am more satisfied with my quality of life (although I don't make as much money now as I once did). It's great to be around people who're concerned about their spiritual journeys.

The sense of community and working within a mission emphasizing the total person and service to others.

As in the latter quote, many additional faculty (22%) similarly stressed their valuing of collegiality, shared mission, and the strong, overarching sense of community they experience at their college/university:

> Atmosphere of community often not found in secular institutions.

> The friendship of people who speak the same language about beautiful things.

> A close family atmosphere with an openness to diversity.

> The community—brings in *all*, not just Catholics, to share in various aspects of college—celebrations, service, academics, etc.

Fourteen percent of administrators did not respond to the open-ended question asking what they like about being at a Catholic college/university. Among those who completed the question (N=156), there was a relatively strong consensus with respect to the aspects mentioned. A substantial proportion of administrators (45%) emphasized their valuing of the freedom to talk about religious and other issues and to integrate this dialogue as part of their work. A further 30% of administrators said they liked the emphasis on values and ethics, 13% said they liked the clear sense of mission and tradition at their college/university, and 12% cited the sense of community.

The following illustrative quotes provide a sense of the administrators' responses:

> The learning and teaching have added values in the context of a tradition that expects students to make the world a better place.

> We focus on *mission*. We *live out* our values.

> Opportunity to implement Catholic values in all decision-making.

Being at home—freedom to raise "my issues"—justice, equality, personal dignity of all; rights and responsibility.

The mission corresponds with my personal convictions.

The open-ended question asking administrators what they dislike about being at a Catholic college/university was unanswered by 13% of the sample, and a substantial 44% of administrators said there was nothing they disliked about being at a Catholic college/university. Of the remainder who mentioned a negative aspect (N=77), one-third, 35%, cited pressures from conservative Catholics and/or from the Church hierarchy with regard to the interpretation of Catholic orthodoxy. The following two quotations exemplify this frustration:

Dealing with the Religious Right in the Church.

Need for caution regarding engagement of speakers and policies, practices that might arouse criticism from the far right and bring about damage to the college.

A further 12% of administrators said that they disliked the lack of openness in discussing doctrinal and other issues, and an additional 9% explicitly cited having to worry about the implementation of *Ex Corde Ecclesiae*. Administrators also said that they disliked the public attacks on and the external image of Catholicism (9%), a lack of financial resources (8%), the Church's conservatism on issues of gender and sexuality (5%), anti-Catholicism among their colleagues (5%), parochialism (4%) and moral hypocrisy (4%). Among the many miscellaneous aspects identified as sources of dislike (9%), administrators commented on the "tension of being a Catholic college for women"; the tendency to be parochial; the "higher level of accountability for behavior," and internal political pressures such as "inserting unqualified religious into administrative positions."

Thirteen percent of the faculty did not answer the question asking what they dislike about being at a Catholic college. Among those who provided written responses (N=409), 77% mentioned some negative aspect, and 23% said there was nothing that they disliked about being at a Catholic college/university. The characteristics identified as being disliked were wide-ranging in scope. Among the negative aspects, however, the two modal categories were faculty perceptions that the administration was too hierarchical, authoritarian, or dictatorial (20%), and low salaries and benefits (14%).

Smaller minorities said they disliked the socio-moral conservatism of the campus atmosphere, including the attitude toward women, and gays and lesbians (10%); the preoccupation with the question of Catholic identity (10%); homogeneity of the students (9%); constraints on freedom of speech and inquiry (7%); lack of intellectual excellence or curiosity (7%); various forms of hypocrisy between rhetoric and practices on campus (7%); and the dominance of dogmatic Catholics (7%). Two percent of the faculty said they disliked the lack of respect shown toward their non-Catholic faith, whereas others cited the core requirements in philosophy (2%), anti-Catholic colleagues (2%), and the public image of Catholicism (2%).

The following quotations provide a sense of the diversity of faculty views on what they dislike about being at a Catholic college/university:

> The stifling of dissent—the right to disagree. The way the structure and spirit of the Church in its secrecy, hierarchy and homosocial, misogynistic cronyism is reproduced in the university structure.

> Students come from an intellectually rigid and authoritarian educational tradition that leaves them passive in the learning process.

> They still have some major blind spots about women. Sometimes their culture of authority seems to be a hindrance to decision-making.

> Fear of discussing abortion, homosexuality, theology in general; current reluctance to call for women in the priesthood.

Its "family shop" obsession with Catholic traditions.

Ex Corde Ecclesiae makes me nervous.

I dislike the continuous debate about Catholic identity that probably would not take place at a secular institution except as an academic discussion.

Roman army type of governance, instead of WASP-type parliamentary governance.

The assumption by certain clergy that they own the higher ground on issues of deep concern to all.

Hiring and Tenuring

Some further significant sources of variation emerged between faculty and administrators in their attitudes toward faculty hiring and tenuring policies. The majority of faculty respondents indicated their opposition to policies that give greater weight to the apparent Catholicism of individual job candidates. In response to the question "Do you think the Catholicism of a candidate for a job at a Catholic college/university is a valid criterion to use in evaluating candidates for non-theological faculty position?" 71% of faculty said no, 24% said yes, and 5% were undecided. Similarly, in response to two further closed-response questions, a substantial majority of faculty respondents said that there should not be an official commitment to hiring (69%) or tenuring (77%) faculty who consider themselves active Catholics. At the same time, the faculty respondents were evenly divided as to whether, in deciding among two "equally well qualified" candidates for a job in a non-theological discipline at a Catholic college/university, the person who appeared to be more committed to the Catholic tradition, irrespective of his or her own religious upbringing and affiliation, should get the job: 47% agreed, 40% disagreed, and 13% were undecided.

Women faculty were significantly less likely than men to agree that the Catholicism of a job candidate was a valid criterion to use in evaluating faculty for non-theological disciplines, and to agree that Catholic candidates should be given preference over others in hiring and tenuring decisions. Significantly greater proportions of Catholic college graduates and of frequent church attendees agreed with employment and promotion policies that would give recognition to Catholicism. Protestant and agnostic/atheistic faculty shared relatively similar views on employment and promotion policies. By substantial margins, both groups were significantly less likely than their Catholic colleagues to endorse as official policy the hiring or tenuring of Catholic candidates. Protestant faculty, however, were significantly more likely than those who were agnostic/atheist to favor the more Catholic-committed candidate in getting an academic position.

It emerged from the regression models that being a Catholic was the strongest predictor of the acceptance of Catholicism as a valid criterion in evaluating job candidates, and of a positive attitude toward an official commitment to hiring Catholic faculty. Church attendance and graduating from a Catholic college, although significant, were less powerful in accounting for variation in faculty attitudes on these questions. Church attendance, on the other hand, was the single best predictor of attitudes favoring the more Catholic-committed job candidate, and in tandem with whether the respondent was a Catholic, also predicted attitudes toward an official commitment to tenuring Catholic faculty.

Many of the reasons offered by faculty in support of the differentiated positions expressed on the issue of recognition for Catholic candidates pointed to the complexity of measuring commitment to Catholicism and incorporating such measures of "qualification" in a fair and reasonable manner. Faculty who favored such policies tended to view commitment to Catholicism as a predictor of subsequent commitment to serving the overall mission of the college/university. As one person in favor said:

> I would take the greater commitment to be indicative of commitment to the school's mission statement.

Another faculty respondent who agreed elaborated that:

> One teaches students not merely in the classroom but also by one's example both on campus and off campus. It also helps in teaching students about living their faith.

Some other faculty respondents took a sharper position intimating that unless both candidates are equally committed to the tradition, then, in fact, "they are not equally qualified."

For still other respondents, what was critical was commitment as opposed to affiliation. In this view:

> No case has two "equally well qualified" candidates. Commitment to (and understanding of) the tradition rather than personal affiliation is the key in my mind.

> None are ever equally well-qualified. I think we need a critical mass of Catholic faculty, not disaffected Catholics.

> That's a tough one! It would also be absurd if the University was Catholic in name only and none of its faculty were Catholic (or even only a few).

> Consider the logic: if a Catholic school has no preference for Catholics, it will with time cease to have Catholic character and will retain only a Catholic name (e.g., Georgetown). Jewish schools prefer Jews, evangelical schools prefer evangelicals etc., and that makes sense. Otherwise you destroy diversity in society and education.

> [It] depends on what aspect of "the Catholic tradition" is in question—service, yes, obedience to outmoded ideals, no.

By contrast with faculty respondents' general reservations about giving preference to Catholic candidates, administrators were more likely to endorse such measures. Forty-four percent of administrators (compared to 24% of faculty) said that a candidate's Catholicism was a valid criterion to use in evaluating a job candidate for a non-theological position. But underscoring the complexity of hiring decisions in general, one administrator added:

> Not the only one, however. Candidates must be excellent and Catholic. We seek out candidates of other faiths too (to be Catholic).

Forty-one percent of administrators said that there should be an official commitment to hiring faculty who are active Catholics, and fewer (26%) agreed that such a commitment should also hold in tenure decisions. It is noteworthy that significantly fewer female than male administrators agreed that there should be an official commitment to hiring (12%, 29%) and tenuring (7%, 19%) faculty who are active Catholics. Once again, as with faculty concerns about the measurement of Catholic commitment, administrators reiterated the complexity involved in evaluating Catholic commitment. One female administrator, for example, added:

> This is very difficult to determine! I've had some "active" Catholics during an interview who were not "Catholic" on campus.

Another administrator pointed out that "Their willingness to engage [the tradition] and not disparage it is important."

Nevertheless, three-quarters of the administrators (74%), compared to 47% of faculty, said that among equally well qualified candidates, the more Catholic-committed person should have preference for a faculty position in a non-theological department. It was clear, however, that many of these administrators were more concerned with the "fit" of prospective faculty with their institution's mission than with a candidate's "Catholicism" per se. The following quotations illustrate the reasoning of the administrators on this question:

> But the Catholicism is less of an issue than the "fit" with the mission of the institution. I would want someone who could support the mission.

I would hire the person who understands and seems most comfortable with our mission statement.

Just as we take students who "fit" in our campuses, so there are also some faculty who are a better "fit." Sometimes this is related to a faith commitment—more often than not. However, faculty who are not Catholic but have a faith commitment are incredibly important to us.

It truly depends on the position and the person. On the one hand, I do think it's important for there to be *Catholics* at a Catholic college. The way this question is framed, hiring a Catholic sounds like an affirmative action category. And I don't quite think of it this way.

Another administrator expounded on why it was important for Catholic-committed faculty to be hired especially for non-theological departments. He stated:

The Catholic intellectual tradition is not confined to, or even primarily centered on theology. The university should contribute to the contemporary development of that tradition, as well as expose students to it. The university needs to be a place where the Church can do some important thinking on all sorts of issues, not just—or even especially—theology.

In sum, answers to closed-response questions indicated that administrators were significantly more likely than the faculty to favor pro-Catholic employment policies. Nevertheless, the majority of both faculty and administrators disagreed with the view that the Catholicism of a job candidate was a valid criterion to use in evaluating job candidates for faculty positions in non-theological departments, and disapproved of an official commitment to hiring and tenuring faculty who are active Catholics. On the other hand, 74% of administrators and just less than half of the faculty (47%) agreed that in deciding between two "equally well qualified" candidates, the more-committed Catholic should get the job. The ambiguities perceived, however, by both faculty and administrators in making clear-cut decisions in this domain were well illustrated in the written responses elaborating on their reasoning about the issue.

Conclusion

This essay has presented research findings on a wide array of questions pertinent to understanding administrators' and faculty members' dispositions toward the institutionalization of Catholic identity in higher education. Like all studies, this study is limited by sample size, non-response rates, and the questions asked. The survey results, nonetheless, provide a reliable overview of the study respondents' involvement in, and attachment to, the Catholic tradition, and of their attitudes toward the various ways in which Catholic identity might be given practical visibility in Catholic colleges and universities. Overall, the findings point to relatively high levels of commitment to the Catholic tradition, notwithstanding substantive differences between administrators and faculty, and differences within both groups. The diverse patterns observed in the data point to the complex and multifaceted interests and considerations that have to be borne in mind in charting the way forward for Catholic higher education in America.

There are three important sets of findings from this survey. First, the results underscore that administrators and faculty have different levels of involvement in the Catholic tradition. This is not surprising in view of the fact that the faculty respondents come from diverse religious traditions—while the majority are Catholic (53%), 17% are Protestant, 4% Jewish, 11% identify as other, and 15% are agnostic or atheist. By contrast, almost all of the administrators are Catholic (88%), and most of them reported daily or weekly Mass attendance, thus highlighting their more intimate connection with the tradition. Administrators were significantly more likely than faculty to say that they give a lot of importance to emphases in the Catholic tradition on the coupling of faith and reason, social justice, liturgical rituals, and communal ethics, and were more likely to have read such papal encyclicals as *Fides et Ratio*, the *Gospel of Life*, and *Ex Corde Ecclesiae*. It is noteworthy, however, that despite these different levels of involvement, administrators do not appear to accentuate the importance of the papacy: as documented, only 12% of respondents in each group said they attach a lot of importance to the papacy. This suggests, perhaps, that both faculty and administrators share a more local than Roman view of the structure and content of Catholicism.

The second set of findings points to the fact that faculty and administrators, because of their different structural locations within the university, bring a different prioritization of interests to academic life. The faculty and administrators in this survey clearly recognize the importance of, and show a commitment to, the pursuit of academic inquiry. Administrators, however, have an almost equally significant mindfulness of their Catholic heritage. Their approach to various policies and campus initiatives, therefore, is necessarily going to be different to, and in some instances no doubt, a source of tension in their relations with, faculty. We saw, for example, that whereas 75% of administrators said that Catholic colleges and universities should give high priority to discussing the question of religious identity, only 32% of faculty agreed with this. Similarly, over three-quarters of the administrators (76%) but only 41% of faculty agreed that it was appropriate for the Catholic tradition to be highlighted in non-theological classes. In general, administrators were significantly more likely than faculty to see the task of maintaining academic freedom and highlighting Catholic identity as being compatible: 45% of administrators compared to 72% of faculty said that it would be difficult to maintain both imperatives.

The third important finding is that faculty who teach at Catholic colleges and universities do not comprise a homogeneous group. One significant source of attitudinal differentiation in this study was gender. Women faculty showed evidence of significantly less involvement in some aspects of the Catholic tradition. They were more likely than their male colleagues to attach no importance to the papacy, and less likely than male faculty to have read *Fides et Ratio* and *Veritatis Splendor*. They also had comparatively greater reservations toward institutional policies that would prioritize discussion of Catholic identity, or accentuate the Catholic content of the non-theological curriculum. Women faculty were also more likely than their male colleagues to oppose policies that would recognize a candidate's Catholicism as a criterion in faculty employment and promotion.

Further research would be necessary to understand the reasons for women's somewhat greater distance from the Catholic tradition and the institutionalization of Catholic identity. It may be, however, that the disaffection evident among women in general with respect to Vatican teaching on various women's issues (e.g., the ban on women's ordination) accentuates the concerns of women faculty over efforts to affirm Catholic identity in higher education. It is also important to bear in mind that women administrators were more likely than their male counterparts to oppose an official commitment to hiring and tenuring Catholic faculty.

Independent of gender, indicators of religious commitment systematically differentiated faculty views. As documented throughout the essay, faculty who were Catholic as opposed to non-Catholic, who graduated from a Catholic college, and who attended church frequently were significantly more likely than their respective counterparts to attach greater importance to the Catholic tradition, to feel more comfortable in talking about it, and to endorse practices and policy initiatives that give greater visibility to the Catholicism of their institutions.

Analyses were conducted to ascertain which of these variables, when the overlap between them was taken into account, remained significant in adding to the amount of variance explained. The statistical models presented in the essay highlighted that in some circumstances the most powerful predictor of faculty attitudes was whether or not the respondent was a Catholic. This was the case, for example, in regard to attachment to the Church's liturgical rituals and to the papacy, having read *Ex Corde Ecclesiae*, comfort in talking about Catholicism to students and to their parents, the hiring of Catholic faculty, and incorporating Catholicism into campus discussion of controversial topics.

In many other instances, however, church attendance contributed significantly more than either religious affiliation or whether the faculty member was a Catholic college graduate, to explaining the variance in the dependent variable. This pattern emerged with respect to the personal importance attached to the coupling of faith and reason, and the Church as publicly engaged; the tendency to report having included Catholic themes in classroom teaching; having read *Veritatis Splendor*; attitudes toward the prioritization and greater effort to highlight Catholic identity on campus; and agreement that Catholicism was a valid criterion in evaluating job candidates. These findings demonstrate that it is not Catholicism per se, but commitment to a religious tradition (as indicated by frequent church attendance) that can be more salient in inculcating a positive disposition toward the integration of Catholic institutional identity in colleges and universities. In still other domains, (e.g., the personal importance given to the Church's emphasis on communal ethics), being a Catholic, attending church frequently (irrespective of religious affiliation), and being a Catholic college graduate were each independently significant in contributing virtually similar amounts to the overall variance. The regression results thus point to the importance of recognizing that different (but interrelated) measures of religious commitment can differentially impact attitudes towards relatively similar aspects of the Catholic tradition and toward different dimensions of the institutional identity of Catholic colleges and universities.

Maintaining the Catholic identity of Catholic colleges and universities presents many challenges. Some of the written responses to the open-ended questions pointed to the diverse internal and external pressures that impact on a Catholic college/university precisely because of its dual commitment to Catholicism and to education. On the other hand, many administrators and faculty spoke eloquently about what they saw as the possibilities for enriching intellectual inquiry within the context of a Catholic college. There also appears to be enough goodwill on the part of many of those involved in Catholic higher education to explore the questions at issue. As we saw in this survey, the vast majority of faculty like being at a Catholic college/university and, in particular, appreciate the freedom, holistic values, and sense of community that it provides. Finally, there is also a shared minimal knowledge of the tradition from which administrators and faculty, Catholic and non-Catholic alike, can begin to talk about their diverse interpretations of how Catholic identity and academic experiences might be integrated. The goal should be to find innovative ways by which themes from a broad and pluralistic Catholic tradition might be incorporated into non-theological (and theological) curriculum offerings and into the communal life of the college/university. Shared recognition of a tradition does not necessarily translate into common ground; it does, however, offer the possibility for discourse and the creation of enriched communal initiatives and experiences.

Notes

1. See, for example, the contributions in *America* by Thomas J. Reese (December 4, 1999), Richard P. McBrien (February 12, 2000), and William J. Watson (May 22, 1999); in *Commonweal*, the special supplement (April 9, 1999), and articles on Catholic identity (April 21, 2000); and *Catholic Higher Education: Practice and Promise* (ACCU, Occasional Papers on Catholic Higher Education, August 1995).

2. There are some exceptions, such as Kathleen Mahoney, John Schmalzbauer, and James Youniss, *Revitalizing Religion in the Academy: Summary of the Evaluation of Lilly Endowment's Initiative on Religion and Higher Education* (Chestnut Hill, Mass., November 2000); and Charles Zech's and Judith Dwyer's study of faculty identification with the Catholic mission of their institutions, reported by Charles Zech, "The Faculty and Catholic Institutional Identity." *America*, May 22, 1999.

3. Significance as used here and throughout the research essay refers to statistical significance. It is based on statistical analyses comparing two or more sub-groups in the sample using the Chi-square test of significance. The probability of the observed difference(s) being due to chance is set at, or less than, one in twenty ($p < .05$). This is the standard level of statistical significance used in social science research.

4. Regression analyses require linear or interval level variables and thus if categorical variables are included in the model they must be transformed into dichotomous variables, such as for sex (female=1, male=0); or religion (Catholic=1, non-Catholic=0).

5. The beta score is the coefficient of determination (or strength of association) of an independent variable on the dependent variable. Beta scores can range from -1 to +1.

6. The purpose of regression, however, is not to construct models that achieve the highest possible amount of explained variance using arbitrarily chosen variables, but to examine the effects of theoretically relevant variables on the dependent variable and how much these substantive variables contribute to the overall explained variance.

DEVELOPING THE TRADITION

CHAPTER SEVEN

The Catholic Intellectual Tradition: Challenges and Resources

MICHAEL J. HIMES

To give some structure to my remarks on the difficulties confronting Catholic intellectual life at the end of the twentieth and the beginning of the twenty-first centuries and the resources within the Catholic intellectual tradition to respond to those challenges, I turn to Saint Paul's statement that there are three things that last: faith, hope, and love (1 Corinthians 13:13). These "theological virtues" are basic attitudes establishing us in a right relationship with God and, as such, may help us locate the most pressing challenges confronting Catholic intellectual life and the resources for dealing with them.[1] In connection with faith, I shall say something about pluralism and relativism. In connection with hope, I will offer a comment on cultural despair and cultural arrogance. And in connection with love, I must speak about what I believe to be the most pressing question among Catholics, especially young Catholics, in the United States today: "Why do I need a church?" Spirituality is a "hot" word on college and university campuses today. If you want to fill an auditorium, include the word "spirituality" in the title of your lecture; if you want to empty the auditorium, add the word "church." So the third part of my remarks deals with the fact that there are many in our culture today who profess deep interest in spirituality but see no necessary connection between spirituality and participation in community.

Pluralism and Relativism

Toward the end of his richly productive life, Karl Rahner advanced the thesis that the Second Vatican Council might best be understood as "the Church's first official self-actualization as a world Church."[2] As such, he suggested that Vatican II marks the second great turning-point in the Church's history. In broad outline, Rahner divided that history into three epochs: the brief period of Jewish Christianity, "the period of the Church in a distinct cultural region, namely, that of Hellenism and of European culture and civilization,"[3] and the new period beginning in our lifetime when the Church is finally becoming in practice what it has always claimed to be in intent: catholic, universal. This means that we are now living through the second great crisis in the Church's history. The first, marking the shift from the brief first to the long second of Rahner's epochs, occurred in the apostolic generation. Then the Church had to confront the question whether it was possible to be a Christian believer, a follower of the risen Christ, and at the same time move beyond the Palestinian Jewish world of Jesus and his first disciples into the wider Greco-Roman world. And if it was possible, how could it be done? That these questions were not easy to answer and caused considerable controversy among Christians is amply demonstrated in the Acts of the Apostles and many of the Pauline letters. Now, at the second great crisis, the emergence of the world Church, the question is whether and how it is possible to be a Christian believer, a follower of the risen Christ, and also be a member of a non-Western culture. Virtually all Christians up to our time have lived within European and European-derived cultures. What happens when the Church becomes fully catholic and embraces peoples of Asia and Africa? Must Asians and Africans be transformed culturally into Europeans in order to be Christians?

This is very similar to the question which Paul and Barnabas and their contemporaries had to answer: Did pagan converts have to become culturally Jewish in order to be Christians? Of course, historical decisions always tend to seem inevitable in retrospect, but Rahner pointed out that the answer might have been otherwise. There might still have been a mission to the gentiles, but its results would have been very different from the churches which emerged from the Pauline mission. But, of course, the answer given to the question was that one did not have to become culturally Jewish in order to accept baptism. We are so accustomed to results of that decision that we can easily fail to recognize how sweeping it was. Indeed, we are still working out its ramifications. Even now, nineteen centuries later, the question of Christianity's relationship to the first covenant remains a much discussed issue. But if the response to the question which marked the first turning-point in Christian history was that one can be Christian without becoming culturally a Palestinian Jew, the response to the question which marks the second turning-point may be that one can be a member of the Church without becoming culturally a Westerner.

But how does the Church make the adjustments and adaptations necessary for that decision to be realized while remaining faithful to its tradition? To rephrase that question, how does one embrace pluralism without falling into relativism? What I mean by "pluralism" I shall explain shortly. As I am employing it, "relativism" is a negative term. Relativism is too easy a response to the question which confronts us. I can summarize what I mean by relativism as a cultural shrug of the shoulders. Cultures are simply incommensurable. *Chacun á son gout. De gustibus non disputandum.* Different strokes for different folks.

What has the Catholic tradition to offer which allows pluralism to be embraced and relativism to be avoided? I suggest that we consider an oft-repeated statement, deeply embedded in our intellectual tradition, a statement which is all too frequently violated as soon as it is made: God is mystery. Let us take that claim with maximal seriousness.

All talk about God, if not idolatrous, is framed by two poles which I will characterize by statements from Ludwig Wittgenstein and T.S. Eliot. Probably the most frequently quoted sentence in twentieth-century philosophy is the last proposition of Wittgenstein's *Tractatus Logico-Philosophicus*: "What we cannot speak about we must pass over in silence."[4] In other words, "If you don't know what you are talking about, be quiet." This is an enormously important caution for anyone who speaks about God, the incomprehensible Mystery which grounds all that exists, for speech about mystery inevitably seeks to make it unmysterious. We must be very cautious not to chatter on about ultimate Mystery as if we know what we are talking about. God demands reverent silence, as the scriptures often remind us. Perhaps the most dramatic instance of this is found at the climax of the Book of Job. When Job, having refused to say that his suffering is the result of guilt which he does not feel, challenges Yahweh to come into court and explain himself, Yahweh answers from the whirl-wind in two powerful addresses, the most magnificent poetry in the Hebrew scriptures. Yahweh hammers Job with a series of questions emphasizing the limits of human knowledge: "Where were you when I laid the earth's foundations? . . . Have you ever in your life given orders to the morning or sent the dawn to its post? . . . Have you visited the place where the snow is stored? . . . Can you fasten the harness of the Pleiades, or untie Orion's bands?" (Job 38:4, 12, 22, and 31) In answer to the first of Yahweh's speeches, Job replies, "My words have been frivolous: what can I reply? I had better lay my hand over my mouth" (40:4). The need for reverent silence is emphasized again in Job's response to the second of Yahweh's addresses: "I know that you are all-powerful: what you conceive, you can perform. I was the man who misrepresented your intentions with my ignorant words" (42:2-3).[5] Laying one's hand over one's mouth when one is tempted to speak of mysteries that are too high, too incompre-hensible for us, is a very Wittgensteinian pose. The first pole framing speech about God is the reminder that we do not know what we are talking about and that silence may well be the best response to Mystery.

But there is another pole. A quotation attributed to T.S. Eliot about poetry holds that there are some things about which we cannot say anything but before which we dare not stay silent. Some things are so important, so crucial to our own being, so necessary to our understanding of who we are and who others are and what the world is like, that we cannot be silent about them even though we know that whatever we say will be inadequate. Think of the words, "I love you." Has anyone ever said those words without the sinking feeling that they do not begin to convey what one feels? But silence is impossible. From

Shakespeare's sonnets to woefully inadequate four-letter words sometimes used as synonyms for love in our society, we go on stuttering new ways to say "I love you." They are all attempts to say what cannot finally be said. Yet we know that we cannot, indeed, that we dare not be silent. Preeminently about God, who is not only ultimate Mystery but also the final destiny of all creation, it is impossible to remain silent. In speaking to undergraduates unenthusiastic about curricular requirements in theology, I often ask whether they think that their lives have purpose, meaning, direction, and if so, whether they produce that purpose, meaning, direction or, at least in part, discover it as already present. If they answer that they find meaning present in their lives, I tell them that they are engaged in talking about God, even though they may never use the word. It is impossible to be silent about God because it is impossible to be silent about the reality of purpose and meaning in our existence.

The religious use of language is carried on between these two poles. The danger for those of us who are professional talkers, "ologists" in whatever "ology" happens to be our specialization, is that all our speaking can mislead us into thinking that finally we know what we are speaking about. If we are speaking about incomprehensible Mystery, about God, then we need to be cautioned frequently about the danger of glibness.

Perhaps this is how we should understand the first two commandments of the Decalogue. When I was a boy, I never worried about the first commandment. Idolatry was not a great problem in the Brooklyn of my youth—or, at least, so I thought. Neither my family nor any of our neighbors were especially tempted to butcher a goat for Odin or offer the odd pigeon to Pallas Athena. But I have come to realize that the first commandment is not of merely historical significance. It's the first precisely because it commands against a continuing temptation for all religiously sensitive people: the temptation to make an image of God. Images are not only made by hands; the most deceptive images may be the product of seductive words or susceptible imaginations. An image of God, however great, powerful, rich, deep, attractive, consoling, scripturally based, or ecclesiastically approved, is simply an image and must never be confused with

God. An image may serve certain important purposes and be good so far as it goes, but it never goes all the way. Nothing can. God remains sovereignly God.

There is a story told of a distinguished theologian who began his first class with new students by standing at the lecture podium and solemnly saying one word: "God." After an impressive pause, he continued, "Whatever came into your head when I said the word 'God' is not God." Whether or not the story is true, it may be the most important caution to give students in theology: whatever you think of when you hear the word "God" is not God.

This is the real import of the second commandment of the Decalogue, that against taking the name of God vainly. This commandment has long been reduced in practice to a condemnation of profanity. Now, I am happy to go on record against bad language, but I suggest that the commandment is concerned with something far more important than the Israelites' use of colorful language. The second commandment follows from the first. If every image, even our best, is inadequate to God, then let us not throw the word "God" around vainly. Let us not chatter on about God as if we know what we are talking about. Indeed, far more than a commandment against profanity, the second commandment might be taken as a caution against preaching and theology. Be very careful not to talk about God in vain, not to claim that one can with perfect adequacy speak about absolute Mystery. The claim to know the "right" way to talk about God, the only "true" way to think about God, is always idolatry.

But does this not throw us into the arms of relativism? If there is no "right" way to think and speak about God, does it follow that we can think and say anything and everything about God? I shall appropriate three terms from H. Richard Niebuhr's extended essay, "Radical Monotheism and Western Culture," which I will use in a way not identical but not opposed to his: polytheism, henotheism, and radical monotheism.[6] "Polytheism" is an attitude of pure skepticism which finally ends in making all conversation about values impossible. Polytheism is not simply the worship of an array of gods; it is the positing of an array of goods, all absolute in their own domains, among which we pick and choose. You are for this, and I am for that; you are interested in X, and I am concerned about Y, and there is no way to adjudicate which is better or more important. Niebuhr quotes Walter Lippman:

> Each ideal is supreme within a sphere of its own. There is no point of reference outside which can determine the relative value of competing ideals. The modern man desires health, he desires money, he desires power, beauty, love, truth, but which of them he shall desire the most since he cannot pursue them all to their logical conclusions, he no longer has any means of deciding. His impulses are no longer part of one attitude toward life; his ideals are no longer in a hierarchy under one lordly ideal. They have become differentiated. They are free and they are incommensurable.[7]

The governing principle of life is *de gustibus non disputandum*. *Chacun á son gout*. Different strokes for different folks. Everyone's opinion on everything is equally valid—or invalid. There is no possibility of genuine conversation, merely juxtaposition. Such relativism saps the *gravitas* of the intellectual life. For, as Thomas Mann wrote, "God is a high and difficult task; but 'the gods' are a pleasant sin."[8]

Henotheism is the absolutizing of one particular historically conditioned perspective. In Niebuhr's words, it is "that social faith which makes a finite society, whether cultural or religious, the object of trust as well as of loyalty and which tends to subvert even officially monotheistic institutions, such as the church."[9] Henotheism elevates one "God" above the ranks of the many "gods" and acclaims that "God" as the only one that matters. There is only *one* God, and he is *our* God. *Our* good, *our* value, *our* creed, *our* doctrine, *our* worship, is the finally and absolutely true one. Henotheism is a subversion of radical monotheism because it is actually an idolatry of the community. Our way of thinking and living is the only true way of thinking and living. That this can "subvert even officially monotheistic institutions, such as the church," is not surprising, for henotheism is, in fact, another form of concupiscence, the absolutizing of a relative good. It is the exaltation of *a* good as *the* good, of one way of formulating the truth as the only way of formulating it. To use a biblical category, henotheism is idolatry, the worship of a humanly produced image instead of the living God.

Over against polytheism, the relativizing of the absolute and henotheism, the absolutizing of the relative, stands what Niebuhr calls radical monotheism, in which "the value-center is neither a closed society nor the principle of such a society but the principle of being itself; its reference is to no one reality among the many but to One beyond all the many, whence all the many derive their being, and by participation in which they exist."[10] If I may be permitted to try and summarize this radical monotheism in a phrase, we do not possess the truth, truth possesses us. Any claim that we possess the truth risks falling into henotheism, into idolatry.

Of course, every theologian worth his or her salt has said this since time immemorial. No one has done so more rigorously than Thomas Aquinas, who insists that speaking equivocally about God tells us nothing and renders meaningful speech about God impossible, that speaking univocally about God is idolatrous, and that, therefore, we must speak of God analogically and so with enormous circumspection.[11] Nicholas Lash has suggested that the very definition of a theologian should be "someone who watches their language in the presence of God."[12] In words that I suspect Saint Thomas would have applauded, Lash writes, "Our words and thoughts concerning God are, indeed, inadequate but, as Newman knew, their inadequacy is acknowledged, their 'insufficiency' confessed, not by talking nonsense, but by talking carefully, by taking great care what we say."[13] This seems to me especially pressing today as the Church becomes what Rahner called "a world Church," which requires that we simultaneously recognize that the Church is situated in a global context and that there is a growing pluralism within the Church. The Catholic community must begin to mine deeply its own profound conviction that even its deepest, richest, most traditional formulae about God are simply *our* formulae. They contain wonderful truths about God, but none of them are *the* truth.

All our doctrinal statements are asymptotic. Like certain kinds of curves on a graph, they draw closer and closer to the axis but never intersect it—or, if they do, it is only in infinity. We must profess our doctrinal beliefs with a bit more Wittgensteinian caution, somewhat more of the spirit of Job before the whirlwind. Only so can we recognize that there may be deep, rich, and profound elements of truth among those who speak—and worship—very differently than we. For truth possesses us; we do not possess the truth. This makes real pluralism, as opposed to relativism, possible and so establishes the ground for genuine conversation. By contrast, polytheism renders intellectual conversation impossible and henotheism makes it unnecessary. (If I simply possess the truth, I may lecture others but I have no need to converse with them.) Only radical monotheism allows us to engage in genuine conversation with the conviction that the conversation is important but can never arrive at an absolutely final conclusion. One of the ways we can see this in the wisdom of the Church over the centuries is our traditional way of formulating doctrinal pronouncements: let anyone who says thus and so be anathema. The doctrine teaches what cannot be said but not an absolutely final way in which something must be said. Our doctrine has traditionally been phrased negatively and so avoided idolatry. We must consider this fact more and more deeply if we are to engage in a pluralistic world without becoming a relativistic church. We need to reappreciate the incomprehensibility of God.[14]

Realistic Cultural and Political Engagement

Relativism is the triumph of Humpty Dumpty. In *Through the Looking-Glass* Humpty Dumpty tells Alice, "When *I* use a word, it means just what I choose it to mean—neither more nor less."[15] This is the high road to cultural despair. Social anthropologist Clifford Geertz has offered an oft-quoted definition of "culture": "an historically transmitted pattern of meanings embodied in symbols, a system of inherited conceptions embodied in symbolic forms by means of which men [and women] communicate, perpetuate, and develop their knowledge about and attitudes toward life."[16] The very notion of a unified culture, i.e., shared values, attitudes, and symbols conveying those values and attitudes, falls apart if for those whom Niebuhr might call radical polytheists words mean whatever they want them to mean. If a symbol is so polyvalent that it can mean whatever we want it to mean, then shared symbols are simply impossible.

The way in which the "pattern of meanings embodied in symbols" is "historically transmitted" is through texts, by which I mean not only written documents but human artifacts which are designed to express meaning, e.g., dance, music, statues, pictures, building, rituals, and so on. One of the alarming aspects of contemporary intellectual life is arrogance with respect to texts. A classic text, i.e., a text which has influenced many people over a long period of time, must be approached with reverence. If some one leaves a performance of *Hamlet* saying, "I don't see anything so remarkable about that play," the person is proclaiming judgment on him- or herself, not on Shakespeare. This is not because Shakespeare is sacrosanct, but because for four hundred years intelligent, responsible women and men have found *Hamlet* to be profoundly moving and insightful. To dismiss the play as trivial or silly is disrespect not for a long-dead playwright but for four centuries of lived human experience. One must be very young or very arrogant or very stupid to do that. Since the church is none of these, it must approach its texts with profound reverence. This certainly does not mean that we should not use every technique available to us to read the text. But those techniques are always in service of the text, not the egoism of the reader. Plato has something interesting to say, and it is far more important for me to discover that than endlessly to find mirror images of what I already think reflected back to me. Reverence for the text is necessary if we are to avoid a cultural polytheism which is, in fact, an incapacity for conversation.

This incapacity of conversation ends by making political life impossible. In election years in this country it has become trite to bemoan the sorry quality of the candidates among whom we are asked to choose. Who produces the slate of candidates? In recent decades, thanks to a system of primaries across the nation, we, the voting public, have created the candidates. To paraphrase Shakespeare's Cassius, "the fault, dear Brutus, is not in our candidates but in ourselves." It is increasingly difficult to act as a responsible electorate when there are fewer and fewer shared symbols of cultural values. Unless the symbols that express our "knowledge about and attitudes toward life" are shared, unless they have a communal meaning which cuts across our private meanings, all real political life grinds to a halt. Without some kind of shared symbol system, civil conversation ceases.[17] Polytheism leads to cultural despair which leads to political despair. Since we cannot speak with one another about our deepest convictions about what constitutes a good human life, we vote for our personal interests, a rule which is usually construed as voting our pocketbooks. We vote for candidates who tell us that they stand for the American way, and that the American way means whatever we think it means. To find out what the majority of people think it means on any given day, candidates poll our opinions, over and over and over again; thus they find out what they stand for.

Cultural henotheism, on the other hand, is the path of cultural imperialism. "We have the truth, and we will tell you others what it is—whether you want it or not. We will impose on you our understanding of the good, the true, and the beautiful. We will make you see the world as we see it, and if you cannot, then you simply will not count as part of that world at all." The American way of life is the highest and finest achievement of human beings to this point in the history of the planet. Our way of living is the only authentic way for human beings to live. Everyone outside the sphere of our culture lives in a less than optimally human fashion, is, in short, a barbarian. We have seen cultural imperialism of this sort again and again. Once a barbarian was someone who did not speak Greek, now it may be someone who does not live in a free-market economy, but always it is the one who is not like us. Sometimes we ignore the barbarians, but all too often we decide to bring them the benefits of our culture— liberty, goodness, knowledge—even if we have to send in the troops to do so. This cultural arrogance is really the flip-side of cultural despair. And to the avoidance of both the Catholic intellectual tradition has something important to contribute: what Karl Rahner called "the forthright realism of Christianity."[18]

This realism is the insistence on both the truth of human

freedom and the fact of its limitedness. Christianity's grasp of both the depth of our freedom and the internal and external limits upon it assures us, in Rahner's words,

> that our freedom is finite, that the restrictedness and stubborn facts of the psychological, historical and sociological material of our freedom can never be abolished in the course of history, not even as a result of the greatest psychological and sociological changes for the better in our state of freedom; as long as our earthly history endures, we are always faced with the unresolved contradictions between the claim of our freedom and its actual opportunities; in this sense we are not free, our freedom can be liberated only by the act of God giving himself.[19]

This realistic appraisal can save us from despair on the one hand and utopianism on the other. These utopias are "the result of an outrageous monomania and assert the impossible claim to construct concrete reality in the light of a single principle, thus ultimately having a destructive influence on man."[20] Such utopianism is closely related to what I have been calling cultural henotheism. Christian realism cautions that all our values are finally inadequate, that all the ways we try to express the good, the true, and the beautiful finally fail to live up to *the* good, *the* true, and *the* beautiful. All the ways we structure our societies—our families, our schools, our businesses, and our churches—are tainted by sin. And yet all these expressions of value, all these social structures, may say something of profound importance, may convey goodness and truth and beauty, because God has incarnated God's self into this human world of ours. Within this world of finite values and fallible social structures God has spoken God's Word absolutely. The fact that one cannot canonize any expression of value does not mean that one can dismiss any such expression. The finite and relative remain finite and relative, but in them the infinite and the absolute may be embodied.

In the second act of T.S. Eliot's *The Cocktail Party*, one character tells her psychiatrist that her upbringing was "pretty conventional":

I had always been taught to disbelieve in sin.
Oh, I don't mean that it was ever mentioned!
But anything wrong, from our point of view,
Was either bad form, or was psychological.[21]

This same attitude, that evil is finally explicable as either "bad form, or mental kinks," can be found on many an op-ed page in our newspapers. If evil is an illness, then the task is simply to find the correct therapy; if evil is bad form, it originates in bad social training which is a form of oppression, and then we must identify the oppressor and join the right liberation movement to overthrow him/her/it/them. I am all for good therapy and for overthrowing oppressors, but after all the illnesses are cured and all the oppressors have met their just desserts, there will still be sin. The price of ignoring sin is denying freedom. The notion of sin presumes that, however confined by limits of time and space, by social and physical, intellectual and psychological factors, we are free and can misuse that freedom. We cannot do everything, and so we reject cultural arrogance and imperialism; but we can do something, and so we also reject cultural despair.

Where sin has abounded, grace has even more abounded. That is the Christian hope founded in realism. Not utopianism: all we need to do is improve schools, balance the budget, protect the environment, provide better housing or health insurance or prenatal care, and then all will be well. No, it will still be a world marked by limits and sin. That is the mess of the human condition. But it is in that mess that grace is found. Rahner insisted, "The Church's gospel of Christian realism is and remains the primary service that Christianity performs for the freedom of the individual and society."[22] The Catholic intellectual life must be rooted in that gospel of Christian realism.

Love and the Need for Community

In 1998, the distinguished sociologist of religion at Princeton, Robert Wuthnow, published *After Heaven*, a book whose subtitle tells us what it is really about: *Spirituality in America Since the 1950s*.[23] He offers extensive demonstration of what I suspect many of us already knew anecdotally. In the United States today many people are genuinely interested in developing their spiritual lives, but that interest is largely unconnected to a desire to participate in communities of faith. Wuthnow writes that "growing numbers of Americans say they are spiritual but not religious, . . . that many say their spirituality is growing but the impact of religion on their lives is diminishing."[24] This is an historic shift in our culture:

> At the start of the twentieth century, virtually all Americans practiced their faith within a Christian or Jewish framework. They were cradle-to-grave members of their particular traditions, and their spirituality prompted them to attend services and to believe in the teachings of their churches and synagogues. Organized religion dominated their experience of spirituality, especially when it was reinforced by ethnic loyalties and when it was expressed in family rituals. Even at mid-century, when the religious revival of the 1950s brought millions of new members to local congregations, many of these patterns prevailed. Now, at the end of the twentieth century, growing numbers of Americans piece together their faith like a patchwork quilt. Spirituality has become a vastly complex quest in which each person seeks in his or her own way.[25]

We live in a society in which increasingly even religiously sensitive and concerned people see religion as a matter of "God and me" rather than "God and us." What are the resources which the Catholic intellectual tradition can mine in order to respond to this enormously pressing challenge?

We are familiar with the notion of a hierarchy of truths. Although the phrase came into use after the Vatican II, the idea that doctrines vary in their connection with the basis of Christian faith has, in fact, long been recognized in Catholic teaching.[26] Rather than the term "hierarchy," which carries with it suggestions of "higher" and "lower" truths, I prefer the image of a series of concentric circles. Some doctrines are closer to the center, others more peripheral. The innermost circle contains those elements which are so central, so key, so much the core of the tradition that without them one cannot pretend to be dealing with Christianity at all. I suggest that at least two doctrines are in that innermost circle: the Trinity and the Incarnation. In these two doctrines the whole of the Catholic intellectual life is rooted.

The doctrine of the Trinity is an enormous elaboration of the core claim of Christianity, a claim repeated again and again in varying ways throughout the New Testament documents but which finds its clearest and most succinct formulation in 1 John 4:8, 16: God is love. I intend merely to suggest one consequence of that central claim: outside the context of a community which makes agapic love experienceable, the word "God" will always be used idolatrously. Let me explain what this means by recalling two stories, the first taken from Nietzsche and the second from Dostoevsky.

Certainly one of the best-known passages in all of Nietzsche's work is "The Madman," from *The Gay Science*.[27] Into the marketplace came a madman carrying a lantern who cried out, "I seek God! I seek God!" Those standing about in the marketplace, who did not believe in God, began to mock him, asking whether God had wandered off and become lost or if God had gone into hiding. The madman fixed them with his stare and replied that he would tell them where God was. "*We have killed him*—you and I. All of us are his murderers." Then in a series of stunning images he shows them the consequences of the death of God:

> Who gave us the sponge to wipe away the entire horizon? What were we doing when we unchained this earth from its sun? Whither is it moving now? Whither are we moving? Away from all suns? Are we not plunging continually? Backward, sideward, forward, in all directions? Is there still any up or down? Are we not straying as through an infinite nothing? Do we not feel the breath of empty space? Has it not become colder? Is not night continually closing in on us?

The madman concludes with a stark summary: "God is dead. God remains dead. And we have killed him." When it becomes clear that his astonished hearers do not know how to respond, the madman smashes his lantern and leaves the marketplace murmuring to himself, "I have come too early . . . this tremendous deed is still on its way, still wandering; it has not yet reached the ears of men."

I believe Nietzsche is on to something of immense import in this parable. Please notice that the encounter is set in the marketplace and that those in the marketplace have lost belief in God before the madman ever appears on the scene. This is not only the classical Greek agora; it is also the unregulated, laissez-faire capitalist marketplace of the nineteenth century. And in such a marketplace, a world governed simply and solely by competition, God who is least inadequately understood as *agape* is dead. In a world under the rubric, "Always take care of number one," the word "God" is a nonsense syllable. Those who live in such a world do not believe in God even if they do not yet realize it as yet.

Perhaps I can underscore this point. I ask you to imagine two people standing next to me. On the one side is the most brilliantly gifted scientist since Einstein, a greater philanthropist than Mother Theresa, a more remarkable poet than Shakespeare, a more talented musician than Mozart, a finer painter than El Greco. On the other side is a mentally retarded child. Certainly, no one advocates cruelty to this child, but let us play "life-boat ethics" for a moment. If we have the time, the energy, the resources to care for only one of these two persons, who will it be? The first who so obviously offers so much to the rest of us, or the second who seems to be a drain? On any ordinary scale the first seems a huge plus and the second, we must reluctantly conclude, a minus. The only way to avoid such a conclusion might be to insist that the two are incomparable, each of infinite value in him or herself. Ah, but to speak of infinite value implies an infinite valuer. That would, of course, be God—but, in the words of Nietzsche's madman, "God is dead, God remains dead, and we have killed him." And if God is dead, our imaginary child is in grave danger. What a terrible world, you say? Yes, and as the madman asks, isn't it getting colder every day? You think that you would not want to live in such a world? Quite right, you probably couldn't.

Human beings need "God" to survive and will crumble in a world without "God." That is why in Nietzsche's next book, Zarathustra proclaims the "superman." The superman is the one who can face the dark, cold, empty universe, and survive. We human beings are simply not up to it.

Let me offer a contrasting but complementary story taken from Dostoevsky's *The Brothers Karamazov*. A woman seeks the help of Father Zossima, an orthodox monk and a spiritual director of great fame throughout Russia, who also happens to be the novice master of Alyosha, the youngest of the Karamazov brothers. She is distraught and tells him that she can no longer bear the suffering with which she has been living. After Zossima promises to assist her if he can, she tells him that she was raised as a believer but that somehow she has gradually lost faith. This was not the result of a sudden crisis of faith sparked by some terrible event in her life, but rather a slow drifting away from belief. Now, however, she realizes that she cannot live without hope of continuance of life beyond death. Life has become dreary and meaningless for her. She asks Zossima for some proof for faith, and he replies that, although proof is impossible, conviction is not. He tells her she must enter upon the way of active love, that she must set out daily to love the people around her in the most concrete and practical ways possible. As she approaches real selflessness in loving others, she will gradually discover that she cannot not believe in God. "This has been tested," he tells her, "it is certain."[28]

What Nietzsche's madman says negatively, Dostoevsky's Zossima puts positively. Both insist that, if one lives in a world in which agapic love is systematically ruled out, the word "God" ceases to have any meaning. One may continue to use the word, one may even pray to "God," but the word will designate at best an idol and at worst a void. Apart from Zossima's way of active concrete love, apart from agape, one can only use the word "God" in vain.

In a world governed solely by competition, whatever is meant by "God" will not be the God and Father of our Lord Jesus Christ. On the other hand, if one works to realize agapic love in the world, one comes to an experience of the living God. With due respect to Anselm of Canterbury and Thomas Aquinas, to Descartes and Kant, and all those wise and learned folk who have labored to find proofs for the existence of God, Dostoevsky's Zossima is right: here proof is impossible, but certitude is not. At best, all proofs for the existence of God, even when they seem to work, lead us to a concept. Zossima's way of active love leads us to an experience, which is something entirely different. There is a vast difference between my giving you a dossier filled with information about someone and my introducing you to that person. The first will give you a very full idea of the person, but the second engages you in a richer and incomparably fuller experience. That is the hinge of on which turns the conviction which Zossima holds out to the woman who lost faith. The experience of a community in which agapic love is celebrated and attempted, a community which confesses its failure and repents when it fails to love agapically, is the precondition for the meaningful use of the word "God." Outside such a community, God-talk is idolatrous. This is the first reason why the Catholic Christian community is convinced of the need for church: outside a community of agapic love, one will not know what the word "God" means. Exploration of the core Christian doctrine of the Trinity leads to the recognition of the need for community as the context in which language about God can be used meaningfully.

The second doctrine in the innermost circle of Christian belief is the Incarnation. To point to the significance of this doctrine for understanding the absolute necessity of community in Christian religious life, let me ask you to consider what may, at first glance, seem the least immediately interesting verses in the Gospel of Luke. The first two chapters of Luke's Gospel are the infancy narratives ending with the finding of the boy Jesus in the temple and his return with his family to Galilee. The third chapter picks up where Mark's Gospel begins, with the mission of John the Baptist and Jesus' baptism by him: "In the fifteenth year of Tiberius Caesar's reign, when Pontius Pilate was governor of Judaea, Herod tetrarch of Galilee, his brother Philip tetrarch of the territories of Ituraea and Trachonitis, Lysanias tetrarch of Abilene, and while the high-priesthood was held by Annas and Caiaphas, the word of God came to John the son of Zechariah, in the desert" (3:1-2). I suggest that this verse is enormously important because it is the very antithesis of "Once upon a time . . ." Its claim is that the story being told is not a timeless tale, an always present myth about anyone at anytime, but rather a narrative of events which happened at a particular time (the fifteenth year of the reign of Tiberius, and soon) in a particular place (the desert beyond the Jordan) to particular people (in this case, John the son of Zechariah). When God enters our world, when God translates his Word into human speech, God takes on space and time. Human being is spatio-temporal being. If the claim of the Incarnation is taken with radical seriousness—and how else can we believers take it?—then the Word's assumption of human nature is also an assumption of spatio-temporality. The Word is in space and time. But space and time is always a matter of particularity: here is not there, and now is not then. If the Word of God becomes incarnate in the reigns of Augustus and Tiberius, then the Word does not become incarnate in the same way in the reigns of Hammurabi or Louis XIV. If the Word of God becomes incarnate in a minor province of the Roman empire at the eastern end of the Mediterranean, then the Word does not become incarnate in the same way in China or Peru. That is the point of living in space and time: if you live in the twenty-first century, you do not live in the tenth or the thirty-fifth centuries; if you are born in North America, you are not born in central Africa or Australia. Spatio-temporality means that you are particular.

That particularity propels us into history. Because historical events are particular, there is only one way to know about them: someone tells you. Historical events cannot simply be deduced. They cannot be argued to. One may deduce the Pythagorean theorem, but no one can simply think his or her way to the conquest of Athens by Sparta in the Peloponnesian War. There is only one way in which we can know an historical event: someone told someone else who, in turn, told another who wrote it down, after which it was read by still another who again told someone else who told us. Apart from a chain of tradition, there is no access to historical knowledge. This is why, if the Incarnation is an historical event, i.e., if it is a particular event at a particular time and in a particular place, we can know of it only by participation in a community of witnesses. The great nineteenth-century Catholic apologist Johann Adam Möhler made this point as strongly as anyone ever has:

> We can never arrive at an external authority, like Christ, by *purely spiritual* means. The attempt would involve a contradiction, which could only be disposed of in one or two ways; either we must renounce the idea, that in Christ God manifested himself in history, to the end, that the conduct of mankind might be permanently determined by him, or we must learn the fact through a living, definite, and vouching fact. Thus authority must have authority for its medium.[29]

The intellectual historian John Nef recounts a story about the great physicist Werner Heisenberg.

> An account was recently given me of an episode that occurred when Heisenberg was visiting Cambridge University. The discoverer of the principle of indeterminacy is a gifted amateur pianist. One evening after dinner in hall with the fellows of a college, he was persuaded to sit down at the instrument. He played the last sonata of Beethoven, opus 111. He finished amid silence produced by the majesty of the music. "There, gentlemen," he remarked, "you have the difference between science and art. If I had never lived, another would have discovered the principle of indeterminacy. Given the evolution of science the discovery was inevitable. But if Beethoven had never lived, no one would have written that sonata."[30]

One could say much the same about the difference between "Once upon a time . . ." and "In the fifteenth year of Tiberius Caesar's reign . . ." A timeless myth may be equally available to anyone and, if forgotten, recreated by another, but unless someone tells you what happened in the fifteenth year of Tiberius' reign, you will never know. That is the second reason why church is necessary: apart from a community of witnesses who tell the story, there is no access to the Word made flesh.

G.K. Chesterton maintained that it is crucially important to belong to a community with deep and rich sense of tradition because it saves us from what he regarded as the most degrading of all forms of servitude: that of being merely a child of one's time. Participation in the tradition of life and thought of such a community preserves us from being merely twenty-first century English-speaking North Americans. Through such a community we are connected to the persons and events of the fifteenth year of the reign of Tiberius, as well as the north Africa of Augustine, the Paris of Thomas Aquinas, Spain of Teresa of Avila, and the England of John Henry Newman. What Acton wrote of the study of history is eminently true of participation in a community with such a sense of tradition:

> History must be our deliverer not only from the undue influences of other times, but from the undue influences of our own, from the tyranny of environment and the pressure of the air we breathe. It requires all historic forces to produce their record and submit to judgment, and it promotes the faculty of resistance to contemporary surroundings by familiarity with other ages and other orbits of thought.[31]

We need to mine the doctrines of the Trinity and the Incarnation if we are to explain to students why participation in the community of the church is absolutely essential to their spiritual lives. If they do not participate in the community of the catholic and apostolic church, they will not know how to speak of God and even less how to speak to God and they will find themselves cut off from the presence of the Word in space and time. They will be unintentional idolaters and merely children of their own time.

Faith, hope, love—these three last. Under the heading of faith, our problem is to enter wholeheartedly into pluralistic conversation without falling into relativism. I have suggested that taking with full seriousness the incomprehensibility of the mystery of God gives us a way to begin addressing that problem. Hope makes possible true engagement in the work of politics, i.e., the forming of communities which foster the truly good life for human beings without succumbing to an all too easy embrace of some utopian "ism" or lapsing into a cynical social despair. To encourage this in ourselves and our students, I have suggested that we must explore ever more deeply the proclamation of the gospel of Christian realism, which sees the human situation as deeply marked by sin but even more radically rooted in grace. And finally, to counter the exaggerated individualism of American culture, we must experience again and again that outside communion with one another we can never know communion with God. To appreciate the full depth of this claim and the full scope of our communal being, we must turn, as believers have always turned, to the core doctrines of the Catholic Christian tradition, the Trinity and the Incarnation. Those are challenges that face the Catholic intellectual tradition today, and these are some of its resources for responding to them.

Notes

1. See Karl Rahner, in *Encyclopedia of Theology: The Concise Sacramentum Mundi*, ed. Karl Rahner (New York: Seabury Press, 1975), 1795b: "the real function of the supernatural, infused virtues is to orientate the whole religious ethical life (which itself expresses the spiritual nature of man) towards the immediate possession of God."

2. Karl Rahner, "Towards a Fundamental Theological Interpretation of Vatican II," *Theological Studies* 40, no. 4 (December 1979): 716-27, at 717. Substantially the same article appears as "Basic Theological Interpretation of the Second Vatican Council," in Karl Rahner, *Theological Investigations*, vol. 20: *Concern for the Church*, trans. Edward Quinn (New York: Crossroad, 1981), 77-89.

3. Rahner, "Towards a Fundamental Theological Interpretation of Vatican II," 721.

4. Ludwig Wittgenstein, *Tractatus Logico-Philosophicus*, trans. by D.F. Pears and B.F. McGuiness, International Library of Philosophy and Scientific Method (London: Routledge and Kegan Paul, 1961), 151.

5. All translations are from *The New Jerusalem Bible* (Garden City, New York: Doubleday, 1985).

6. H. Richard Niebuhr, *Radical Monotheism and Western Culture, with Supplementary Essays* (New York: Harper and Row, 1970).

7. Walter Lippman, *A Preface to Morals*, 111, quoted in Niebuhr, *Radical Monotheism and Western Culture* 31; in the most recent edition of Lippman's book (New York: Time-Life Books, 1964), the passage is located at 103-04.

8. Thomas Mann, *Joseph and His Brothers*, trans. by H.T. Lowe-Porter (New York: Knopf, 1983), 1133.

9. Niebuhr, *Radical Monotheism and Western Culture*, 11.

10. Niebuhr, *Radical Monotheism and Western Culture*, 32.

11. *Summa theologiae* I, q. 13, a. 5.

12. Nicholas Lash, "Reality, Wisdom and Delight," in his *The Beginning and the End of "Religion"* (Cambridge: Cambridge University Press, 1996), 49-72, at 58.

13. Lash, "Reality, Wisdom and Delight," 58.

14. See the seminal articles by Karl Rahner, "Thomas Aquinas on the Incomprehensibility of God," in David Tracy, ed., *Celebrating the Medieval Heritage: A Colloquy on the Thought of Aquinas and Bonaventure, The Journal of Religion* 58 (1978) Supplement, S107-S125, and "An Investigation of the Incomprehensibility of God in St Thomas Aquinas," in Karl Rahner, *Theological Studies*, vol. 16: *Experience of the Spirit: Source of Theology*, trans. David Morland (New York: Seabury Press, 1979), 244-54; see also the excellent study by Richard W. Miller, "Karl Rahner on Naming God," a paper delivered to the Karl Rahner Society at the Catholic Theological Society of America convention, June 10, 2000 (unpublished).

15. Lewis Carroll, *Through the Looking-Glass and What Alice Found There*, ch. 6, in Lewis Carroll, *The Annotated Alice: The Definitive Edition*, introduction and notes by Martin Gardner (New York: W.W. Norton, 2000), 213.

16. Clifford Geertz, "Religion as a Cultural System," in his *The Interpretation of Cultures* (San Francisco: Harper Collins, Basic Books, 1973), 87-125 at 89.

17. For development of this point, see Michael J. Himes, "Public Theology in Service to a National Conversation," in Edith L. Blumhofer, ed., *Religion, Politics and the American Experience: Reflections on Religion and American Public Life*, introduction by Martin Marty (Tuscaloosa: University of Alabama Press, 2002).

18. Karl Rahner, "The Church's Responsibility for the Freedom of the Individual," in *Concern for the Church*, 51-64, at 53.

19. Rahner, "The Church's Responsibility for the Freedom of the Individual," 53.

20. Rahner, "The Church's Responsibility for the Freedom of the Individual," 54.

21. T.S. Eliot, *The Complete Plays of T. S. Eliot* (New York: Harcourt, Brace and World, 1967), 187.

22. Karl Rahner, "The Church's Responsibility for the Freedom of the Individual," 56.

23. Robert Wuthnow, *After Heaven: Spirituality in America Since the 1950s* (Berkeley: University of California Press, 1998). This is many ways a sequel to his influential book of a decade before, *The Restructuring of American Religion: Society and Faith Since World War II* (Princeton: Princeton University Press, 1988).

24. Wuthnow, *After Heaven*, 2.

25. Wuthnow, *After Heaven*, 2.

26. The phrase appears in the Vatican II decree on ecumenism, *Unitatis redintegratio*, section 11.

27. Friedrich Nietzsche, *The Gay Science*, trans. Walter Kaufmann (New York: Random House, Vintage Books, 1974), 181-82.

28. Fyodor Dostoevsky, *The Brothers Karamazov*, trans. Peter Pevear and Larissa Volokhonsky (San Francisco: North Point Press, 1990), 56.

29. Johann Adam Möhler, *Symbolism: Exposition of the Doctrinal Differences between Catholics and Protestants as Evidenced by Their Symbolical Writings*, trans. James Burton Robertson; introduction by Michael J. Himes (New York: Crossroad, 1997), 266.

30. John U. Nef, recounting a story told by Erich Heller, in *The United States and Civilization*, 2nd ed. (Chicago: University of Chicago Press, 1967), 83-84.

31. John Emerich Edward Dalberg, Lord Acton, *Lectures on Modern History*, ed. John Neville Figgis and Reginald Vere Laurence (London: Macmillan, 1952), 44.

CHAPTER EIGHT

Polytheism, Henotheism, and Idolatry

FRANCIS X. CLOONEY

It is daunting to find oneself having to offer a response to a presentation by so eloquent and wise a speaker as Michael Himes. I am fundamentally in agreement with his general position and sentiments about the Catholic tradition; I share most of the values he commends and worry about most of the dangers he signals. This should not come entirely as a surprise: I come from Brooklyn too, and from a similar religious background; I did Ph.D. studies at the same university; I teach in the same department. Many of the points he makes are simply what I would have tried to say in my own words were I in his position. So I will not be proposing any sharp disagreements in substance.

My expertise is in the study of India and comparative theology, so I was naturally intrigued by Himes's discussion of monotheism and the temptation to settle for easier and less authentic alternatives. In particular I enjoyed observing his use of the categories of polytheism, henotheism, and radical monotheism, which H. Richard Niebuhr had introduced in his *Radical Monotheism and Western Culture* to sort out and explain the core of Christian identity and the temptations which dilute it. Luckily, since there are three of us who have been asked to respond, I feel authorized in narrowing my response to a particular issue: How are we to think about monotheism in relationship to polytheism, henotheism, and idolatry, and how might this affect how we teach the wisdom of our own tradition in relation to that of other religious traditions in today's world?

Let us recall how the terms are used in Himes's presentation of Niebuhr's ideas. First, he quotes Niebuhr, "Polytheism is an attitude of pure skepticism which finally ends in making all conversation about values impossible."[1] Himes adds:

Polytheism is not simply worshipping an array of gods, polytheism is positing an array of absolute goods and you pick and choose among them. You think this, I think that. You are for this, and I am for that. I am concerned about this issue, and you are concerned about that issue and they are all simply incommensurable. There is no way to discuss them; it is simply different values for different people; different strokes for different folks. It is a pure relativism which says everyone's opinion on every issue is as good as everyone else's opinion. It is a kind of democracy of the intellectual life. Whatever anyone thinks is equally valuable with what everyone else thinks. There is no possibility of genuine and meaningful conversation.

In Niebuhr's essay, as Himes cites it, henotheism is "social faith which makes a finite society, whether cultural or religious, the object of trust, as well as of loyalty, and which tends to subvert even officially monotheistic institutions such as the Church." Himes interprets Niebuhr this way:

Henotheism is the approach that says there is only one best value. Out of all the possible values, there is only one. Out of all of the many gods, only one matters, and believe in him. It is our God, our good, our value, our creed, our liturgy, our doctrine which is the finally and absolutely true and one. It subverts radical monotheism because, in fact, it becomes a kind of idolatry of the community.

Finally, Niebuhr suggests that "radical monotheism speaks of a situation in which the value center is neither a closed society nor the principle of such a society, but the principle of Being itself. Its reference is to know one reality above the many, but to one beyond all the many whence all the many derive their being and by participation in which they exist." Himes adds later on, "If I may be permitted for a moment to try and summarize the deep and rich perspective that Niebuhr offers in that article, it would be this: we do not possess the truth; the truth possesses us. Any time we speak as if we possess the truth, we are falling into henotheism, we fall into idolatry."

Thus far Niebuhr, and Niebuhr as used by Himes. It is easy to agree with them both—though a detective (writing a longer essay) might notice differences in their views—since none of us will in principle favor religious consumerism or clumsy and artificial substitutes for God. But I would like to raise a few questions about the genealogy and use of the terms "polytheism," "henotheism," "monotheism," and "idolatry" in Himes's paper. As Catholic intellectuals, after all, we need to ponder both the explicit and implicit effects of the words we speak, as well as the sources of those words.

Niebuhr himself does not tell us where he gets the terms "polytheism," "henotheism," and "monotheism." In a footnote he refers vaguely to Emile Durkheim's *The Elementary Forms of Religion* as a source for ideas on mythologies and cults, but at least in that work Durkheim does not use the terms we are interested in. The likely source, though not mentioned by Niebuhr, is F. Max Müller, the great nineteenth century scholar of religion and pioneer Indologist who was generally considered the first to make widespread good use of "henotheism." In one of his 1878 *Hibbert Lectures*, for instance, Müller took up the topic of "Henotheism, Polytheism, Monotheism, Atheism."[2] He begins the lecture with the question, "Is monotheism a primitive form of religion?" Drawing on examples from the ancient Vedic religion of India, Müller argues that henotheism—derived from the Greek "hen" (one) rather than "monos" (one only)—was the oldest form of religion evident in the Vedic cult which had already diverged from a thorough polytheism (if it had ever embraced it previously). According to Müller, henotheism aimed at acknowledging divine presence in specific single objects recognized as particularly and compellingly worthy of respect. Ritually, this attitude functions as "a successive belief in single supreme gods" which must be kept "distinct from that phase of religious thought which we commonly call polytheism, in which the many gods are already subordinated to one supreme god, and by which therefore the craving after the one without a second has been more fully satisfied."[3] In Müller's essay, monotheism, in which the multiplicity of gods is banished, succeeds both henotheism and polytheism, as one God becomes not only the immediate but also enduring and perpetual object of worship, to the exclusion of all others. We can also note though that for Müller atheism, in which the personality of particular deities and even of a supreme deity is put aside, goes beyond monotheism. His interest heads in this direction since he is interested too in non-theistic Indian thought, particularly the great Vedanta traditions, some of which are not theistic but instead nondualist. Obviously, neither Niebuhr nor Himes engages Müller's whole project of theorizing about where monotheism and atheism came from in the first place; both have a specifically Christian theological notion of monotheism in mind, even if Niebuhr's monotheistic apprehension of "the principle of being" does not seem identical with Himes's God-language.

In a longer and very learned response with copious footnotes someone might also, as Müller himself did, turn again to the study of ancient India, in order to (re)gain insights into what henotheism, polytheism, monotheism, and atheism meant in that context. Such would be a worthy service to this discussion, since ancient India has preserved for us so many interesting aspects of the religious history of the human race in general, and it would be worthwhile to balance our considerable knowledge of the West with more knowledge of other cultures and traditions. Here I will offer only a few summary observations based on my own reflection on the gods and worship of gods in India, as found in ancient Indian ritual texts such as the hymns of the three thousand year old *Rg Veda.*[4]

To be a Hindu polytheist, as distinct from a Niebuhrian polytheist, is to be aware of multiple divine presences in the world. This awareness opens up opportunities to apprehend the numerous arrivals of the Divine in our experience, in our world, and through our rituals, in our practice and worship. It seems that very many Hindu polytheists over many millennia have dealt with the multiplicity of gods by reinterpreting it as symbolic, or as a complex manifestation of the one. In some cases, the many gods are servants of the single highest and true deity. The reason why a polytheist does not immediately become a monist or a monotheist, insofar as people might be imagined to be stepping back and making conscious choices in this regard, has something to do with honoring the possibilities and not denying the fact that there are many different ways we can encounter the Divine. The polytheistic claim, even if formalized as a claim about divinities, is not at all the same as a loss of the possibility of saying anything definite nor need it be "a pure relativism which says everyone's opinion on every issue is as good as everyone else's opinion."

We should be able to honor the polytheistic insight at least as a general principle in our theology and our teaching: there is not just one possibility, but many, and even the apparently best possibility need not eradicate the multitude of good ones. Filtered through a monotheistic perspective, for instance, a polytheistic perspective might nonetheless be honored as asking us whether God, who has spoken to us in certain ways, might also speak to others in other ways; whether the truths we apprehend in certain concepts and words and images might be rendered thinkable to others by other concepts and words and images; and whether the tradition which makes sense to us and gives us life need be taken as the only successful life-giving tradition. Whatever our answers, no or yes, we are the better off for the asking of the questions as real questions.

Concerning henotheism, it is surely possible for people in any culture to have contempt for views other than their own, and to reduce everything to what one happens to believe right now. But it is not clear that "henotheism" is the word to characterize such attitudes or that monotheism is the sole antidote. As I understand early Indian worship, the dynamic of henotheism was not to deny the other, but rather to appreciate and immerse oneself in whichever encounter one experienced at any given moment, without being distracted by other possibilities, even better ones. Every word, even in blame of others, is subsidiary to praise of the one before whom one stands in worship. At appropriate moments in a ritual performance, the god or goddess being invoked is addressed with high praise and reverence, as *the* deity best suited to help the performer at *this* present time. The experience is total, one is not looking over the deity's shoulder to see if someone more influential might be passing by.

A henotheist might then be taken as reminding us not to be paralyzed by the multiplicity of possibilities, the tyranny of the generic "better" or the tyranny of the generic "best," and not to conclude immediately that to make a good choice I must deny that other choices might be made, by myself or others, at other times. Rather, one is challenged to stand in humility before the various presences of the divine in the world, and to offer full commitment, here and now, as we are able. Although modern Americans and Christians may not be able to be henotheists in an ancient Indian sense, we certainly should be able to discuss how imperfect, incomplete, and finite choices can still be honorable and holy, and how my firm affirmation of the truth as I see it now does not preclude different affirmations in different contexts. This interpretation seems more fruitful than saying that henotheism "says there is only one best value. Out of all the possible values, there is only one. Out of all of the many gods, only one matters, and believe in him . . . Any time we speak as if we possess the truth, we are falling into henotheism, we fall into idolatry."

Perhaps this is the point at which I should include a comment on idolatry. I have known some fine and virtuous idolaters, Hindus deeply devoted to consecrated embodiments of a deity dear to them, in temples large or small, on Indian mountaintops or on street corners or in American suburbs. One of the things I have learned about idolatry is how idolaters are able to affirm that a particular image—this stone carving or that wooden figure or that image painted on a wall—can, even in the context of obvious fragility and limitation, be loved, chosen, and worshipped as holy, as a gift of divine immediacy. Idolaters I know do not think that every block of wood or every stone is God (or a god), even if for some of them, as for us, God is everywhere and in all things; they do not expect images to start talking or to defend themselves if struck by a zealous skeptic; they do not forget that God is more than stone and wood. For the majority of Hindu idolaters who are theists, idolatry is also about divine vulnerability: to be near to devotees, God chooses to be vulnerable and limited, confined by love to particular very small places. There is something profound and very powerful in idol worship, and Catholics at least should be able to recognize this kind of love and recognition, as at least similar to the Eucharist. There would be no shame in saying that Hindu idolaters and Catholics devoted to the Blessed Sacrament have a great deal in common. In any case, idolatry need not be taken as a defense of the view that "we alone possess the truth"—an attitude to which iconoclasts have yielded as often as idolaters.

Finally, let us consider monotheism. Here too, I agree with most of what Himes has to say. The self-manifestation of God—Father, Son, and Holy Spirit—is a gift, a terrifying gift, something God reveals to us, not something we figure out on our own. To stand on the brink and yield to the monotheistic intuition opens us to the mystery of the Divine, teaches us to be silent, at best to speak with a kind of stutter because we know we can never say properly what God is and has done for us. We can fill out this story too, confessing that for the people of Israel discovering the one true God was also to acknowledge the pain of slavery, alienation in a foreign land, the celebration of Passover, crossing the Red Sea and receiving those great first and second commandments at Sinai. We are blessed if we can remember and honor this great gift in our lives.

But one can do well or poorly in speaking of monotheism, and it is important to consider the uses to which we put the term. Niebuhr works with his own sense of radical monotheism, the confidence "that Being is God, or, better, that the principle of being, the source of all things and the power by which they exist, is good, as good for them and good to them."[5] In a footnote in his book, Niebuhr concedes that he does not want automatically to extend his thoughts on monotheism to other cultures: "In confining the ensuing discussion to Western culture I do not wish to imply that radical monotheism has emerged nowhere else. The question of the relation of this form of faith to the monisms of the East is left aside partly because I am not prepared by intimate knowledge to explore it, partly because the present situation seems to require first of all critical self-knowledge on the part of Western man if his encounters with the East are to be fruitful."[6]

Himes seems to be talking more directly about God and God as present in our thinking, praying, and worshipping, but it seems fair to ask Himes whether there isn't at least a hint of Catholic self-congratulation at work when he says:

> Because the truth possesses us, we do not possess the truth. We cannot be polytheists because that renders all intellectual conversation impossible. We cannot be henotheists because that renders all intellectual conversation unnecessary. Only monotheism allows us to engage in genuine conversation with insistence that the conversation is important, but never absolutely final. One of the ways that the Church has recognized this over the centuries, is the traditional way of formulating doctrine—the *via negativa*. Let anyone who says thus and so be anathema. The doctrinal formulae told us what could not be taught: you cannot go beyond this point and you cannot go beyond that point. If you teach anything beyond this, you are outside the circle of belief; if you say anything beyond that, you are out. But in here—all is possible and should be prayerfully pursued. The attempt to claim to speak with positive precision always leads to idolatry. The Church needs to explore that much more richly and deeply.

But I cannot resist intruding with my own rhetorical flourish here, observing that more than once there have been problems with monotheism and those who live by monotheism, problems not resolved simply by stating that monotheism is fine while monotheists remain sinners.[7] The interesting issue of anathemas aside, it would be naïve for us and not credible with our students were we to give the impression that the story of radical monotheism in the Bible is simply a happy and wise celebration of The Great and Gracious Mystery. There is the problem of the slaughter of the first born of the Egyptians and the soldiers in the Red Sea, the slaughter of the Amalekites and the Moabites, the indigenous peoples God smites on behalf of his own people, and there is the problem of I Kings 18, wherein Eli'jah challenges the four hundred and fifty prophets of Ba'al and the four hundred prophets of Ashe'rah to a contest in which they will demonstrate whose divinity is more attentive and more active. After the priests of Ba'al and Ashe'rah have failed, despite their best efforts, to bring down divine fire on their altar,

> Eli'jah said to all the people, "Come near to me"; and all the people came near to him. And he repaired the altar of the Lord that had been thrown down; Eli'jah took twelve stones, according to the number of the tribes of the sons of Jacob, to whom the word of the Lord came, saying, "Israel shall be your name"; and with the stones he built an altar in the name of the Lord. And he made a trench about the altar, as great as would contain two measures of seed. And he put the wood in order, and cut the bull in pieces and laid it on the wood. And he said, "Fill four jars with water, and pour it on the burnt offering, and on the wood." And he said, "Do it a second time"; and they did it a second time. And he said, "Do it a third time"; and they did it a third time. And the water ran round about the altar, and filled the trench also with water. And at the time of the offering of the oblation, Eli'jah the prophet came near and said, "O Lord, God of Abraham, Isaac, and Israel, let it be known this day that thou art God in Israel, and that I am thy servant, and that I have done all these things at thy word. Answer me, O Lord, answer me, that this people may know that thou, O Lord, art God, and that thou hast turned their hearts back." Then the fire of the Lord fell, and consumed the burnt offering, and the wood, and the stones, and the dust, and licked up the water that was in the trench. And when all the people saw it, they fell on their faces; and they said, "The Lord, he is God; the Lord, he is God."

Neither a polytheist nor a henotheist, Eli'jah adds a final touch:

> And Eli'jah said to them, "Seize the prophets of Ba'al; let not one of them escape." And they seized them;

and Eli'jah brought them down to the brook Kishon,
and killed them there. (I Kings 18.19-40)

Such texts are part of our tradition, and reflection on monotheism
would be incomplete without some discussion of them. What
might a polytheist or henotheist or idolater say about Eli'jah? Our
students should know this kind of report too, if our educational
institutions are to stand for both "intellectual" and "Catholic."

The point of course is not to turn things around and suggest
that we monotheists are nasty, while polytheists, henotheists, and
idolaters are the nicest of people. Different people do well and
poorly in different contexts, and no single rule covers all cases. I
am talking rather about the claims we end up making or seem to
be making about people in other traditions as we sort out the
claims we wish to make about ourselves. Our Christian monotheistic commitment is a precious gift from God and should not
lead to contempt for the other, intolerance, or violence. But if we
are to encourage our students to think through the issues discussed
by Himes at the heart of his presentation, we cannot afford to
give them even the impression that monotheism is intelligent and
virtuous, while polytheism, henotheism, and idolatry are narrow-
minded, mistaken, and vicious. Even if we believe that the gift of
knowledge of God has a profound effect on our lives, we cannot
convincingly draw a straight and exceptionless line from
"monotheism" to "good" and "true" or from "henotheism" and
"polytheism" to "bad" and "false." Unless disclaimers—such as
Niebuhr's footnote cited above—are explicit, a claim about us
(such as Himes intends) may very well seem to be also a claim
about people quite different from ourselves. It is too likely that
some of our students at least will begin to think of other real
people, such as Hindus, to be precisely the polytheists,
henotheists, and idolaters who are obscured in our shadow. Even
if some critical assessments of others are true, the task in the
classroom is to indicate how we could possibly know this, and
what lessons are to be drawn from our discovery of the failures of
others. We want our students to think, not to congratulate
themselves at the expense of people unlike ourselves.

My point then is a practical and pedagogical one. If Himes has so finely used the India-Müller-Niebuhr series of concepts and words in order to say something very wise and important about what we need to remember and what we need to resist if we are to be humble and intelligent Catholics, he and we still need to remind ourselves that we have not said something humble and intelligent about the polytheists, henotheists, and idolaters of the world. But if their story is unheard and their theories unthought, ours too are incomplete. If we Christians are by the grace of God monotheists, then too, by the grace of God and out of respect for the intellectual life, we need to make it clear that we have much to learn before we draw conclusions about "henotheists" and "polytheists" and "idolaters." Who knows: some may find their way into our classrooms, and it would be a shame to overlook them.

Notes

1. F. Max Müller, "Henotheism, Polytheism, Monotheism, Atheism," in *The Hibbert Lectures on Origin and Growth of Religion, Collected Works*, vol. 6 (London: Longmans, Green, and Company, 1898). 260-316. More briefly, see for instance, F. Max Müller, *Introduction of the Science of Religion: Four Lectures Delivered at the Royal Institution in February and May, 1870* (London: Longmans, Green, and Co., 1899), 80-82. Except where noted, my quotations from Niebuhr are from passages cited by Himes. Page references can be found in his text.

2. Müller, "Henotheism, Polytheism, Monotheism, Atheism," 277. Müller's understanding polytheism as dependent on monotheism differs from my own, since I would posit a polytheism in which the multiplicity of gods remains multiple and unsubordinated to a single supreme deity.

3. For a sampling of Vedic hymns, see Wendy Doniger, *The Rg Veda: An Anthology* (New York: Penguin Books, 1981); and Raimundo Panikkar, *The Vedic Experience Mantramanjari: An Anthology of the Vedas for Modern Man and Contemporary Celebration* (Berkeley: University of California, 1977).

4. H. Richard Niebuhr, *Radical Monotheism and Western Culture* (New York: Harper Torchbooks, 1970), 38.

5. Niebuhr, *Radical Monotheism and Western Culture*, 38, note 1.

6. See Regina M. Schwartz, *The Curse of Cain: The Violent Legacy of Monotheism* (Chicago: University of Chicago Press, 1997).

CHAPTER NINE

On the Goals of Catholic Education

Louis Dupré

I am very happy that I did not receive even the two-page outline of Professor Himes's lecture because I would be in a bad situation if I had. I would have to criticize something with which I agree 100 percent. I would have tried to match an eloquence, the like of which I have never seen. What we heard is actually Catholic common sense raised to a level of wisdom, insight, eloquence, and art. All the time he was speaking, I was thinking of G.K. Chesterton. Maybe Chesterton would also qualify this a little bit. I am, as you might suspect, a monotheist, but not a radical monotheist. Radical monotheism is too radical for me. I leave that to our Protestant brothers and sisters. As a Catholic, I know what is the essence of Catholicism for me. It is in Chesterton, "if a thing is worth doing, it's worth doing poorly." That is a very comforting thought to me.

I believe in the communion of saints, as Fr. Himes would say. We are together here, and we are many people out together, and there is a mess. Many people are starving, stumbling to a common end and they never really get there. But this is part of why I like to be a Catholic and could never be, if I may say so, a Protestant, as Mr. Niebuhr was.

First of all, what is education? Briefly, education has traditionally consisted of integrating and incorporating the young into the structures and values of a particular society for better or worse. We know what Socrates had to say about it. In the modern world, that means that we have to incorporate them into a tradition that gets longer and longer. There are more and more books to be read, there is more to be known, and the pace has accelerated in the last fifty years beyond compare. Education has become so revolutionized in scientific and technical terms that to speak of a humanistic education in the same way that we spoke about it in the past makes no sense at all. One is not a humanist today if one does not know something about science or modern technology. So this is the new incorporation.

Second, for the Catholic student there is an additional task, which may well be the central task, mainly to raise the young within a Catholic tradition—a tradition which also, as you know, is in full change. As Archbishop Rembrandt Weakland put it very clearly—but threateningly—our generation wants all institutions of higher education to be academically excellent, to form leaders in American society, who have vision and values, to work hard at the larger and greater Catholic tradition of learning. We want our graduate students to know the Catholic tradition, even when they decide to reject it. Most of us are convinced that such tradition is not just one of private religion but also that has something to say to this world and to American society. I could not agree more. But this is a very tall order. It is not easy.

Allow me to approach the purely intellectual task, the education of the young into the modern world and into the humanistic tradition. We Catholics have to do a lot of catching up to do. One may remember that about fifty years ago, Monsignor John Tracy Ellis said, "Catholics in America are not non-intellectuals, they are anti-intellectual." I believe when I first immigrated to this country, this was to some extent still true. Of course, we had great Catholic intellectuals, whom we already had in the nineteenth century. But there was a great deal of catching-up to be done. At this point, this is no longer true. We have a great Catholic intellectual tradition, and we are being recognized, which we were not at that time. No Catholic institution, not even Notre Dame, Boston College, Fordham, or Georgetown were taken seriously. Today they are. But they are also being recognized within the secular academia. It is rather remarkable that the Divinity school at Yale and the Religious Studies Department at

Harvard, both fortresses in the past of anti-Catholic thinking, now have Catholics as their leaders.

So the situation is obviously changed. But what does this mean and what is the lesson? We are there? No. The lesson is this: we can no longer invoke the lame argument in the past that we can do whatever we want to because they do not recognize us. It is true that there has been, and continues to be, anti-Catholicism. But we have proven ourselves and cannot fall back into mediocrity with the excuse of an anti-Catholic environment. It does exist, but not in terms of quality. They expect that if we are running a university, we had better run a good university.

From an intellectual point of view, we in the United States are in a particularly favorable position. If one takes just the order of the Jesuits, they have twenty-eight universities in the United States alone. This is incredible, by any standards. That means that this single religious order is a more widespread infrastructure than anything else in the country. So why don't we use it? Because I still feel that there is still too much mediocrity. We are still too rapidly satisfied with what we have done, and we still think too easily "It's good enough for us because we have Catholicism, we have the truth anyway." That does not work. We have to continue to prove ourselves to God and to each other. What is particularly disturbing is that we, by the very nature of our religion and by the very nature of our training in Catholic schools, we are too inclined to take things for granted, not to criticize them, and not to investigate them.

This brings me to the point of the Catholic identity. As you know, there is a general feeling that we are losing our identity. I do not think I reveal any secrets when I say that some universities have lost it in such a way that it will be very difficult to retrieve. This is a matter of great concern to me.

The question is, what is it to be Catholic? Here again, I think we take it too lightly. We take too much for granted. To be Catholic does not consist of simply repeating formulas that we find in the *Catechism*, or in papal encyclicals, not even in the most recent ones. Those things are fine, but they are not sufficient. I think that we must be more Catholic in a far more fundamental sense. Yesterday, we spoke about Catholic literacy and the example of the Real Presence. I do not think it is going to be particularly helpful if one explains to hisor her students, those who are involved in theology, "Well, that is very simple, that means transubstantiation." I must admit, and my field is philosophy, I do not know what a substance is, so even I would have real problems with this. Is it something like what Spinoza said? I do not think that most Catholic sacramental theologians would be very happy with that. Or is it something like what Descartes said, who was in this trouble already in his lifetime and had to explain that this substance could be reconciled with the Eucharist? That is not the point. Let us not simply repeat formulas. But at the same time it is extremely important, whether you put it this way or another way, that we believe in the Real Presence, that we explain what is the Real Presence. To me it means that we have to make a personal and creative effort to understand what we are talking about.

Fr. Himes has done us all a great service by reminding us about common sense. There are many things that we have known all along and at the end of the day they all looked different. I believe this. Perhaps one of the helpful things about being a Catholic educator is to believe in Catholicism. And that means not repeating, but digesting it. It has to become part of us. These formulas have to be surrounded by a spiritual halo, by the spiritual life, by the concrete spirituality of thought. It is not sufficient for a Catholic school to say it has a tremendous theology teacher or an excellent department. It is a matter of penetrating the whole faculty with this kind of meaningfulness of the Catholic mystery. In other words, if I teach English literature, or French literature, I have to be inspired by the same Spirit. This is a very tall order, and I do not know how I can accomplish it completely, but at least I would like to try to do it.

I remember in earlier days saying to my students, most of whom are idolatrists at best, "Now look, I'm not going to apologize here for belonging to the religion of Pascal, Descartes, Mozart and Cardinal Newman. Shed your inferiority complex, it's high time for being Catholic. Do you know that you come from a tradition which is not just poor immigrants, but which is the tradition of some of the greatest minds of history?" Catholicism is a wonderful thing as long as one has the courage to accept it, to think it through, to let it radiate and penetrate everything. But to do that, we have to be absolutely free. We Catholics keep saying *veritas vos liberabit.* We say that, but does it? Why do we so quickly go back to a formula, an encyclical or something else that denies the free expression and creative searching of the truth? We must be free to think and challenge in order to find the deepest of truths.

CHAPTER TEN

A Critical Look at
the Catholic Intellectual Tradition

URSULA KING

I am here because I have contributed a chapter to the first
volume on the Catholic intellectual tradition. I see myself as
both an insider and an outsider. I feel I am an insider in the
Catholic intellectual tradition because I am a professor of Theology
and Religious Studies. I have been brought up in the Catholic
tradition, and I have worked in research for more than forty years.
I am actually the previous generation to Fr. Himes. My childhood
was in the 1940s, not the 1950s. But the more I live in this tradition,
the more I hear such brilliant speeches, presented like seamless
garments, I feel that the beauty, the majesty, the glory of the Catholic
tradition is all there. Yet, I am also deeply uncomfortable and hurt.

Looking at the program I am the only speaker here from outside
America—from Europe—unless Professor Dupré is also counted as
being of European extraction. But I look at the Catholic intellectual
tradition somewhat differently than you.

The Catholic intellectual tradition is not identical with
Catholic institutions, especially not with American institutions.
My experience with the Catholic intellectual tradition comes from
different places in Germany, France, and England, where part of
the tradition developed historically, and also from India, where I
lived, studied, and taught for five years.

Looking at the Catholic intellectual tradition critically, I think
we need a new paradigm. Fr. Himes spoke about the crisis we are

in, and to deal with that requires a new paradigm. I think Hans Küng has clearly shown how many different paradigm shifts have occurred throughout the history of the Church in his book about global theology, and it is imperative that we look at the Catholic intellectual tradition from a global perspective.[1]

Allow me to present some statistics. According to a report in the German *Frankfurter Allgemeine Zeitung* (May 5, 2000), the Vatican published *The Statistical Yearbook of the Catholic Church* in the year 2000, but the data are from December 1998. According to this source, Catholics represent 1.04 billion people worldwide (that is 17.4% of the global population), of which 49.5% live in the two Americas. That is to say that 28.4% of all Catholics live in Latin America alone, which is just a little more than in Europe, where 27.8% of all Catholics live today. In other words, there are more Catholics living in South America alone than in Europe, and there are far more Catholics living in the whole of the Americas than in Europe. In other words, Catholicism as a living tradition is now far more represented in other parts of the globe than in Europe.

What does that say about developing the Catholic intellectual tradition? We may be too concerned with being too past-oriented by always looking backwards. We have to look forward instead. What is this tradition going to produce? In this brief talk, I could have said something about faith, hope, and charity, as I had originally intended to do. But I have decided otherwise because I now feel much more uncomfortable with the Catholic intellectual tradition since I realize its ambivalence far more than when I wrote my chapter for the first volume on the Catholic intellectual tradition. There I outlined the global challenges, the gender challenges, and the spiritual challenges that are put to the intellectual tradition of Catholicism. Based on my earlier work on spirituality I asserted that if there is a future for the Church, it will be a Church for the mystics.

It must also be a Church where women are more equally represented and take a fuller part than is the case now. Kathleen Mahoney points out that there is a lack of an adequate representation of women in the Catholic Church. And that is one of the greatest injustices and deepest hurts. Can you hear the violence of abstraction in theological speech? Michael Himes mentioned it at the very end of his brilliant lecture where he referred to just two women, Catherine of Siena and Teresa of Avila, as part of the ongoing intellectual conversation. But what are two women within an entire theological tradition marked by a great oppressive patriarchal expression?

If we look at the Catholic intellectual tradition not from a universal point of view where everybody is meant to be included, but from a women's point of view, then women have been marginalized and assumed to be invisible in much of the tradition. There are many women's resources in the Catholic intellectual tradition. We have had great women theologians in the Middle Ages, and we have had not only Church Fathers, but also Church Mothers.[2] Many of these women leaders have never been brought fully into speech nor have they been made equal, recognized, and been welcomed in the Church. Through my forty years of teaching and research, I have experienced personally, physically, mentally and spiritually what it means to be a woman in intellectual life—and there are many traces of hurt and pain. I spoke about this very briefly in a lecture I recently gave in Oxford, and an American Catholic woman student came up to me afterwards and said, "I feel so liberated when I hear a woman speak. Until now, I have only heard men speaking here."

Only men in theology? Where are the women? You know that a lot of women among the audience here carry a lot of the educational and missionary tasks of the Church. Women do so much for the Church: they work at parish level, catechetical level, and liturgical level. But officially they do not seem to be there, or they are only half there in terms of official representation and recognition. I think this absence of women reflects very badly on the Catholic intellectual tradition. If the Church does not meet the challenges of gender equity and justice, if it does not respond to the cry of women, there will be no Church in the twenty-first century because women will leave and seek their spiritual nourishment and fields of activity elsewhere.

In previous years I, like several other women theologians, have held the office of President of the European Society of Women in Theological Research. We have sought to have a dialogue with Cardinal Ratzinger about women's theological work, but with little success. We have especially tried to stand up for women theologians to get jobs in German universities, which has been somewhat more successful. The situation is extremely difficult since the Vatican is full of fear and ignorance as far as women's theological development and work are concerned. Many church representatives actually do not know what is happening in terms of creative breakthroughs in feminist theological circles today. There exist many creative and inspiring developments which can be truly affirming of women, men, and children through promoting justice, peace, and the dignity of creation.[3]

The intellectual as well as existential and experiential developments among Christian women have to do with faith. They have to do with hope. They have to do with love, and with community building. We really have to give this more thought. In a way, this links up with the theme of pluralism which encourages the diversity to rejoice, to celebrate life in all its diversity. This celebration proceeds from the great panorama of biological evolution to the wonderful web of life with all its different levels and its diversity of people, to the diversity of religious faiths and the many mysterious expressions of the spirit with their disclosure of divine mystery.

When you look at the Church, I think pluralism is the foundation of the Catholic intellectual tradition. When speaking of the Catholic intellectual tradition, there often seems to be a strong temptation to think of the monolithic medieval European Church, or post-Tridentine absolutist and centralized Church teaching, as if we were all standing *en bloc* like a military regiment, all marching in the same direction behind the same banner and the same general. Well, the Christian church did not start like that. The Jesus movement of the early church was quite different. It was far more complex and diversified. For example, when one looks at the letters of St. Paul to the Corinthians, there was in the colony of Corinth a melee of Greeks, Romans, Egyptians, people from all over the ancient Middle East, as there were in many other cities around the Mediterranean. Pluralistic foundations were there from the very beginnings of the New Testament, in the early church and throughout the history of the church. Pluralism is really at the heart of the Christian tradition. As Christians we are following a vision, a call, a mission, but we can come to it from very different directions indeed. It is essential for the Catholic Church and the Catholic intellectual tradition to rethink its own identity and history, and also to dialogue with contemporary culture and all its revelatory moments, which can be seen as signs of the times, as when the Second Vatican Council was called.

Yet we have a problem. We can see that the Catholic intellectual tradition gives us a glorious inheritance. Today, this inheritance is particularly precious, but also exceptionally vulnerable in the context of our profoundly changing culture. We are at a critical threshold in the development of human evolution and that of growing globalization. I think we have to reconceptualize what it means to be a Catholic intellectual. We need to carefully consider not only what we are handing on and handing over, but how does this tradition make sense to our lives, how does it feed our spirit, and how does it nourish our community? I know the Church needs structures for transmitting teachings, experiences, and visions. But whether the structures we have in place are actually sufficiently flexible, sufficiently open as Francis Clooney mentioned so beautifully in his paper, I am not so sure.[4]

How do we transmit the fire of the Spirit, the message about God? Father Robert Imbelli spoke about the loss of a robust Christic center. I fully agree. But what do you understand by a Christic center? Is it merely a central focal point, a rarefied doctrinal teaching, or even an ideology? Or is part of a deep religious and mystical experience where we encounter a Christic center as the heart of the world, a center which radiates outwards, which is dynamic, which is living, which is present wherever you are, in the way that Teilhard de Chardin spoke about the heart of God at the center of the world?[5]

I have written a great deal about Pierre Teilhard de Chardin.[6] It is sad, if not tragic, to see that the publicly acclaimed Catholic intellectual tradition, which is fed in many different ways, does not seem to include him, perhaps because he was not an insider of Catholic institutions. After he left the Catholic Institute in Paris, he worked always in secular institutions. But he certainly was a great Catholic intellectual, and a great Catholic mystic of the twentieth century. Why is it that a man of such deep spirituality, Christ-centeredness, and deep Christic mysticism—where everything came together in the fiery heart of Christ, where the fire of the spirit runs through his entire vision of the world—has officially been taken so little note of? Why is it that Catholic intellectual institutions today make so little use of such a splendid resource?

I leave you with that question. Perhaps its answer lies in living with greater faith, hope, and love.

Notes

1. See Hans Küng *Theology for the Third Millennium: An Ecumenical View* (New York: Doubleday, 1988).

2. See, for example, Laura Swan, *The Forgotten Desert Mothers. Sayings, Lives and Stories of Early Christian Women* (Mahwah, New Jersey: Paulist Press, 2001).

3. See, as one example among many other publications, the volume edited by Elisabeth Schüssler-Fiorenza, *The Power of Naming: A Concilium Reader in Feminist Liberation Theology* (Maryknoll, New York: Orbis Books, 1996).

4. Francis X. Clooney, "Polytheism, Henotheism, and Idolatry," in this volume, 105-15.

5. See Pierre Teilhard de Chardin, *The Heart of Matter* (New York: Harcourt Brace Jovanovich, 1978).

6. See my books *Spirit of Fire: The Life and Vision of Teilhard de Chardin* (Maryknoll, New York: Orbis Books, 1996); and *All Things in Christ: Exploring Spirituality with Teilhard de Chardin* (Maryknoll, New York: Orbis Books, 1997).

HANDING ON THE TRADITION

CHAPTER ELEVEN

The Jesuit Ideal of a Teacher:
A Complex and Developing Tradition

GERALD A. McCOOL

Although Jesuits have been working in the classroom for several centuries, their founder, Saint Ignatius of Loyola, did not set out to be an educator. Before his wounding at Pamplona, Ignatius had been a soldier by profession, and, after his conversion at Loyola, he chose the life of a pilgrim and a penitent. Indeed, even after the founding of the Society of Jesus, neither Ignatius nor his first companions thought that their corporate work would include long hours at the teacher's desk. Their aim was to serve their Church as a group of free-lance apostles, placed at the disposition of the Holy See, ready for any task assigned to it. Sanctification of their neighbor, rather than his intellectual improvement, was to be the goal of their apostolate. Jesuit educational work was undertaken only when Jesuits found themselves drawn into it through their answer to an urgent apostolic call.[1] Ignatius had been asked to found a college at Messina and he felt compelled to do so. But as haphazard as that initial commitment to education might appear, once Ignatius had made it, it turned into a decisive option. In the final years of his own life, Ignatius opened thirty-five colleges; and, as each school was founded, he followed every step in the process with personal interest. He wanted detailed information about the administrative structure of the school and the program of studies to be followed in it; and no decision of consequence was to be made about these matters without his knowledge and consent.[2] There can be no doubt then that the Jesuit interest in education and the Jesuit willingness to commit the best resources of their order to that work goes back to their order's founder, Ignatius of Loyola.

Jesuit Schools in the "Old Society"

That interest never flagged. Successive Superior Generals continued Ignatius' support for the Jesuit apostolate of education; and, as the order grew, the institutional base of that apostolate expanded. By 1599, the year in which Claudio Aquaviva ended decades of discussion by approving the definitive *Ratio Studiorum*, the uniform program of studies to be followed in every Jesuit school, there were 245 schools. By the first decade of the eighteenth century, the number of Jesuit colleges added up to 612, and by the middle of that century their number had reached 669, without counting another 176 seminaries under Jesuit direction.[3] Unfortunately, however, success can have its price, and a quarter of a century later, there were no Jesuit schools at all. For, in 1773, under the pressure of the Bourbon monarchies, Clement XIV suppressed the Society of the Jesus and the history of education in what Jesuits would later call the "Old Society" came to its close.[4]

The schools of that "Old Society" were in a class by themselves, not only because of their large number, unified control, and identical curriculum but also because of their strategic location over the broad expanse of Europe, Asia, and the Americas. In almost every land to which the Jesuits had come they seemed to have opened schools. There were Jesuit colleges and universities in Italy, Spain, Portugal, France, the Low Countries, the German and Austrian lands, and Poland. Even in turbulent seventeenth-century Ireland the Jesuit college at Kilkenny had managed to stay in operation for a while; and in the Spanish Netherlands, Robert Persons had opened the Jesuit college at Saint Omer, to which for more than two centuries young English Catholics came across the channel for their education.[5] The Apostle of the Indies, Saint Francis Xavier, had opened a college at Goa, and other Jesuit apostles had done the same in Mexico, Brazil, Argentina, Peru and, across the Pacific, in the Philippines.[6] Even in our own Maryland, breaking the law, of course, John Carroll, the founder of the American hierarchy, and his cousin Charles, the signer of the Declaration of Independence, had attended a small Jesuit school at Bohemia Manor before they were sent abroad together to continue their education at Saint Omer.[7]

Jesuit history tells us that in the centuries between the foundation of their order and its suppression, the priests and scholastics of the "Old Society" had been able to keep in operation, through their tightly woven network of colleges and universities, an influential, effective, uniform, highly organized, international system of Catholic education. In its heyday, the Jesuit system had no equal. In Europe, Asia, and the American colonies of Spain and Portugal, thousands of students of many nationalities were able to receive their secondary and higher education completely free of charge in colleges and universities fully endowed by benefactors of the Society.[8] For many a poor boy in Europe and the Americas, the Jesuit college in his town had become his gateway to opportunity.

This did not mean, of course, that everybody was a friend of the Jesuit schools. Influenced as they were by Ignatius' *Spiritual Exercises* and by the theology of Saint Thomas, which Ignatius had ordered Jesuits to make their own, Jesuit educators took an optimistic view of human nature and of its possibilities. It followed then that, as teachers, preachers, and confessors, Jesuits showed themselves staunch defenders of the freedom of the will. Like Ignatius, who had received a humanistic education at Paris, Jesuits were partisans of Renaissance literary humanism.[9] Following the Paris model, which Ignatius had prescribed for their own education, the Jesuits made the pagan authors of Greece and Rome, judiciously expurgated, the core of the graded sequence of courses in grammar, poetry, and rhetoric that prepared their students for the subsequent study of science and philosophy.[10] In advising their students or in guiding the penitents who came to them for counsel, Jesuits had been taught to respect the liberty of the individual conscience.[11] In consequence, the Jesuit style of teaching, preaching, and counselling, as we know from our reading of Pascal's *Provincial Letters*, was of the sort which was bound to scandalize the morally rigid Jansenists of seventeenth- and eighteenth-century Europe; and unfortunately for the Jesuits, the Jansenists were both numerous and influential.[12]

The Jesuits made other enemies as well. The curriculum of the Jesuit colleges and universities, the theology taught in them, and the internal administration of each school were completely in the hands of an international religious order subject only to the Holy See. The Gallican theologians of the seventeenth and eighteenth centuries and their allies in the legal bureaucracies of the European monarchies felt that the educational independence which the Jesuit schools enjoyed was an intolerable challenge to the firm control that officials of the crown, the courts, and the institutions of the national church should have over education in a well-run state. Exceptions of that sort, they felt, were dangerous.[13]

In the age of the Enlightenment, when deism and skepticism began to spread among the upper classes of Europe, the classes from which the advisers of its kings and queens were drawn, a new complaint was made about Jesuit education. Exception was now being taken to the supernatural viewpoint of Jesuit teachers and administrators. Jesuits taught in their schools as part of their Apostolic service to the Church, and, as a result, the aim of their teaching was to prepare their students to live a life of faith and of Christian service to their neighbor. For the Enlightenment *philosophes*, however, that was not the scientific type of education that the modern world required. Modern education should be guided by what the *philosophes* conceived to be the philosophical worldview of Locke and Newton. This meant that education should be completely secular in outlook and that its aim should be to prepare an enlightened, free-thinking citizen for the service of his state. The national state then and not an international religious order should have control of the education given by the state to its future citizens.[14]

The Jansenists, the Gallicans, and the Enlightenment intellectuals and bureaucrats had no great love for one another, but they were united in their hatred of Jesuit education. In the third quarter of the eighteenth century, then, they cemented their alliance and their orchestrated campaign for the suppression of the Society of Jesus got under way. When that campaign succeeded, as it did in 1773 with the suppression of the Society of Jesus, the system of Jesuit schools went out of existence.

Jesuit Schools in the "New Society"

Jesuit schools appeared again with the restoration of the Society in the early nineteenth century; but neither in number nor in quality could these nineteenth-century schools rival the Jesuit schools of former days. Trained Jesuit teachers were in short supply, as their order struggled to re-establish itself, in a Church whose religious and educational institutions had suffered greatly in the turmoil caused by the French Revolution.[15] Nineteenth-century civil governments were often hostile to the Church, and even when their leaders were willing to tolerate other Catholic institutions, their toleration did not extend to the Society of Jesus. All through the century, a series of expulsions and the forced closings of their schools hampered the Jesuits' work in education. Russia, France, Italy, Spain and Prussia, on various occasions, drove out the Jesuits; and so, in continental Europe, anything like sustained development in Jesuit education became impossible.[16] Progress could be made, however, in the English-speaking lands. For although the Catholic minority found prejudice enough against its faith in the British Empire and America, Catholic schools there were allowed to go about their work in peace. Exiled European Jesuits were able to cross the ocean and join their American colleagues in laying the foundations for the system of Jesuit schools and colleges which we find today in the United States.[17]

While making needed adaptations to their time, the nineteenth- century Jesuits tried to retain, as best they could, the basic curriculum of Aquaviva's *Ratio Studiorum*.[18] The result was that, although it may surprise us now, the program of studies in Jesuit schools and the curriculum prescribed for the continental *lycées* still had much in common. The Jesuit school was the *collège*, a European institution whose range of classes ran from the grammar grades to what would be the sophomore year of an American four-year college. In his Jesuit *collège* or in its secular equivalent, the state *lycée*, a student could follow the same set of courses in grammar, classical and vernacular literature; and in either one of them, the student would be given the same solid grounding in mathematics.[19] The reason for the similarity is obvious enough. The Enlightenment intellectuals to whom the state system of education looked for inspiration had never complained about the Jesuit program of humanistic studies. After all, Corneille, Moliére, Buffon, Fontenelle, and many another distinguished man of letters had been formed by it. Even Voltaire and Diderot, for all their dislike of the Jesuits, gave credit to their Jesuit education for their own love of literature. Not without reason. For in the great days of the Collège-Louis-le-Grand, from which both of them had graduated, a single professor of rhetoric, the famous Father Porée, had seen nineteen of his former students become members of the French Academy.[20] The *philosophes* may have talked a good deal about science, but they were not really scientists themselves. They were men of letters and they had no desire to see eighteenth-century science take the place of literature in their scheme of education.

The crucial distinction between the Jesuit *collège* and the secular *lycée* would not be found in their programs of literature, mathematics, and science. The crucial distinction between the two types of school would emerge rather in the nature of the philosophy taught in them and in the different approach which the *collège* and the *lycée* took to Christian revelation. The Jesuit *collège* and the state *lycée* both intended to be first-class schools, in the classical tradition, from which their graduates would emerge well-prepared for higher studies in the university or for a commercial or professional career.[21] The reason for which Catholic parents chose the *collège* in preference to the *lycée* was the vision of man, the world, and God communicated to its students by the *collège*. That Christian vision of reality, which a corps of teachers, united in their belief, could communicate to their students in the atmosphere of a Jesuit school community, was the worldview which Catholic parents hoped that their sons would make their own.

In the politically divided France of the nineteenth century there was a difference as well in the approach to history taken by the Jesuit *collège* and the anti-clerical *lycée*. In the state *lycée*, for example, students were supposed to learn from Professor Jules

Michelet's *Histoire de France* that the Revolution and the secular state were two of France's greatest blessings. In the Jesuit *collège*, on the other hand, the sons of Royalist parents would be assured by Father Jean-Nicholas Loriquet's *Histoire de France* that nothing good could come from either of them.[22] Father Loriquet, we may remark in passing, was a figure of no small importance in nineteenth-century Jesuit education. The plan of studies which he had devised for the Jesuit school at Saint Acheul became the model which other French Jesuit schools would follow, and which Jesuits trained in France would carry with them to America. Father Nicolas Point, known later for his paintings of the Northwest Indians, made it the norm for the teaching at the Jesuit college at Grand Coteau, Louisiana, when he was Rector there;[23] and William Stack Murphy, an Irish-born member of the French province, brought it with him in 1846 when the French Jesuits came up from Kentucky to establish themselves at Fordham. Later in his career, in his terms as Vice-Provincial of Missouri, Father Murphy endeavored to impose the Loriquet plan of education on the reluctant Flemish Jesuits of the American mid-West.[24]

In order to survive in the nineteenth century, Jesuit schools were forced, for the first time, to charge tuition.[25] That change in policy, together with their classical curriculum, made European Jesuit schools educational institutions for the Catholic middle and upper classes. The Old World's class distinctions were still quite rigid and upward mobility was rare. In America, on the other hand, the land of immigration and of commercial expansion, society was fluid; and for the bright boy from an immigrant family or his friends from the same parish the Jesuit high school in his town and later on the Jesuit college could be his road to economic and social advancement. Tuition was kept low, and Jesuits, together with the sizeable corps of lay colleagues who now taught alongside of them, had taken it as their mission to prepare the sons of Catholic immigrants to make their way up the economic ladder and adapt themselves to the ways of American society without losing their inherited religious identity. In the atmosphere of a Jesuit school, the religious and moral worldview which these young Catholics brought with them from their homes and parishes would be supported.[26] They would learn to understand for themselves the evidence which supported it, and to live their lives under its direction in a reasonable and responsible way. Young men from working and lower-middle-class families would be made familiar with the literature of Greece and Rome, their classical heritage from Europe, and would become familiar as well with the English literature of their new home. Immigrants' sons would be shown how to analyze a problem and give their solution to it in clear and cultivated English. Reasons would be brought forward in support of the moral code which, up to now, these young men took only on faith. At the end of their Jesuit schooling, they would emerge as decent, believing, educated Americans. Then they could make their way in their own career and give moral leadership to the society in which they lived.

Jesuits in the nineteenth century and in the earlier years of the twentieth had reason to believe that dedication to the work of teaching in a Jesuit high school or college was a worthwhile lifetime commitment. Jesuits and laymen alike, they were working as a team in the communal enterprise of a Jesuit school, and they were giving the type of education which, in its essential thrust at least, was still in the tradition of Aquaviva's *Ratio Studiorum.*[27] That was why, they could still believe, they were able to form in their students the same type of mind which their own Jesuit education had formed in them. For from its beginning, the aim of Jesuit education had been the systematic development of a cultivated Catholic mind: a mind whose range was broad enough to embrace the realm of human knowledge as an articulated whole, yet sufficiently familiar with the diverse branches of knowledge to unify the multitude of disciplines without confusing them. That ideal of perspective, discipline of mind and imagination, analytic skill, and ability to see things as a whole was the integrative habit of mind which a community of broadly educated teachers, working in the light of their common faith, could develop in their students. Their Jesuit ideal of teaching, in other words, came fairly close to the ideal of education, which Cardinal Newman had proposed in *The Idea of a University.*[28] In the nineteenth century and in the early years of the twentieth, that ideal could still recommend itself rather readily as a goal capable of realization. *"Age quod agis"* ("Keep on doing what you are doing") had been an adage of Saint Ignatius, and in the nineteenth century, Ignatius' adage could still be applied to Jesuit education.

Jesuit Colleges and Universities Today

Jesuit schools, however, can no longer operate today as they operated from the sixteenth through the nineteenth centuries. They have ceased to be part of an international network of colleges and universities under unified and autonomous control. Furthermore, the expansion of human knowledge in the natural and social sciences, history, and religious studies, has made the integration of knowledge at which the traditional Jesuit curriculum was aimed a controverted goal.[29] European humanistic education, built around classical and vernacular literature, mathematics, science, and philosophy, is no longer acknowledged as generally as it used to be as the acceptable way to prepare a student for a professional career. Indeed, whether cultivation of the mind or the acquisition of marketable skills should be the aim of a college education is now a matter for dispute. Research universities promote the ideal of specialized inquiry, and the influence of their research ideal on undergraduate education is readily observable. Generalist teachers, whose ideal of education is the integration of knowledge through an interdisciplinary style of teaching, may find themselves at a disadvantage in colleges whose basic unit of instruction has become the individual department. For departments are often at war with one another today to secure a place for their own specialty in the undergraduate curriculum. State and professional agencies as well have their own demands to make on that curriculum, and as a result, anything like the academic independence, which Jesuit schools enjoyed in that respect from the sixteenth through the nineteenth centuries has become impossible.

American colleges and universities are also asked today to promote a broad diversity in the educational background of their professors, and once Jesuit colleges and universities had opted for their present legal status as secular institutions, they could no longer be operated on the confessional basis on which Jesuit schools had been conducted for the previous four centuries. One consequence of this change of legal status in our colleges and universities might be that the common bond, which used to form a school's corps of teachers into a Jesuit educational community may cease to be a distinguishing mark of Jesuit education. For that earlier bond of unity among the teachers in a Jesuit school was an interpersonal one. It came from the faculty's shared worldview, the similarity of its intellectual formation, and its shared understanding of the nature and goal of a Jesuit education.[30]

Another casualty of the shift of Jesuit schools to secular status might also be the bond of religious service, which in former times linked the corps of teachers in a Jesuit institution to the larger Catholic community around them. Conscious attachment to the larger Catholic community often helped the faculty of a Jesuit school to appreciate the religious and social value of their work. That sense of religious service was certainly present in the Jesuits who taught in the schools of the seventeenth and eighteenth centuries; and it could be found as well in the teachers, Jesuit and lay, who taught in the Jesuit schools of nineteenth-century Europe and America.[31] The vision of their work as a religious vocation gave these teachers firm support for the high esteem in which they held their own profession. Their work in the classroom, as they saw it then, was their share in the mission entrusted to their Jesuit school to educate men, and later women, who would be able to promote the teachers' own religious and social values.[32] When teaching can be looked upon as a vocation of that sort, the teacher's devotion of his life to it can well appear to be a gift of self well worth the making.

It would not be true to say that the traditional bond which linked the Jesuit college or university to the religious community about it must now be severed. Nevertheless, Jesuit colleges and universities must operate today within the stringent legal limits required of them by their civil status as secular institutions. Furthermore, in our own time the Catholic Church has come to look on members of other religious orders in a more ecumenical light as diverse religious groups have learned to interact with one another in a less embattled way. In these changed circumstances the character of the religious service which a school in the Jesuit tradition should render now stands in need of clarification and perhaps of redefinition. But clarification and redefinition can be a lengthy process and, unfortunately, while it is going on, a good deal of ambiguity can ensue over what that bond, in practice, would mean today. Ambiguity or perhaps communal disagreement about the nature of a school's religious service can easily weaken the strength of the commitment which individual teachers are willing to make to it. Should that ambiguity persist, then, as indeed it may, one of the strongest motives which moved teachers of high quality to make great personal sacrifices in the interest of Jesuit education may cease to operate.

Some Characteristics of Ignatius' Educational Ideal

A good deal of reflection more systematic and sustained in character than we have seen to date will be called for if the Jesuit ideal of the teacher is to retain its viability today. Consideration of the ideal's content might suggest lines along which some of that reflection might proceed.

Ignatius' ideal of education was the fruit of his own prayer and experience, and of the subsequent reflection which he had made on both. It is set down explicitly in the Fourth Part of his Jesuit *Constitutions*,[33] and we can see it work implicitly in the instructions which Ignatius gave for the staffing of the Roman College, the flagship school of his educational system.[34] Many years later, as the result of further prayer, experience, and reflection by a good number of topflight early Jesuits, the Jesuit ideal of education was definitively formulated in Claudio Aquaviva's *Ratio Studiorum*.[35]

For Ignatius and the early Jesuits, the aim of their educational work was service to God and to their fellow men, and they wanted it to be, like the rest of their apostolic work, distinguished service. Distinguished service in education, however, would call for the formation of a group of capable teachers who could work for God's greater glory in a first class system of schools.[36] Personally humble though Ignatius was in the sight of God, Ignatius, as an apostle, was never humble in the scope of his ambition. His aim was not simply to do good but to achieve the greater good, and that meant that the aim of his Jesuit schools was to provide the sort of education which its contemporary critics would call elitist.

The greater glory, which God would receive through the work of a well-educated disciple, had been the motive which carried Ignatius through his long and difficult years of study at Alcalà and Paris. During these years he had seen with his own eyes the damage done to students by the aimless and disorganized program of studies under which he had studied at Alcalà; and later on he had seen what a well-planned intelligently organized series of courses had been able to do for him and for his first companions at Paris. Since the members of his Society would be called upon to work for God's greater glory, Ignatius believed that a first-class, coherently organized program of studies, such as he had followed at Paris, would be required to prepare them for their future work. The same sort of education, he also thought, should be given to the lay students who came to the Jesuit colleges. For these students too were intended to emerge from their Jesuit schooling as educated Christians well prepared to give intellectual and moral leadership to the society in which they lived.[37] The lasting good which well-prepared students of that sort would be able to accomplish through their influence upon the world about them justified in Ignatius' eyes the allocation of his order's best resources to its schools, even though at times the needs of other Jesuit apostolates might appear to be more pressing.[38] The priority given to educational work in the Society of Jesus was never challenged until quite recently. Now, however, some Jesuits at least believe that the urgent social problems of our time have a greater claim on the resources of their order than its traditional apostolate of education. In that case, since the Society's resources are not unlimited, the work of education could well be left to others. Firm defenders of Jesuit education can still be found, of course, in the Society of Jesus; but if its priority is to be retained today, education will have to defend its claim against the counterclaims of other and more direct apostolates.

Jesuit education has always made great demands on the resources of their order. Schools run in the Jesuit tradition were expected to be run as well as possible, since for Ignatius the Jesuit commitment to education meant a commitment to do the job of teaching in a highly professional way. Expert instruction by well-trained Jesuits who had made a name for themselves in their own field was the standard which Ignatius set for the Roman College, since instruction there was meant to be the model which his other schools would follow. Great weight was placed on the selection of Jesuit professors, on the preparation given to them for their future work, and on their willingness to devote their lifetime to it.[39] If Jesuit education were to measure up to the hopes which Ignatius himself had entertained for it, it would have to be an education in which a high degree of competence in its teaching staff would be a mark of its distinctiveness; and by and large, Jesuit schools have tried to meet that standard. In our day, professional competence of that sort may no longer be prized as highly as it used to be. Critical standards are less demanding and the skills which Jesuit professionals cultivated in their students are less esteemed. Education has become much more egalitarian, and teachers who make the Jesuit ideal of education their own may find themselves swimming against the tide.

Jesuit education was never meant to be either a free flowing or a passive affair. It called for a clear sense of direction in its teachers and a focused process of self-development in its students.[40] Jesuits were never believers in the discipline of the rod, and Jesuit teachers were forbidden to lay their hands upon a student.[41] But they were firm believers in disciplined activity in their classrooms. Three centuries after its promulgation, Aquaviva's *Ratio Studiorum* still impresses us by the emphasis which it places on education through self-activity and the measures recommended to foster it. Diverse forms of self-expression, from contests, games, and small group repetitions in the lower grades, to essays, discussions, and debates in the academies or seminars attached to the higher classes, were central elements in the *Ratio*'s program of education. The classroom teacher was urged to stimulate personal activity in every student, and in order to do that well, he was encouraged to know each student personally.[42] Knowing them well, he could then guide their intellectual, moral, and religious development by his own personal example.[43] Education, in the ideal of the *Ratio*, was a dynamic process carried on through the personal interaction of students and their professors.

The optimistic view of human nature implied in the Jesuit ideal of education, as we have seen, scandalized the rigid seventeenth-century Jansenists; and its openness to Christian revelation, as we also saw, displeased the rationalist *philosophes* of the Enlightenment. Pessimism, skepticism, and irreligion have become more radical today, and the consequences of that development for liberal education have manifested themselves in an alarming way. A number of educators have not only proclaimed their loss of faith in God and their lack of belief in a free human nature; they have even questioned the intelligibility of the world encountered in human experience. Mankind should no longer look for meaning in his world, they tell us, since meaning can be no more than a product of his own human making. Once its contingent nature has been recognized, the claim of objective universality, which Eurocentric culture has traditionally made, can no longer be recognized. The inherited culture of Europe and America, and their traditional liberal education, can no longer occupy the place of honor, which even Enlightenment thinkers were willing to give them. They can no longer claim to be grounded on mankind's universal experience of self and world. Far from being grounded on tested experience, accessible to every mind, Western culture has been exposed for what it is, the product of political power and ethnic prejudice. Power, rather than tested knowledge, is the real source of the meanings, values, and ideals honored in our Western schools.

This radical attack on traditional culture and on liberal education, religious and secular, has been met with consternation in academe. Even educators otherwise quite sympathetic to non-European cultures have been repelled by it, and a heated discussion is now going on over the nature and value of liberal education. One outcome of that discussion could well be a more sympathetic understanding of Jesuit education by academics who, up to now, have shown little interest in it.

The Continuing Value of the Jesuit Ideal

Jesuit educators' knowledge of history, philosophy, and theology has equipped them well to defend traditional liberal education. In many ways, the present century has been a golden age of Jesuit scholarship. Jesuit historians, like Hugo Rahner, Joseph de Guibert, William Bangert, James Hennesey, and Gerald Fogarty, have made great contributions to the history of their order and of the Church. Jesuit philosophers and theologians, such as Henri de Lubac, Karl Rahner, Bernard Lonergan, and Michael Buckley, have reflected on the pluralism of modern culture and the challenge which it presents to the unification of knowledge under the guidance of philosophy and theology, and through their efforts some possible new approaches have been suggested. Jesuits, therefore, are far from unaware of the problems which the rise of atheism, the growth of historical consciousness, and the explosion of scientific knowledge have created for twentieth-century liberal education. Jesuits have thought about them at some depth, and a defense of liberal education drawing on their work could give support to a number of educational values which are under attack today. Indeed, if the defense of Jesuit liberal education were carried out with any skill, secular educators might become more aware of the contribution which a religiously oriented approach to it can make to their own form of liberal education. For, as Jesuits who know their history could point out, the crisis in liberal education today is the end result of a growing conflict between the earlier religious approach to education and an opposition to it which has grown progressively more radical during the past three centuries. In our own day, opposition to the intellectual presuppositions of the old world view has become so radical that even the foundations of secular liberal education, with its roots in the Enlightenment, have been challenged by it.

Jesuit educators have lived through the whole history of that conflict; and, under fire as they have been, they have been forced to reflect on the reasons for their own stand toward education. As heirs to a living tradition, Jesuit educators know whence they have come, why their opponents have attacked them, where they stand today, and the reason why they stand there. Jesuit education has never been a paper theory; it has always been a network of real schools in which Jesuit educators worked often with great self-sacrifice. If then these Jesuit educators can still feel confident of the value of their work, and if they can make a case for it, that should be good news for today's hard-pressed defenders of liberal education. And certainly, as far as their traditional worldview is concerned, Jesuits see no reason yet to give up that confidence.

The religious faith and the realistic philosophy of the first Jesuits grounded the worldview of their education. European culture has evolved considerably in the past four centuries and Jesuit philosophy and theology have evolved along with them. Through these changes, however, Jesuit philosophers, theologians, and educators have found no reason yet to give up their Christian faith or to abandon their sturdy confidence in human reason. Even today, they still find their conviction that our world has an intelligent creator to be a reasonable opinion; and they still find good reasons to treat all people as human persons endowed with a free and intelligent human nature. For them, as for the earlier Jesuit educators, God's created world can still make sense, and mankind's inquiring mind, purifying its knowledge through a constant process of self-correction, can arrive at some under-standing of it. Given their view of mankind and nature, Jesuit educators can defend their belief that objective, discoverable norms govern the process of healthy self-development. Literary self-expression need not be reduced to weaving a tapestry of language over a meaningless universe in the fashionable deconstructionist way. Literature, like morality, can still be judged by intelligible norms of meaning, truth, and value, which authentic self-expression cannot ignore. The ideal teacher of their Jesuit tradition can still be defined as the teacher who can recognize these norms, appreciate their value, and then communicate them to students by the way in which he or she teaches them the arts or the sciences.

As far as these Jesuit educators can see, no compelling argument for atheism has yet been mounted; nor has any philos-opher been able to prove to them that agnosticism should be taken as the only intellectual approach to revelation acceptable today. Does not religious belief, then, remain as reasonable an approach to education, they might ask, as the unbelief which the radical opponents of liberal education profess today? Determinists have been arguing their case for centuries, but they have not succeeded yet in silencing the defenders of free will. Is it not still reasonable, then, for a Jesuit educator to assume that his or her students are free and capable of responsible self-development?

What convincing evidence has yet been brought forward, they might also ask, to show that their acceptance of a meaningful world is less reasonable than the radical despair of meaning displayed by the radical opponents of liberal education?

They see no reason then to believe that the advances made in science or philosophy have undermined the plausibility of their Jesuit ideal of education. A tradition rooted in religious faith, philosophical realism, and respect for the freedom of the will still deserves a respected place in American education. Indeed, even to educators who do not share the early Jesuits' religious faith, a very good case for the survival of the Jesuit ideal can be made on the basis of its consequences for liberal education. For the Jesuit ideal of education justifies a number of values which educators, of other faiths or of none, believe to be sound and worth preserving. Among these values are the focus of education on the formation of the total person, the ideal of the integration and distinction of the disciplines, the emphasis on personal influence in teaching and the demands which that emphasis places on the teacher, the belief that the work of teaching is a vocation, and not just a job, and the appreciation of the school as a community of personal influence.

The Jesuit ideal of an integrative whole in knowledge as the goal of liberal education, even if we take it today as an asymptote, preserves education from a number of distortions. Faith in the presence in the world of a creating and redeeming God is a protection against a narrow, this-worldly secularism or a despairing resignation to an unintelligible universe. Conviction that the human person has a divine call to wholeness is a defense against a narrow professionalism in education or the tyranny of a single discipline. Interdisciplinary cooperation is neither a sacrilege nor an imposition. Fidelity to an old and coherent tradition frees the educator from slavery to the present or to the immediate future.[44]

Conclusion

Educators in the tradition of Saint Ignatius today are heirs to a long tradition of humanistic education, open to the God of revelation, confident in the soundness of the human mind, respectful of human freedom, and, despite all the difficulties which the task involves today, still optimistic about the work of integrating human knowledge. The God to whom Ignatius prayed made the world and gave it meaning. The God who made Ignatius' human mind gave it a drive to find that meaning and return to him by finding it. Even if that Jesuit vision is taken only as a hypothesis or a hope, it is an optimistic vision, and a vision whose consequences for education are fruitful.

Educators in the tradition of Saint Ignatius have good reason to respect themselves and the work they do. They are generous men and women, called to the service of their students, of the community around them, and, consciously or not, of God. The service they are called to give is the work of teaching, done as professionally as they can do it. Teaching in the ideal of Ignatius means stimulating self-activity and conveying through personal influence the intellectual and moral values which have become the teacher's own. In the tradition of Saint Ignatius, there is something sacred about the work of teaching; it is a vocation, and a lofty one at that.

If Ignatius' ideal of the teacher is to survive, the faculties of our Jesuit schools and colleges will have to make a conscious effort today to keep it alive and well. One of the greatest obstacles to their doing that may well be the lack of knowledge of the Jesuit tradition which we often find today in Jesuit schools and colleges, including the history of Jesuit education, of its worldview, or of the intellectual presuppositions which have shaped it. Greater knowledge of that tradition would help the teachers in Jesuit institutions to appreciate the distinctive character of Jesuit education and to understand the value of its preservation. With a better understanding of Ignatius' ideal of a teacher and of the contribution which the schools which share it can make to American education, teachers could gain a better sense of a Jesuit faculty's corporate identity and of the pride which they could take in serving on it. At times, their academic decisions might be wiser and more in harmony with the tradition from which their school has come. If that were to happen, the consequences for Jesuit institutions, and for liberal education in general, I am convinced, would be happy; and the future of Saint Ignatius' ideal of a teacher would be more assured. To make some of that knowledge more available, in summary form, has been the aim of this article.

Notes

1. Allan P. Farrell, S.J., *The Jesuit Code of Liberal Education: The Development and Scope of the* Ratio Studiorum (Milwaukee: Bruce, 1938), 25.

2. Farrell, *The Jesuit Code of Liberal Education*, 138.

3. Farrell, *The Jesuit Code of Liberal Education*, 365.

4. William V. Bangert, S.J., *A History of the Society of Jesus* (St. Louis: Institute of Jesuit Sources, 1986), 398.

5. Bangert, *A History of the Society of Jesus*, 145; William J. McGucken, *The Catholic Way in Education* (Chicago: Loyola University Press, 1962), 45.

6. Farrell, *The Jesuit Code of Liberal Education*, 16, 378.

7. Thomas O. Hanley, *Charles Carroll of Carrolton*, 2 vols. (Chicago: Loyola University Press, 1982), I:15.

8. Farrell, *The Jesuit Code of Liberal Education*, 438.

9. Aldo Scaglione, *The Liberal Arts and the Jesuit College System* (Philadelphia: John Benjamins Publishing Company, 1986), 85.

10. George E. Ganss, S.J., *St. Ignatius' Idea of a Jesuit University* (Milwaukee: Marquette University Press, 1954), 30, 306.

11. Bangert, *A History of the Society of Jesus*, 116.

12. Bangert, *A History of the Society of Jesus*, 78, 202 ff.

13. Bangert, *A History of the Society of Jesus*, 311.

14. Farrell, *The Jesuit Code of Liberal Education*, 379; Scaglione, *The Liberal Arts and the Jesuit College System*, 133.

15. John W. Padberg, *Colleges in Controversy: The Jesuit Schools in France from Revival to Suppression, 1815-1880* (Cambridge: Harvard University Press, 1969), 47.

16. Padberg, *Colleges in Controversy*, 273.

17. Padberg, *Colleges in Controversy* 13; McGucken, *The Catholic Way in Education*, 76, 82; Scaglione, *The Liberal Arts and the Jesuit College System*, 158.

18. Farrell, *The Jesuit Code of Liberal Education*, 387.

19. Padberg, *Colleges in Controversy*, 154.

20. Farrell, *The Jesuit Code of Liberal Education*, 374.

21. Padberg, *Colleges in Controversy*, 154.

22. Padberg, *Colleges in Controversy*, 30, 186.

23. Cornelius M. Buckley, S.J., *Nicolas Point, S.J.: His Life and Northwest Indian Chronicles* (Chicago: Loyola Press, 1989), 146.

24. Buckley, *Nicolas Point, S.J.*, 434.

25. Farrell, *The Jesuit Code of Liberal Education*, 439.

26. John W. Donohue, S.J., *Jesuit Education: An Essay on the Foundations of Its Idea* (New York: Fordham University Press, 1963), 209.

27. Donohue, *Jesuit Education*, 355.

28. Gerald A. McCool, S.J., *Jesuits and Education: The Society's Teaching and Practice, Especially in the United States* (Milwaukee: Bruce, 1932), 28.

29. McCool, *Jesuits and Education*, 93.

30. Donohue, *Jesuit Education*, 87.

31. McGucken, *The Catholic Way in Education*, 155.

32. McGucken, *The Catholic Way in Education*, 267.

33. Farrell, *The Jesuit Code of Liberal Education*, 143.

34. Farrell, *The Jesuit Code of Liberal Education*, 72.

35. Farrell, *The Jesuit Code of Liberal Education*, 314.

36. Farrell, *The Jesuit Code of Liberal Education*, 71.

37. Ganss, *St. Ignatius' Idea of a Jesuit University*, 18.

38. Ganss, *St. Ignatius' Idea of a Jesuit University*, 41.

39. Farrell, *The Jesuit Code of Liberal Education*, 200.

40. McGucken, *The Catholic Way in Education*, 37; Donohue, *Jesuit Education*, 68; Farell, *The Jesuit Code of Liberal Education* 52.

41. Farrell, *The Jesuit Code of Liberal Education*, 74.

42. Ganss, *St. Ignatius' Idea of a Jesuit University*, 79.

43. Ganss, *St. Ignatius' Idea of a Jesuit University*, 194.

44. McCool, *Jesuits and Education*, 36.

CHAPTER TWELVE

Teaching as Vocation: Faith and Literacy

FRANS JOZEF VAN BEECK

In my twenties I read quite some Chesterton and Belloc. One of Chesterton's essays, I recall, was titled "On Pigs as Pets."[1] I reread it before I got too far into this paper, to be sure I was not going to fool myself—or worse, you.

Why am I bringing this up? The title I was given, I submit, involves an interesting logic. In Chesterton's title, it is assumed that we are familiar enough with both pigs and pets (if probably from different angles) to find the idea of pigs as pets entertaining; still, below the surface the title implies that we understand pets better than pigs, and so, that the burden of proof is on Mr. Chesterton; he will have to show that pigs, unbeknownst to us, make fine (or at least acceptable) pets. Thus, the logic of the title is predicated on the assumption that we know about pets, and that it is up to the author to show us that there is a lot more to pigs than we know.[2]

"Teaching as Vocation" is the title I was given, and my first job is to caution you: the logic I just described does not apply. Why not? "In my experience"—a much-overrated claim I promise not to repeat[3]—the noun "vocation" is imprecise in the extreme. At the age of six I wanted to be a priest. I quickly learned this meant I "had a vocation"—a fact I did not always wish to remember when I was sixteen. By the time I was in my twenties, Catholics, encouraged by Popes Pius XI and XII, were saying that lay Catholics had a vocation, too, especially the married. The problem is, of course, that if everybody has a vocation nobody does; and in regard to marriage, many of us eventually realize that it is not so much a vocation as a widespread convention, nowadays competing with divorce; the only vocation I can see in marriage (and I confess I stand in awe of it) is for this particular person to stay married to this other particular person. Finally, being a frequent visitor to Southwest Wisconsin, I know that Southwest Technical College in Fennimore is best known locally as "the Vocational School"—"VoTech" for short. It reminds us that in many walks of ordinary life "having a vocation" simply means knowing one's trade.

I conclude that the word "vocation" is unlikely to enlighten us on teaching as vital to the Catholic intellectual tradition, which is what I have been asked to clarify.[4] So let us start elsewhere.

Learning and Teaching:
Their Origin in the Desert of the Nations

The words "teaching," "learning," "imitating," and "portraying," along with their cognates occur in the New Testament with striking frequency—not to mention words of related semantic significance, like "witness," "read," and "write."[5] Yet in this regard the New Testament is far outdone by the literature produced by later Judaism. Between the second and twelfth centuries, the substance of the Jewish life of faith gradually came to consist in the development of commentary on the Talmud and of observance of *Halakhah*. Jews lived by the Talmud and an array of laws and rituals celebrating God's *Shekinah*[6]— God's Holy Presence (originally dwelling outside the camp[7]) accompanying his people wherever they were dispersed.[8] Jews memorialized the twists and turns of Jewish history, the blessings and disasters that had befallen the Jews since the Temple was ruined in the year 70 C.E. In this, the rabbinate functioned as a (very flexible) *magisterium*.

All this is all the more surprising as we notice how rare words like "teaching," "learning," "imitating," and "portraying" are in the older Hebrew Scriptures, especially the Pentateuch, Joshua, and Judges. It is true, teaching does appear in Deuteronomy and gets genuine attention in the prophetic literature, early, classical, and exilic. It occurs with some frequency in the late-exilic and post-exilic prophets; it comes into its own in early wisdom literature and in some later Psalms, to become the chief theme only in the apocryphal wisdom literature, much of it originally composed in Greek.[9] This affinity between the Christian and the late-Jewish Scriptures invites examination. Just what gave rise to the Jewish talent for learning, teaching, and professional and intellectual tradition-building, right down to our own day?

The answer is not far to seek: it was in the Assyrian-Babylonian exile that Jews first learned how to make a home abroad,[10] how to "sing to God in the teeth of the idols,"[11] how to marvel at, and wonder about, the whole wide world, how to think and pray in universalist terms—i.e., eschatologically. In this way, Jews came to appreciate learning, and so, teaching. As the Bible conveys the story, this was an extremely slow process; literacy never comes fast, neither does faith in the One True God—our own God indeed, yet by the same token the God of each and every creature, at the expense of none of them.

Abram was a stay-at-home, "a wandering Aramean,"[12] a nomad on the edge of the desert, until he heard the Living God's Word, believed, and became Abraham, the patriarch animated by faith and the promise of plenty. Six centuries later, it was all of Israel's turn to be uprooted from Egypt's fertile soil at the orders of Moses, "God's friend."[13] Again, they heard the Word; in the desert, they became a true nation—God's. And not till it was deracinated once again and lost in "the desert of the nations"[14] did Israel—or what was left of it—become the chosen people in diaspora, with a matchless Torah— God's own Living Wisdom, the Eternal Blueprint for Creation—to guide them in a world wide desert.[15] In this way, so the author of the Letter to the Hebrews points out (well aware that the Temple was now the dead center of a heap of ruins), the Jews were slowly preparing us Christians for "the assurance of things unseen."[16] True believers have no homeland to fall back on;[17] habits of wayfaring keep us on the way to the City of God; all we do is keep a record—"road markings"[18]—to recall the sites where we learned our lessons, usually by suffering and thus coming to true life.[19] Humanity's forced journey out of Eden will go on till the Heavenly Jerusalem comes down to meet us and takes us in.[20] The Bible is a prophetic travelogue—a guide away from a garden gone to seed forever and toward God, who "has built a city for them."[21] Was it not outside the glorious but ensconced city that Jesus became "the pioneer of faith and its fulfillment"?[22] Prophets are not heard in their birthplaces; witnesses must testify to what others more familiar with the locale have overlooked or failed to hear, and so, find hard to believe. We Christians are essentially God's people in transition,[23] and transients must be quick studies, inquirers both inquisitive and discerning, appreciative guests, hard to discourage, slow to take offense, and ready to relate and participate. Diaspora Jews have grasped this for centuries: squatters remain outsiders, even when treated, to quote Daniel Patrick Moynihan, with "benign neglect"; in fact, they have demonstrated this for close to two millennia and a half, even if their thirst for a homeland never wholly died down, as we know only too well today.[24]

In this particular regard, Christians have been different from most Jews, ever since the New Testament. Never since the Gospels and the Acts of the Apostles were composed have we viewed dispersal among the nations as a curse; we have always (or at least most of the time) considered it a blessing and indeed, a mission.

In light of this, there is no need to explain that in the history of dogma, the sixteenth-century maxim *cuius regio illius et religio* was a huge setback—one far worse than the establishment drawn up by Constantine in the fourth century and sealed by Justinian in the sixth. Thank heavens, the Roman empire had soft boundaries from the start. Early, and even high medieval Europe, "unquiet souls"[25] and all, was still a well-functioning sounding board.[26] The Desert Fathers were read in the monasteries at the mouth of the Rhône and in the churches further up the valley;[27] the Mediterranean, even if ridden by pirates, was as yet more of a marketplace than a war theater; rulers and bishops had scholarly representatives at the court of the Caliph at Cordoba; Francis of Assisi could visit the Sultan and preach to him. In this fashion, the Christian West learned to associate faith with literacy. Its earliest schooling had come from Augustine's *City of God*, of course, with its brilliant counterpoint of Scripture and the classics.[28] In its wake, a fifth-century polymath like Orosius (a native of Braga in what is now Portugal) clearly thought that theology, geography, and world history made perfectly good company between the covers of one huge work, *Historia adversus Paganos*. In ninth-century Lower Saxony, Walafrid Strabo ("the Squinter"), undeterred by terrible eyesight, wrote voluminously on every subject.

There was no "no-man's" land between sacred and profane writing; religious poetry and the (pagan) courtly love tradition could learn and even borrow from each other—both idioms and melodies[29]. The *Carmina burana* may be irreverent, but they obviously belong to the same cultural world as the Bible, not unlike the indelicate hints at Saint Joseph's delicate predicament in some medieval Christmas plays. This is the Europe where John Scottus Eriugena wrote his wide-ranging experiment in fundamental theology *Periphyseon*,[30] where Fulbert introduced Aristotle's logical writings at the School of Chartres as early as the late tenth century,[31] and where Alan of Lille, another polymath—poet, theologian, and preacher all rolled into one—taught first in Paris and then in Montpellier, only to end up an old monk at Cîteaux. In this cloud of witnesses we also have Peter Lombard, "the Master of the Sentences," who introduced the Latin West to John of Damascus' *Fount of Wisdom*, and thus, kept the Greek Fathers alive in the West until well into the seventeenth century,[32] when the Benedictine Maurini made a fresh start, along with Richard Simon (1638–1712), the first modern, critical reader of the Scriptures. Andrew of Saint-Victor learned Hebrew and the Talmud from learned Jewish Rabbis in a Paris yeshiva;[33] Hadewijch of Antwerp could treat her women friends to letters of spiritual direction in an elegant vernacular, betraying a deep familiarity with both the catholic tradition and the systemic injustice being done to notable women by men of rank in the Church; in London, Geoffrey Chaucer could lament Petrarch's recent death;[34] and the most gifted of them all, Dante Alighieri, could base his *Divina Commedia* on both Scripture and classical mythology, obviously regarding the two as fonts of equal illuminative power to interpret current morals and politics—both secular and ecclesiastical—on the Italian peninsula.[35] If these people were anything at all, they were *Catholics*: they recognized food for faithful thought and thoughtful faith wherever it occurred.[36]

Almost a century after Dante, Chaucer was to sum up the idea behind this marriage of faith and literacy by ending an animal fable like this:

> But ye that holden this tale a folye,
> As of a fox, or of a cok and hen,
> Taketh the moralite, goode men.
> For Seint Poul seith that al that writen is,
> To our doctrine it is ywrite, ywis;
> Taketh the fruyt, and lat the chaff be stille.
> Now goode God, if that it be thy wille,
> As seith my lord, so make us alle goode men.
> And brynge us to his heighe blisse. Amen.[37]

No wonder the cathedral and abbey schools and the universities are the creation of the Middle Ages. No wonder two noble pagans, Plato and Aristotle—the former a contemplative canonized by Plotinus and baptized by Augustine, the latter a metaphysician with an astonishing eye for detail embraced and unfolded by Aquinas—could become their guiding lights.

Let me interrupt myself. In giving these examples of the synthetic forces at work in the Middle Ages, I have no wish to keep alive the nineteenth-century Ultramontanist myth that the Middle Ages were Catholicism at its best.[38] Yet I do wish to show how what lies at the root of what we know as the tradition of Catholic education was a thin, very fragile network of plucky Catholic institutions that fostered Catholic talent steeped in culture and tradition sacred and profane in the broadest sense of the word.[39]

This *habitus* was firmly rooted in the early Church. In second-century Rome, Justin Martyr treated the classics of his day in the same way. Born a pagan in Nablus on what is now the West Bank, he became a seeker who finally found the "true philosophy" in Ephesus—a key Christian hub from the late first century onward.[40] Eventually he settled in Rome—a theological tutor, orator, and author. In his first *Apology*, he professes with startling clarity how, by virtue of the wisdom Christians have gained from the knowledge of Christ, they have the ability to discern vestiges of the divine *Logos*, "of whom all humanity has received a share." Examples are the wisdom of "Socrates and Heraclitus among the Greeks, and others like them," and among the foreigners "Abraham, Elijah, Ananias, Azarias, Misael, and many others."[41] In his next *Apology* he makes the same point. After appreciatively mentioning "Plato, . . . Stoics, both poets and prose writers," he ends on a confessional, explicitly Christian-philosophic note, by stating that "the seed and pattern of a reality is given according to a person's capacity, and that is one thing. But the reality itself is something else: sharing in *it* and portraying *it* are bestowed according to his [= the *Logos'*] grace."[42] What is this "reality"? I propose it is the sense of high, unowed privilege, which encourages Christians to interpret humanity and the world and respond to them in the light of God. Clement of Alexandria, Origen, Basil, Gregory Nazianzen come to mind. The latter two left rural Cappadocia to go to Athens. Students at the Platonic Academy, they became close (if never quite compatible) friends.[43] Later on Gregory put the theme of their companionship in a nutshell:

> This I considered part of training in philosophy:
> Not to be seen working hard for a first-rate life,
> But *to be, rather than be seen to be, God's friend.*[44]

My point must be plain by now: in the Great Tradition of the undivided Church, the love of God, faith, eschatology, catholicity, discerning love of this universe-in-process and this humanity for the sake of the God who makes them so, mobility, hospitality, and the cultivation of learning are sheep of the same wool.[45]

Dissociation of Sensibility and Differentiated Consciousness

Let us move on before I lose myself any further. If there is one century that has had a huge impact on learning and teaching—one I wish to urge you both to admire and to pick a bone with—it is the sixteenth. In my opinion, its first four decades invite comparisons with the forty years that we have just behind us.

A few moments ago, I alluded unfavorably to the sixteenth-century *maxim cuius regio illius et religio.* In my judgment, the phenomenon of the state church is only one of the many varieties of an interest that became all-powerful in the course of the sixteenth century: a mistaken confidence in definition. Is not the practice of religion within assured political boundaries analogous to reducing Christian doctrine to certified propositions? Late medieval nominalistic scholasticism had conspired with secular humanism to drive its worry about the nature of verbal and nominal reference to the point where precision-by-dint-of-subtle-but-unreal-distinction had prevailed over reasonable understanding; exact truths had become more prominent than Truth. My venerable friend Giuseppe Rambaldi, S.J., at the Gregorian University in Rome, now in his nineties but alive and thinking, puts it as follows: they forgot that we need not *verità* (truths) but *verità vere* (true truths). How could late-medieval Christendom expect to dissect its faith in ways that Erasmus and Luther were to find repulsive without eventually cutting itself to bits as well? In doing so, it was beginning to force itself to settle, eventually, for the umbrella-word "Christianity."[46] By the mid-seventeenth century, the question "Which is the true Church?" had become the nightmare of the West.[47]

The unity of Christians had become an abstract, non-incarnate universal named "Christianity." "Church" conveyed institutionalized division and a world of religious war, invective, and argument, serving no purpose but to "tire the truth."[48] In this standoff, forces bent on control took over. *Forced* judgment was set to oust *true* judgment; authoritative *magisterium*—whether of the local, puritanical vestry kind or the prelatical, papist variety—put itself on a par with Scripture. No wonder this inaugurated the disintegration of the university, a development already foreseen and dreaded by Jean Gerson (1363-1429).

Before I go any further, let me hasten to assure you that I have no wish to disparage the early sixteenth century's uncommon fertility: the great European vernaculars (jealous of Italian, as it were) came into their own, finding themselves capable of prose—I mean, prose not only of the narrative and expository kinds (hitherto dominated by Latin) but of the reflective kind as well. Much of the latter built on medieval ascetical and mystical writings in the vernacular,[49] and on Latin philosophic classics like Seneca and Cicero.[50] Added to this, we must mention the unprecedented early sixteenth-century aptitude for matters of consciousness, self-consciousness, and conscientiousness; in many ways, the word "I" developed a meaning unknown before, with the possible exception of Petrarch, who had died in 1374.[51] "I" came to signify the conscious, self-conscious, self-moving, searching, striving self, what Maurice Blondel was to call *le sujet.*

What we mean nowadays when we say "authentic" was first experienced in the years between 1490 and 1540. Luther, Calvin, Ignatius Loyola are as unthinkable without it as Henry VIII, Charles V, and Francis I.[52] So are Erasmus' highly personalized *Enchiridion* and the *Spiritual Exercises* of Ignatius Loyola—the latter neither a thinker nor a writer but a voluminous correspondent, as well as a mystic with a "way with people."[53] Erasmus and Ignatius were mentors, teachers of how to discern and decide personally.[54]

But there is a cloud to every silver lining. Contemporary historians now consider the late fifteen-twenties a historic turning-point.[55] To them, it looks as if the outburst of creative energy associated with the new humanism, the spurt toward reform of the Church, the rise of the merchant class and the modern sovereign state, the mobility toward the big cities on the part of the new entrepreneurial trading-and-banking class all over Europe, the opportunities for international trade as well as colonial expansion occasioned by the discovery of the earth's actual rotundity (and the navigational skills and the mappemondes needed to make the most of it) and perhaps more than anything else, the development of the printing press—all these excitements appear to also have struck the movers and the shakers with the prospect of chaos. Control became a watchword; order had to be. In a seminal book with the ominous title *Ramus: Method and the Decay of Dialogue*, Walter Ong has shown that the period is also marked by a harsh change in educational method: *encounter* with persons and things gave way to *analysis* of texts and concepts.[56] In a dazzling passage in a dazzling book, *The Presence of the Word*, Ong writes:

> In a world . . . taken up with the human or quasihuman . . . , impartiality will be the chief form of objectivity. In this world, man's relation even to inanimate nature is imbued with quasihuman relations. Another kind of objectivity does not get involved in human values as such. This objectivity, essential for scientific explanation, becomes possible when one envisions the world as set off from oneself as essentially neuter, uncommitted, and indifferent to the viewer. Study of such a world is felt to be not a response to the world but an operation upon it.[57]

In other words, "objective objectivity" acceded to the throne, but, being still a minor, "method" became its tutor.[58] Everything had to be consistent and fixed in the mind, preferably visually. Cajetan turned Aquinas' thought into a closed system; everything got defined—i.e., locked up in its conceptual "nature"—even humanity itself: our native openness to God and the World began to be overlooked.[59] Philip Melanchthon and his voluble Catholic opponent Melchior Cano assumed that it was imperative to capture Christian orthodoxy in a number of doctrinal exhibits that could be viewed and visited, respectively, in Reformed and Catholic *musea* full of articles of faith.[60] By writing their respective *loci theologici* they demonstrated it was possible to do just that. Professing one's faith almost became a matter of affixing one's signature to a bill of lading, under oath if necessary.[61]

In this impasse of at least potentially global proportions, the traditional catholic penchant for literacy-*cum*-faith and faith-*cum*-literacy found itself stretched to the point of breaking. This is where Ignatius Loyola came in.

Jesuit Education at the Dawn of Modernity

It has been cogently shown that the foundation of Jesuit schools, starting with the college at Messina in 1549 and picking up at a speed of four or five foundations a year in the next seven years, was not a deliberate, strategic initiative on Ignatius' part:

> What is still surprising . . . is how easily the first Jesuits glided into a decision of this magnitude and how little account they seem to have taken of its manifold impact upon them.[62]

This is all the more surprising if we recall that before he was thirty-three Ignatius had never gone to school. This implies he had no Latin, the recognized language of instruction in the sixteenth century. He first went to school to learn it in Barcelona, in 1525, when he was thirty-four; he had concluded that if he was serious about his mission to "help people advance spiritually"—*ayudar a las animas*[63]—education was a must. Still, at a deeper level, education did fit the new world revealed to him at Manresa to a fault. What world? In his *Autobiography* he says:

> Once, out of devotion, he was going to a church which was just over a mile distant from Manresa (I think was called St. Paul), and the road runs close to the river. Thus moving along intent on his devotions, he sat down for a moment with his face towards the river running down below. And as he sat there, the eyes of his understanding began to open. And it was not as if he beheld a vision of some kind, but he saw and understood many things, things spiritual as well as things concerning faith and learning, and this with so great an illumination that all things appeared new to him. And it is impossible to point out the particulars he then understood, although they were many; but he received a great clarity in his understanding, so much so that, it seems to him, in the whole course of his past life right up to his sixty-second year, if he should gather all the helps he has received from God, and everything he has come to understand, even if he should add them all together, he has received not as much as at that one time alone.[64]

The year is 1521. Ignatius, a fine penman but spiritually illiterate, has his first glimpse of what was to become the universe of Jesuit education: "He saw and understood many things, things spiritual as well as things concerning faith and learning, and this with so great an illumination that all things appeared new to him." Ignatius became a Catholic teacher without benefit of academic literacy; his vision was Catholic; so was his sense of mission. Always a Catholic of the elementary kind, he had inherited integrity of intention and generosity toward the world. To this had been added an all-encompassing, all-suffusing vision of a generous, all-loving, all-enabling God. It guided him to the age-old Catholic meeting-place of faith and literacy: he became a student at the Sorbonne. There he would discover the *modus parisiensis:* a coherent curriculum, discussion exercises in groups, and the quiet, disciplined theological reasonableness of the *devotio moderna*, which he had already tasted in Spain.[65]

He arrived in 1528. John Calvin was just finishing up; conceivably, the two just may have met. But a world of difference was to separate the cool assertiveness of Calvin's *Institutes*[66] and the generous affect that feeds the no less assertive Constitutions of the Society of Jesus, and their sense of mission.[67]

At the risk of sounding unecumenical, let me suggest a complex of causes for this difference. It would be ludicrous to suggest that the sixteenth-century Reformers had no interest in learning; they did. Luther knew his Bible and his liturgy; Calvin knew his church fathers, his scholastics, and assuredly his Augustine. Yet they did decide, sadly, that (in Melanchthon's famous phrase) "to know Christ means to know his benefits"; true enough, except they understood this truth restrictively.[68] In this way, soteriology—the doctrine of fallen humanity's salvation by divine grace in a theologically neutral cosmos—became the centerpiece of the Reformation's Christian faith.[69] Thus, Nature, this immense theater of tangible reasons to praise God, became an appendix to the Christian faith. Never did the pursuit of Christian humanism cut itself off from humanity's cosmic matrix in as short-sighted a manner as the Reformation did, alas, under invocation of the Holy Spirit. Luther and Calvin acclaimed the study of the Bible and theology and even renewed it; yet they insisted that the world, and every form of understanding or managing it, even philosophic contemplation, was theologically irrelevant.[70] This critically impoverished the Christian faith—its flair for theological imagination, its eschatological doxology in liturgical worship, its "mysticism of gladness at the world."[71]

In his great essay on the Metaphysical Poets, T.S. Eliot has described the "dissociation of sensibility" that gradually transformed the mood of the Christian West in the wake of the extraordinary cultural shifts of the early sixteenth century.[72] Modern humanity came at a price: the cultivation of freedom of initiative, individuality, freedom, literacy, the storage and retrieval of knowledge by means of print (which enabled individual learning and research), and the displacement of traditional authority by free, allegedly purely rational, objective, "scientific"[73] inquiry and discovery caused growing pains in the human area. Christianity suffered from new discordances; unsurprisingly, the polemics between faith and literacy became neuralgic. They still are.[74]

However, it would be a mistake to overlook the liberating aspects of these neuralgic developments: they marvelously stretched the range of potential human learning and human skill, and thus also demonstrated the depth and the breadth of humanity's capacity for fulfillment.[75] Dissociation of sensibility eventually gave birth to differentiated consciousness—and where would we be without that today? In this sense, through the synthetic humanism of the Jesuit schools, Ignatius ended up affecting catholic intellectuality as much as Ramus did. The catholic tradition in education began to include modern objectivity, by coupling it to the Christian tradition of discerning interest in, and love of, the world; at the same time—and here is a truly novel factor—it began to embrace the cause of sociopolitical, civic leadership with its gift for modernity and enterprise. With the monarchies still flourishing, often with Jesuit advice (but often without Jesuit consent), the death-knell of the divine right of kings had rung. Jesuits became missionaries, in India, Japan, and the areas we now know as Quebec, New England, New York, Florida, Colombia, Brazil, Paraguay; here, the novelty was that they were also explorers, linguists, and students of culture, and especially that they wrote home to explain themselves, well aware that their letters were not just going to be filed. They were Catholics: learning and teaching—i.e., receptive and responsive openness to God's world—was in their blood.[76]

Catholic Education in America:
Then, Now, and in the Future

In making this point I have quietly taken a giant leap across the Atlantic. In Europe, a merchant breed, self-conscious, conscious of a mission, and set to be educated, had entered the lists. Its mission became international, and eventually global, a development which in the end put this country—yes, these United States—at the center of the globe, along with its "activism, which [gives] great emphasis to science and technology."[77]

But if anything has demonstrated the depth of the Catholic instinct in the United States, it is not technology but the startling development of a Catholic school system paralleled nowhere in the world. In my judgment, it is only partly based on the natural immigrant communities' instinct for self-preservation; after all, Georgetown started in 1798. It is also only partly based on the interesting affinity between American optimism of the apocalyptic kind[78] and Catholic humanism of the universalistic kind.[79]

True, the Catholic identity of our institutions of higher education was too defensive for decades, but in the early 'sixties we did catch up, not in the last place thanks to the G.I. Bill of Rights. Braced by this challenge, American Catholics walked into the educated American mainstream in fifteen years; before World War II, the Catholic lag still looked like a thirty or forty years' haul. We now know from experience that Catholic identity has been a function of anxious dependence on borderlines; but frankly, we are also witnessing the liability of Catholic identity to uncritical "charismatic" openness.[80] Cardinal George's words "liberal Catholicism is an exhausted project" should give us pause.[81] We need to recover both the Catholic mystique of total abandon to God and the Catholic politics of discerning love of the world.[82] But we are part of a literate-technological culture addicted to quantification, means, tools, and "info"; we are fairly untutored when it comes to quality, ends, understanding, and humane decision-making.[83] Catholic education must cultivate discernment in the midst of a skillful but pretty undiscerning culture.

There are reasons to feel encouraged. It was an event of high symbolic significance when Karl Rahner explained, in a prophetic address first heard in the United States in 1979, at the Weston Jesuit School of Theology in Cambridge, Massachusetts, how the Catholic Church, universal by dint of faith from the start, had in our lifetime become empirically universal.[84] No less symbolically, fifteen years before, it had been an American pen, wielded by one "Xavier Rynne," that had given the world a vibrant account of the Second Vatican Council as it was taking place.[85]

I submit that these two symbolic events raise the issue of the Catholic intellectual tradition with a vengeance. At this moment in Catholic church history, lack of resolution or suspended animation on the part of Catholic intellectuals would be suicidal. So, Where do we come from? What are we? Where are we going?[86]

I have two views to offer.[87] They come from a heart and mind shaped by thirty-eight years of the best European pre-judgments, but matured and decisively "modernized" by thirty-two years of study in two Catholic American universities, chiefly by teaching.

Let me start with a neuralgic matter that leads up to a point I wish to make. For us Catholic intellectuals, my friend Garry Wills's recent book, *Papal Sin*, should be a warning signal.[88] Let me explain. One virtue long claimed by Neo-Protestantism and deism is sincerity.[89] It has bequeathed to our culture an abhorrence of formalism, especially of the Byzantine kind. So, when a thoroughly traditional Catholic intellectual like Wills is irritated enough to take exception to the Vatican culture of systemic insincerity (i.e., the cultivation of diplomacy at the expense of truthfulness and competence), he is doing a very American thing, and one we Catholic intellectuals have to learn how to do as confidently—if also more reasonably and accurately. It is not un-Catholic to decry fudging in high ecclesiastical places. It is time to put "Rome" on notice. If the Enlightenment's claim to sincerity was at least partly hypocritical, it is also true that Roman habits of scoffing at sincerity as indelicate are not a case of Christian virtue. The recent furor about *Dominus Iesus* may help give us pause. Why should Pope John Paul II have to explain a document that he commissioned (but did not sign) to celebrate the Jubilee, yet which, once published, excelled at alienating both Catholics and non-Catholics?[90] The world of American Catholic intellectuals is entitled to making pertinent representations when Roman practices *de facto* jeopardize the credibility of our Catholic faith by their lack of intellectual integrity. But—and here comes the point I wish to make—how serious (and how generous) are we when we in our turn get to tackle the issue of Catholic identity? Are we still afraid of being accused of parochialism, of being called intolerant? Are we open to the suggestion that we'd rather be too tolerant than be thought of as intolerant? Are we reluctant to embrace a frank catholicity that has discerningly made a demanding peace with North American pluralism—not a peace at cut rates, let alone at any price?

Secondly, in our culture, intellectual integrity as a Catholic virtue implies an intellectual creed that reflects the Great Tradition of Christian love of the world. Let me try one:

The human spirit, natively (if largely unthematically) attuned to the living God, is also attuned to the countless "presences" that surround it in the cosmos—presences to which it must keep itself responsive. Inspired by this basic (and, in the last resort, mystical) intuition, the human spirit has the inner resources to handle the knowledge explosion which it has unleashed in recent centuries, especially in the form of natural and social science. It can face the vehemence and even violence it has discovered, both in the universe and in humanity; it can face even the violence humanity has positively inflicted on itself and the cosmos. As for the proliferation of information so characteristic of modernity, if dubious at times, it need not daunt us; it is even possible to welcome it, provided we take it as an invitation to understand its dynamics— that is, the fierce dynamics of human communication in word and gesture. Given that understanding, we can afford to open ourselves to all that is particular, specialized, curious, strange, far-fetched, and even barbarous, because (if only we persevere) we will discover that the forces of harmony, integration, and coherence run deeper, both in the universe and in ourselves, than the forces of contention, dissipation, and disintegration; that, finally, all this is within our reach because all that exists finds its unity and reconciliation in God, to whom we are more deeply attuned than we are to the universe or even to ourselves and each other, and who, therefore, is capable of enlightening honest seekers in such a way as to keep them from getting lost.[91]

I must conclude. I think of teaching as a profession, loved by all of us who found, perhaps as early as the first grade, that we belonged to the tiny minority of kids who simply loved school. But in the Catholic tradition, learning and teaching are a matter of mission. So, those of us who have continued to love school had better seek to become unashamedly Catholic—discerningly open to everything in God's world, heart and soul. For openers, I recommend a rereading of *Lumen Gentium* and *Gaudium et Spes*. Who knows, we may end up feeling teaching is a vocation after all, perhaps even one to holiness.

Notes

1. See *Essays by G.K. Chesterton* (London: Collins, 1939), 224–28.

2. For clarity's sake, here is an example of the same logic. If I were to offer you a paper on Napoleon as a lyrical poet, my assumption would be that all of you know what lyrical poetry is, but that Napoleon's poetic gifts are a well-kept secret. Again, the logic of the title rests on the assumption that we all know about lyricism (an unsafe assumption these days: as more professors talk about poetry, they seem to read less of it). In any case, the charm of the title lies in its promise to teach us that there is more to Napoleon than we think we know.

3. Years ago, Hans-Georg Gadamer told me in a conversation he was convinced that *Erfahrung* was "one of the least clarified sources of authority of our day" (*einer der am mindesten aufgeklärte Begriffe der Gegenwart*). On the subject, see George P. Schner's interesting essay "The Appeal to Experience," in *Theological Studies* 53 (1992): 40–59.

168 / *Frans Jozef van Beeck*

4. For the range of meanings of "catholic," see Avery Dulles, *The Catholicity of the Church* (Oxford: Clarendon Press, 1985), 185. To prevent misunderstandings, "Catholic," in this essay, is synonymous with "Roman Catholic"; "catholic" means "characterized by catholicity."

5. Let me put together a rough-and-ready, entirely impressionistic checklist. "To teach": Matthew 14x [that is, 14 times]; Mark 17x; Luke 16x; John 10x; Acts 16x; Pauline corpus 15x. "Teacher": Matthew 12x; Mark 12x; Luke 16x; John 8x; Acts 1x; Pauline corpus 7x. "Teaching": Matthew 4x; Mark 6x; Luke 1x; John 3x; Acts 4x; Pauline corpus 25x. "To learn": Matthew 3x; Mark 1x; John 2x; Acts 1x; Pauline corpus. "Learner, disciple": Matthew 71x; Mark 45x; Luke 37x; John 33x; Acts 28x. "Make disciple(s)": Matthew 3x; Acts 1x. "To remind"; reflexive "to remember, recall": Matthew 3x; Luke 4x; John 4x; Acts 2x; Pauline corpus 2x. "To imitate, imitator": Pauline corpus 7x; Hebrews 2x. "To read": Matthew 7x; Mark 4x; Luke 3x; John 1x; Acts 8x; Pauline corpus 8x; Revelation 1x. "To write" (but excluding "it is written"): Matthew 1x; Mark 3x, referring to Moses; Luke 11x; John 13x; Acts 5x; Pauline corpus 27x; 1 John 13x; 1 + 2 John 5x; Revelation 28x.

6. *Š°kinah* is related to *maškîn*, which means "tent" and specifically, esp. in Exodus, the Tent of Meeting. The root *škn* means "inhabit, dwell." The Greek word for "tent" is *skn*; coincidentally, the Greek and Hebrew roots have the three consonants s-k-n in common, which makes it attractive to hypothesize that "dwelled among us" (John 1:14) is a pun, hinting that the *Logos*, or divine Wisdom, came to "tent" among us, just as the *Š°kinah* "tented" with Israel in the desert. This hypothesis is corroborated by a phrase in the Book of Tobit, which was originally written in Hebrew or Aramaic (Tobit 13, 11c LVV): "so that his tent may be rebuilt for you with joy," an obvious reference to the Temple. Is this the reason why Paul's two chief images of the Christian community are "Temple" and "Body" (cf. also John 2:19), conveying what we call "Community" and "Incarnation"?

7. See Exodus 33:7-8. In the same way, the Jerusalem temple overlooks the Old City of David; see Hebrews 13, 13.

8. As the experience of defeat made God's closeness to Israel (and hence, God's Lordship over history) very questionable, God's transcendent glory began to look more and more like mere impenetrability and remoteness. But rabbinical Judaism resisted the temptation to choose between the two—that is, it refused to let the forbidding riddle of God's ways push it into a denial of God's intimate presence. Israel's faith-tradition prohibits the playing off of God's transcendence against God's presence, the glory against the tenderness, the

awe against the intimacy. In insisting that God was now sharing Israel's suffering, the rabbis also pointedly refused to teach that faithfulness to Israel made it incumbent upon God to abandon the divine mercy and crush the powers that be with a decisive show of power. Instead, they patiently taught that the great disaster of God's apparent absence, while a most severe test of faith, was the decisive sign of God's favor in the midst of a world estranged from God. That is, God was the same God as the God who had looked down on Israel in Egypt: God was once again the God of the poor and the downtrodden. Note that a modern Jewish author, Zvi Kolitz, in his short story *Yossel Rakover's Appeal to God*, shows the same depth of theological insight in his interpretation of the religious meaning of the Holocaust. See F.J. van Beeck, *Loving the Torah More than God?* (Chicago: Loyola University Press, 1989), 13-28.

9. Here is a rough-and-ready count of the LXX, as listed in Hatch and Redpath's concordance. "To teach": Deuteronomy 9x; Judges 1x; 2 Samuel 2x; Hosea 1x; Isaiah 3x; Jeremiah 7x; Ezzekiel 1x; 1 + 2 Chronicles 5x; Esdr + Nehemiah 7x; Job 14x; Psalms 22x; Proverbs 7x; Ecclesiastes 1x; Song of Solomon 1x; Wisdom 4x; Sirach 7x. "Teacher": LXX 2x. "Teaching": Psalms 1x; Proverbs 1x; Sirach 2x; Isaiah 1x. "To learn": Exodus 1x; Deuteronomy 7x; Isaiah 9x; Jeremiah 4; Psalms 4x; Proverbs 4x; Wisdom 4x; Sirach 5x. "Learner, disciple," "make disciple(s)": not in LXX. "To remind"; reflexive "to remember, recall": Genesis 11x; Exodus 4x; Leviticus 4x; Numbers 3x; Deuteronomy 15x; Isaiah 21x; Jeremiah 11x; Ezekiel 15x; Esdras + Nehemiah 14x; Tobit 10x; Job 8x; Psalms 48x; Sirach 27x; 1 + 2 Maccabees 13x. "To imitate, imitator": Psalms 1x; Wisdom 2x. "To read": Heptateuch 5x; 2 Kings 6x; Isaiah 3x; Jeremiah + Baruch 19x; Daniel 6x; Esdr + Nehemiah 13x; Job 1x; Sirach. "To write": Exodus 9x; Numbers 2x; Deuteronomy 21x; Joshua 7x; Judg 1x; Samuel + Kings 49x; Isaiah 8x; Jeremiah + Baruch 23x; Ezekiel 7x; Daniel 17x; 1-2 Maccabees 39x; Chronicles 29x; Esdras + Nehemiah 44x; Tobit 5x.

10. Jeremiah 20:1-14.

11. E.g., Psalms 138:1b. See Norbert Lohfink, *Lobgesänge der Armen* (*Stuttgarter Bibelstudien* 143; Stuttgart: Verlag Katholisches Bibelwerk, 1990), 103, note 1.

12. Deuteronomy 26:5.

13. Exodus 33:11. On this theme, Emmanuel Lévinas writes: "The oneness of [God's] Name means the oneness of the language and the Scriptures and the institutions. It implies the end of naïveté and rootedness. The Church remains faithful to a deep-seated Jewish impulse when it seeks the religious emancipation of humanity by (as Simone Weil

complains) 'imposing the Jewish Scriptures everywhere.' All speech means being uprooted. Every rational institution means being uprooted. The establishment of a genuine society is a form of being uprooted—it marks the end of an existence where 'being at home' is an absolute, where everything comes from inside. Paganism means rootedness, almost in the etymological sense of the term. The arrival of writing/scripture means, not the spirit being subordinated to a letter, but the letter replacing the soil. In the letter, the spirit is free; in the root, it is tied down. It is on the arid soil of the desert, where nothing holds, that the true spirit descended into a text, so as to seek a universal fulfillment." "Simone Weil contre la Bible," in *Difficile liberté: Essais sur le judaïsme*, 2nd ed. (Paris: Albin Michel, 1976), 178–88, quotation at 183.

14. Ezekiel 20:35.

15. Cf. Proverbs 8, 22–9, 6; Sirach 24, 1–12.

16. Hebrews 11:1b.

17. Cf. Hebrews 11:1–40.

18. See Dag Hammarskjöld, *Markings*, trans. Leif Sjöberg and W.H. Auden (London: Faber and Faber, 1964); originallly published as *Väg märken* (Stockholm: Bonniers, 1963).

19. See Hebrews 5:7–10.

20. Revelation 21:2.

21. Hebrews 11:16b. Incidentally, this is why it is fair to say, especially after over two centuries of historical-critical study of the Bible, that the Scriptures as we have them are the record of the history of their own interpretation.

22. Cf. Hebrews 12:1–4, 13:12–14.

23. See F.J. van Beeck, *God Encountered: A Contemporary Catholic Systematic Theology*, vol. 2 (Collegeville MN: Liturgical Press, 1993), §76.

24. I have tried to argue that Jews and Catholic Christians have a taste for civilization in common, in *Loving the Torah More than God?: Towards a Catholic Appreciation of Judaism* (Chicago: Loyola University Press, 1989, esp. 67–83.

25. See Richard Kieckhefer, *Unquiet Souls: Fourteenth-Century Saints and Their Religious Milieu* (Chicago: University of Chicago Press, 1984).

26. I found this broad characterization of the Middle Ages nicely supported by Willemien Otten. See her "The Role of Theology in the Third Millennium: Views from the Perspective of Medieval Christianity," in *In Quest of Humanity in a Globalizing World: Dutch Contributions to the Jubilee of the Universities in Rome 2000* (Leende, Netherlands: Damon, 2000), 321–38.

27. See Robert A. Markus, *The End of Ancient Christianity* (Cambridge: Cambridge University Press, 1990), 199–211.

28. Peter Brown, *Augustine of Hippo* (Berkeley: University of California Press, 1969), 306–07.

29. See C.S. Lewis, *The Allegory of Love: A Study in Medieval Tradition* (London, Oxford University Press: 1936).

30. See Willemien Otten, *The Anthropology of Johannes Scottus Eriugena* (Leiden: E.J. Brill, 1991). See also *Eriugena: East and West*, ed. B. McGinn and W. Otten (Notre Dame: University of Notre Dame Press, 1994).

31. See Richard W. Southern, *The Making of the Middle Ages* (London: Hutchinson University Library, 1967), 184–94.

32. Aquinas' *Summa theologiae* (arguably the stroke of genius that ended up cutting the Latin West off from the Greek Fathers) did not displace Lombard's *Sentences* until the sixteenth century, when Sylvester of Ferrara and especially Thomas Vio "Cajetan" turned the *Summa* into a coherent system.

33. See Beryl Smalley, *The Study of the Bible in the Middle Ages* (Notre Dame: University of Notre Dame Press, 1964), 112–95.

34. Cf. *The Clerk's Prologue*, in *The Canterbury Tales*, ll. 26–38.

35. By contrast, we moderns classify books: literary, philosophical, theological, spiritual, geographic, historical, and what have you; Dante and Chaucer viewed the written word as such as part of Christian formation.

36. While the instances where the authority of the Christian faith was really contested, therefore, were few and far between, they were nonetheless real. In the case of the extravagant, brilliant thirteenth-century Emperor Frederick II, the claim to have transcended Christianity (which earned him a reputation for atheism, among many other things) may have been mainly a matter of swagger. But there are good reasons to think that the medieval Church had to deal with undercurrents of sophisticated critique, in a variety of quarters. Leaving aside the numerous instances of proletarian, rural anti-clericalism (see Norman Cohn, *The Pursuit of the Millennium*, rev. ed. [New York: Oxford University Press, 1970], 19–126), there was the philosophical daring at the universities, the creative independence found in literary circles, and the increasing claims to secular authority voiced among the merchant class stimulated free thought not always compatible with Christian orthodoxy. In philosophy, there were tendencies toward Averroism and rationalism, sometimes feebly defended by means of the theory—frequently attributed to Siger of Brabant, Aquinas' colleague and adversary in Paris—that there exist two

independent realms of truth, reason and faith. A good deal of medieval literature, including some religious literature, owed more to pagan philosophy than to faith. It is also hard to imagine that there was nothing serious behind the aesthetic charm—often merely elegant, sometimes delightfully naughty—with which many medieval and early Renaissance authors proposed not a few pagan ideas which, if seriously entertained, would be quite offensive; for example, the courtly love tradition. Petrarch, Chaucer, and Boccaccio come to mind; even Dante has not escaped suspicion (see E.L. Fortin, *Dissidence et philosophie au Moyen Age: Dante et ses antécédents, Cahiers d'études médiévales*, 6 [Paris: J. Vrin, 1981]). The advice of the humanist Clelio Calcagnini, "speak with the many, think with the few," was widely taken long before it was formulated. At least for the record, therefore, it must be noted that real dissent, all the more careful for having to be cautious, was far from unknown in the otherwise very Catholic Middle Ages.

37. *The Nun's Priest's Tale* (3438–46), in *The Canterbury Tales*; the reference is to Romans 15:6. The priest winds up the fable of Chauntecleer and Pertelote by telling his listeners not to stop at the bare story, its *sensus historicus*, but to draw the moral lesson from it. Elsewhere, Chaucer, speaking on his own behalf, turns the end of *The Parson's Tale* into a little homily to entreat his readers, on the authority of the same Pauline text, to believe in his good intentions and so, to put a favorable construction on his writings, even where they find them morally objectionable (1080–85).

38. Peter Raedts has argued that nineteenth-century Ultramontanist ideology succeeded in reforming the Catholic Church in the image of a medieval culture that never existed. See "De christelijke middeleeuwen als mythe: Ontstaan en gebruik van een constructie uit de negentiende eeuw" (with a summary in English) *Tijdschrift voor Theologie* 30 (1990): 146-80.

39. See Willemien Otten, "The Role of Theology in the Third Millennium," 335–37.

40. From Gk. *Neapolis*, the Shechem of the patriarchs.

41. *Apol.* I, 46, 2–4; Goodspeed, 58–59; *FC* 6, 83–84 (Bettenson, 5). I long wondered why Heraclitus shows up in Justin's enumeration until I found the substantial *florilegium* of (alleged) Heraclitus quotations in Hippolytus' *Philosophumena*, bk. 9 (*Refutatio omnium haeresium* [Berlin: Walter de Gruyter, 1986], 341-78) The find was occasioned by Hans-Georg Gadamer's fine essay "Zur Überlieferung Heraklits," in *Der Anfang des Wissens* (Stuttgart: Philipp Reclam jun., 1999). Gadamer grants that one fragment in Hippolytus (IX, 11, 348, ll. 56–59), taken as we have it, has to be the fruit of Christian adaptation. Hermann Diels, too, had

come to this conclusion; accordingly, the fragment is absent from *Die Fragmente der Vorsokratiker,* vol. 1 (Berlin: Weidmann, 1951), 139–90). Still, Gadamer argues that this particular fragment is crystallized around a typically Heraclitean philosophical aphorism, for which he submits, by way of hypothesis: "One is justly called father when one has become son of oneself"—meaning that father and son are father and son only by virtue of being relative to each other, so that only by having a son is a father made (note the passive voice) father. In context, Hippolytus is controverting Noetus; he is a heretic, since he appeals to Heraclitus to deny that the Son is truly Son of the Father.

42. *Apol.* II, 13, 3–6; Goodspeed, 88–89. This understanding is reminiscent of the Gregory of Nyssa's insistence that although we are naturally equipped to see God, the actual vision is a gracious gift; in fact, only the gift awakens us to the awareness of our natural ability. For a good example of this, see the sixth of his *Homilies on the Beatitudes,* in *The Lord's Prayer: The Beatitudes* (Westminster, MD: Newman Press, 1954), 143–53. *The Cloud of Unknowing* (ch. 34) gives a similar account of this idea: "The nature of this activity is such that its presence makes a soul able to possess it and to experience it. And that ability is not available to any soul apart from it [the activity]. The ability to perform this activity is united with the activity itself, inseparably; hence, whoever experiences this activity is able to perform it, and no one else—so much so that apart from this activity a soul is, as it were, dead, and unable to crave it or desire it. For as much as you will it and desire it, so much you have of it—no more and no less; and yet it is neither will nor desire, but something you-know-not-what, that stirs you to will and desire you-know-not-what."

43. Basil was resolute, became the father of Eastern monasticism, but equally resolutely took the See of Caesarea. Gregory, forever torn between a desire for contemplation and his sense of duty, ended up resenting Basil's stratagems on his behalf, which eventually got him to the Patriarchal See of Constantinople. After a few months he panicked and fled.

44. *Carmen de sua vita,* 322–24 (emphasis added), in Gregory of Nazianzus, *Autobiographical Poems,* ed. C. White (Cambridge: Cambridge University Press, 1996). Plato's classic distinction between truth and appearance is apparent.

45. Paul Claudel and Arthur Honegger, *Jeanne d'Arc au bûcher,* scene II: "Dominique, Frère Dominique, nous sommes des animaux de la même laine" (Jeanne d'Arc to Frère Dominique).

46. John Bossy, *Christianity in the West, 1400-1700* (Oxford and New York: Oxford University Press, 1985.

47. Cf. John Donne, Sonnet xviii:
Show me, dear Christ, thy spouse, so bright and clear.
What, is it she, which on the other shore
Goes richly painted? or which rob'd and tore
Laments and mourns in Germany and here?
Sleeps she a thousand, then peeps up one year?
Is she self truth and errs? now new, now outwore?
Doth she, and did she, and shall she evermore
On one, on seven, or on no hill appear?
Dwells she with us, or like adventuring knights
First travail we to seek and then make love? (ll. 1-10)

48. Cf. Georges Braque: "Les preuves fatiguent la verité."

49. I am thinking of linguistic pioneers like Aquinas' slightly older contemporary Hadewijch of Antwerp (and Jan van Ruusbroec (1294-1388). See R.W. Chambers, *On the Continuity of English Prose from Alfred to More and His School* (London: Oxford University Press, 1957).

50. Unforgettable in this regard are Leonardo da Vinci, Niccolò Machiavelli, Francesco Guicciardini, Francisco Jiménez de Cisneros, Teresa of Avila, Juan of the Cross, Brother Martin Luther and his splendid Bible, François Rabelais, John Colet, John Lyly, Thomas More (who wrote a history of Richard III in English, probably in his mid-thirties)—to mention just the more important.

51. See Charles Taylor, *Sources of the Self: The Making of the Modern Identity* (Cambridge: Harvard University Press, 1989), esp. 127-42, 495-521.

52. At this point, I am tempted to drop another raft of names, of artists this time. Let me just mention one, who incorporates the subjective mood of the period at its most tortured: Mathias Grünewald, the painter of the masterpiece known as the *Isenheimer Altar* (1515; Colmar, France).

53. His formula is *forma agendi cum hominibus eosdemque tractandi* (*Constitutiones Societatis Iesu*, P. X, 3 [814]).

54. In comparison with Erasmus and Ignatius, famous fourteenth- and fifteenth-century works on the discernment of spirits such as those by "Henry of Hessia" (i.e., Heinrich Heinbuche von Langenstein, 1325-1397) and *De discretione et examinatione spirituum* (in *Doctoris ecstatici Dionysii Cartusiani opera minora*, vol. 8 [*Opera Omnia*, vol. 40 (Tournai: Cartusia S.M. de Pratis, 1911), 261-319] by "Denis the Carthusian" (i.e., Denys van Leeuwen, *alias* Denys Ryckel, 1402/3-1471) are cumbersome and arid.

55. See Robert Bireley, *The Refashioning of Catholicism, 1450–1700: A Reassessment of the Counter Reformation* (Washington: Catholic University of America Press, 1999), 6–8.

56. Walter J. Ong, S.J., *Ramus: Method and the Decay of Dialogue* (Cambridge: Harvard University Press, 1983).

57. Walter J. Ong, S.J., *The Presence of the Word: Some Prolegomena for Cultural and Religious History* (New York: Simon and Schuster, 1970), 223.

58. See F.J. van Beeck, *Christ Proclaimed: Christology as Rhetoric* (New York: Paulist Press, 1979), 66–69.

59. Henri de Lubac has provided us with a keen analysis of Cajetan's betrayal of Aquinas on this point: *The Mystery of the Supernatural* (New York: Herder and Herder, 1967), 181–216.

60. They were also referred to as *theatra:* "viewing places." In modern English we still say "operating-theater."

61. Interestingly, the *professio fidei tridentina* (DS 1862–1870) is one of only two sixteenth- and seventeenth-century professions of faith that open with the Nicene-Constantinopolitan creed (albeit with the *filioque* addition). Only the (Lutheran) *Book of Concord* (1580) features the three creeds properly so called—the Apostles', the Nicene-Constantinopolitan, and the Athanasian—before featuring the early (1527–39) Lutheran consensus documents and the *Formula Concordiae* (1577). In all the professions of faith of the various scions of the Reformation, the creeds are marginalized to the point of disappearance. Instead, their truth is now predicated on the "articles" of faith, sometimes with the addition of a phrase like "since they can be proved from Scripture." It is fair to say, therefore, that the (baptismal, and thus, liturgical) creed was implicitly supplanted by "articles of faith," even in the Catholic Church, insofar as the catechism (as against the liturgy) became the ordinary tool for religious instruction, and where only the clergy were obliged to attest to their orthodoxy by a formal acceptance of the *professio fidei tridentina.* An example of the effect of this development is the title of John H. Leith's useful *Creeds of the Churches: A Reader of Christian Doctrine from the Bible to the Present,* 3rd ed. (Atlanta: John Knox Press, 1982). In this title, "creed" means any profession of Christian faith. The problem is that, as E.J. Bicknell rightly points out, "Articles are primarily 'tests for teachers.' They set a limit to official teaching. Creeds are for teachers and learners alike." See his classic *A Theological Introduction to the Thirty-nine Articles of the Church of England,* 3rd ed. (London: Longmans, Green, and Co., 1955), 19.

62. John W. O'Malley, *The First Jesuits* (Cambridge: Harvard University Press, 1993), 200 (italics added for emphasis).

63. Alternative expression: *aprovechar a las animas.*

64. Ignatius of Loyola, *Autobiography*, in *The Spiritual Exercises and Selected Works*, ed. George Ganss (New York: Paulist Press, 1991), 80–81.

65. See John W. O'Malley, *The First Jesuits*, 134–64, 215–25, 264–66.

66. This qualification characterizes not only the definitive edition of the *Institutes* (1559), but also the very first, written when Calvin was a mere twenty-seven years old, and published in 1536.

67. Most recently published as *The Constitutions of the Society of Jesus and Their Complementary Norms* (Saint Louis: Institute for Jesuit Sources, 1996).

68. Here is the full text: "But as for one who is ignorant of the other fundamentals, namely, 'The Power of Sin,' 'The Law,' and 'Grace,' I do not see how I can call him a Christian. For from these things Christ is known, since *to know Christ means to know his benefits*, and not, as they [i.e., the Scholastics] teach, to reflect upon his natures and the modes of his incarnation. . . . In his letter to the Romans, *when he was writing a compendium of Christian doctrine*, did Paul philosophize about the mysteries of the Trinity, the mode of incarnation, or active and passive creation? No! But what does he discuss? He takes up *the law, sin, grace, fundamentals on which the knowledge of Christ exclusively rests.*" See *Loci communes von 1521*, ed. Hans Engelland, in *Melanchthons Werke*, vol. 2, ed. Robert Stupperich (Gütersloh: C. Bertelsmann Verlag, 1952), 3–163, quoted at 21–22 (italics added for emphasis).

69. See F.J. van Beeck, *God Encountered: A Contemporary Catholic Systematic Theology*, vol. 1, 2nd ed. (Collegeville, MN: Liturgical Press, [1997]), §20, 2. It might be added that Neo-Protestantism was to end up treating the cosmos as morally indifferent as well, Immanuel Kant being the supreme example.

70. It could perhaps be argued that here lies the root of the failure to remain professedly Christian on the part of those North American institutions of higher learning that were started under Protestant auspices.

71. See "Die ignatianische Mystik der Weltfreudigkeit," in *Schriften zur Theologie*, vol. 3 (Einsiedeln: Benziger Verlag, 1956), 329-48; ET, "The Ignatian Mysticism of Joy in the World," in *Theological Investigations*, vol. 3 (London: Darton, Longman and Todd, 1966), 277-93.

72. T.S. Eliot, *Selected Essays 1917-1932* (New York: Harcourt, Brace and Company, 1932), 241-50.

73. In the sense of *wissenschaftlich*, "scholarly."

74. For an eloquent as well as competent autobiographical witness to this, see Guy Consolmagno, *Brother Astronomer: Adventures of a Vatican Scientist* (New York: McGraw-Hill, 2000).

75. See F.J. van Beeck, *God Encountered: A Contemporary Catholic Systematic Theology*, vol. 1, 2nd ed. (Collegeville, MN: Liturgical Press, [1997]), §28, 6, c–d.

76. A splendid yet by no means uncharacteristic monument to this practice is *The Jesuit Relations and Allied Documents: Travels and Explorations of the Jesuit Missionaries in New France, 1610-1791; the Original French, Latin, and Italian: Texts, with English Translations and Notes*, ed. Reuben Gold Thwaites (Cleveland: Burrows Bros., 1896–1901).

77. See James Hennesey, *American Catholics: A History of the Roman Catholic Community in the United States* (New York: Oxford University Press, 1981), 7, where Hennesey appeals to the sociological studies of Elizabeth Nottingham.

78. The clearest indication to the fact that North American Protestantism has always been different from classical European Protestantism is the inclination to theological gloom of the latter and the moral optimism of the former. Total depravity may have been taught and even professed this side of the Atlantic, but it hardly ever made its mark on the soul.

79. On this theme, see two revealing articles by Thomas E. Wangler: "The Birth of Americanism: 'Westward the Apocalyptic Candlestick,' " *Harvard Theological Review* 65 (1972): 415–436; and "American Catholic Expansionism: 1886–1894," *Harvard Theological Review* 75 (1982): 371–393. Needless to say, "Americanism" was a negative European-Catholic construction put on an America which to established European Catholicism looked implausible as well as heretical; obviously, the many immigrants who were moving here to work for a living thought otherwise. Most puzzlingly to Europeans, Americans claimed that being American was positively compatible with being a Catholic. The reason behind it was that the U.S. were politically allied neither with Europe's Enlightenment anti-Catholic liberalism nor with modern anti-Christian socialism.

80. See F.J. van Beeck, *Catholic Identity after Vatican II: Three Types of Faith in the One Church* (Chicago: Loyola University Press, 1985).

81. See www.commonwealmagazine.org. The soon-to-be Cardinal Francis George gave a homily at Chicago's Old Saint Patrick's Church on January 17, 1998. It included the phrase "liberal Catholicism is an exhausted project." Cardinal George agreed to explain what he meant, which he did at a *Commonweal* Forum held on Wednesday, October 6, 1999 at Loyola University Chicago. The Forum was subsequently published in *Commonweal*. In my judgment, it is of high relevance to the present conference.

82. On this issue, see Johann Baptist Metz, *Zeit der Orden: Zur Mystik und Politik der Nachfolge* (Freiburg: Herder, 1977); and ET, *Followers of Christ: Perspectives on the Religious Life* (London: Burns and Oates; New York: Paulist Press, 1978).

83. See F.J. van Beeck, *God Encountered: A Contemporary Catholic Systematic Theology*, vol. 2/4A: *The Revelation of the Glory*, part IVA: *The Genealogy of Depravity: Morality and Immorality* (Collegeville, MN: Liturgical Press, 1999), §132.

84. "Towards a Fundamental Theological Interpretation of Vatican II," *Theological Studies* 40 (1979): 716–27; cf. "Theologische Grundinterpretation des II. Vatikanischen Konzils," in *Schriften zur Theologie*, 14 (Einsiedeln, Köln: Benziger Verlag, 1980), 287–302.

85. *Vatican Council II* (New York: Farrar, Straus and Giroux, 1968). Xavier Rynne, it turned out, was Rev. Francis X. Murphy, C.Ss.R., a long-time resident of Rome.

86. This is a translation of the title of a painting by Paul Gauguin in the Boston Museum of Fine Arts: *D'où venons-nous? Que sommes-nous? Où allons-nous?* The present reference means to convey contrast, not affinity, for the painting conveys a sultry atmosphere, and what chiefly contributes to this is the near-oppressive ambiguity of the scene and everything in it. It is impossible to tell the direction of the light, let alone the time of day; the age of the figures is hard to determine; it is even harder to determine what (if anything) they are doing. Most remarkably, the difference between men and women is hard to tell. Indeterminacy reigns supreme. The painting is neither sad nor happy. It makes one wonder, and wonder without much hope for a resolution.

87. One of the more salient being that there is really no such thing as popular art, or even popular culture.

88. Garry Wills, *Papal Sin: Structures of Deceit* (New York: Doubleday, 2000).

89. See F.J. van Beeck, *God Encountered: A Contemporary Catholic Systematic Theology*, vol. 1, 2nd rev. ed. Collegeville, MN: Liturgical Press, 1997), §28, 1-6.

90. See *L'Osservatore Romano: Weekly Edition in English*, October 4, 2000, 1, 12.

91. See F.J. van Beeck, *God Encountered: A Contemporary Catholic Systematic Theology*, vol. 2 (Collegeville, MN: Liturgical Press, 1994), x–xi.

CHAPTER THIRTEEN

Teaching as Vocation

MONIKA K. HELLWIG

Father van Beeck's remarkable paper demonstrates from history under what conditions Catholic intellectual life can flourish, and hints at the end to some internal conditions under which it can most certainly not flourish.

Teaching as a vocation was a concept accepted as meaningful by such great Christian thinkers as Paul of Tarsus, Origen of Alexandria, Thomas Aquinas, Ignatius of Loyola, not to mention a great multitude of founders and foundresses of teaching congregations in modern times. Vocation in the Christian context is in the first place the calling to follow Christ in discipleship, a calling that is common to all of us by virtue of our baptism. That this vocation belongs to all the baptized does not diminish its meaning for each of us. Further, within that general shared calling, each of us is called to some specific task related to the coming reign of God. As Paul expresses it in I Corinthians, chapter 12, we are called according to the gifts we are given to be apostles, prophets, teachers, miracle workers, healers, and so forth. That some are called to be apostles does not take away the vocation and dignity of those who are called to be teachers or healers. It is in the complementarity of gifts and tasks that fullness of the presence of the risen Christ in the world is realized. This is a matter of calling, of vocation. That is surely not a problematic claim. It would be extraordinarily unfortunate if the shaping of awareness, alertness, knowledge, and attitudes of the future generations of young people were not seen as Christian vocation. What, after all, is closer to the building of the church, the work of the redemption, the reaching towards the Reign of God in the world than the passing on of the heritage and the formation of the People of God of the future?

The vocation of teaching in the Christian tradition begins with the rather extraordinary Hebrew way of initiating young people into their tradition. That context of narrative and celebration, of festival and pilgrimage, of blessings and prayers, of customs and patterns of life, of family observances and synagogue gatherings must have shaped Jesus. To be a teacher of tradition, of wisdom, of the good and godly life, was and is a highly esteemed calling, vocation, in the Hebraic tradition. The title of rabbi is one of the ways that the disciples expressed their understanding of Jesus' own vocation and mission. He is presented as the teacher *par excellence,* never as ruler or commander, and never as priest, except in the Letter to the Hebrews, which turns the prior notion of priesthood upside down. His vocation is presented as that of teacher. Even in his death he is above all the teacher. Moreover, the gospels and the early tradition are at pains to tell us much about Jesus' own way of teaching, based on the tradition he inherited but internalized and reflected so that it has become essentially his own. He models in himself what he asks of his disciples: to be like a householder who is able to bring from his storehouse both old and new riches. Jesus' own way of teaching, his adult education project in his public ministry, for such it was, is recognizable today as consciousness raising, liberating, challenging his listeners to trust their own experience, to reflect critically on their own experience. Always the great literature and learning of the Hebrew tradition is in the background, but he cuts to the heart of the issues past the sophistry. This surely is also what he expects of his followers, whose vocation is first discipleship, that is to say, learning from the master teacher, and secondly teaching, that is to say the sharing of the fruits of learning and experience contemplated.

Our rich tradition of teaching as a vocation includes in the second Christian century the wonderful Greek apologists with their critiques and syntheses of wisdom traditions in the pagan and

Hebrew worlds. But our tradition of teaching includes also, from the second century on, a catechetical and theological tradition from Irenaeus to Origen to Augustine. These were great thinkers for whom no aspect of their Christian lives was more important than their vocation of teaching. When they engaged in scholarship it was so as to share the gifts of wisdom and insight, certainly not to gain eminence for themselves as scholars or Fathers of the Church. That was merely a byproduct of their principal aim to clarify the meaning of our faith, hope, and way of life for others. From Irenaeus, who shaped the salvation-history pattern of handing on the faith and theologizing about it, to Clement and Origin, who brought Scripture and philosophy together in a new way of organizing theological thought, to the great catechetical and mystagogical works of the fourth century, and the magnificent syntheses in philosophical and doctrinal theology of Augustine, the focus of the church as been on the vocation of teaching.

In the medieval era we have not only the great scholastic debates and architectonic constructions, directed to the inner circle of privileged scholars, and becoming by the early fourteenth century quite obscure and effete. We have also the monastic tradition of *lectio divina.* In addition to the benefits of this tradition for individuals, it produced a great copying and treasuring of manuscripts. This copying, compiling, maintaining, and cherishing of manuscripts was surely all with the intent of sharing and passing on, in other words, as a project of teaching. In this aspect of medieval scholarship and teaching, we should not forget that women, while excluded from the cathedral schools, from the *studia generalia,* and from the subsequent universities, were very much engaged in the monastic tradition, with its educational combination of prayer, work, and study. We have some extraordinary testimonies about this, for instance from Hildegarde of Bingen, who in our times has suddenly been remembered and brought out of relative obscurity among scholars.

Even the great scholastics bear significant testimony to the Christian vocation of teaching. Among other developments, they invented schools where large numbers of people were taught simultaneously in a certain progression of subject matter. When we notice the extent to which the early mendicant friars, especially Franciscans and Dominicans in the first fervor of their congregations, became involved in the schools, it is clear that they saw this involvement as a matter of Christian vocation. Our greatest, best known, and most quoted scholar of this time, Thomas Aquinas, tells us of his concern with the scholar's vocation of teaching. In the introduction to his *Summa Theologica,* we learn that when he arrived in Paris he was distressed and indignant because the scholars there were having so much fun, arguing with one another, that they were ignoring the students. They were throwing the students into the middle of the scholastic argument where they could not possibly get a foothold because they had not heard what the debate had been about before. And that motivated this very great work of Aquinas.

By the time of the Reformation, Ignatius of Loyola found that Paris was still carrying on the tradition of Thomas in that respect. Loyola had found in his studies in Spain that they were still playing the games and not paying attention to the students while Paris was the place where they had a decent curriculum and held their professors to it. In the same way Ignatius and his early followers in their turn recognized teaching as a sublime vocation to which the very best minds and the most competent people could justly devote themselves after discerning what for them might be the *magis* of their service to Christ and the Church. So much has this been recognized by the Church in modern times that devoting oneself to the education of the young has even at times become part of the formula of vows in which the response to vocation is expressed. Even among the practices and exhortations of the Reformers, Catholics can find inspirational examples of the Christian vocation of teaching. In the Catholic post-Tridentine community the recognition of teaching as a vocation flourished in the emergence of a multitude of vowed congregations of women and of men for whom teaching was the central apostolate of their calling. It became evermore evident that education, not only in the faith but in secular fields, was the key to refinement of conscience and responsibility, the hope of the poor and despised for a more fully human existence, and the means of engaging the privileged in concern and action for the common good. Education was clearly the basic need for a peaceful and just society and for the cultivation of civility and mutual consideration.

In the contemporary Western industrialized world, however, teaching is not greatly respected. It is common knowledge that our future professors coming out of the graduate schools define themselves by expertise on some topic on which they can publish—in which they can be noted by fellow scholars. It is only a few of the liberal arts four-year colleges that doggedly value and promote the importance of teaching. There are a number of reasons for that. We have all blamed the graduate schools; we have also blamed the Germans for the research university model. But why has it invaded our college corridors so badly? Is it perhaps that even among us who call ourselves Christian, money, power, and prestige are the dominant operational values? Could that be the reason that while the religious congregations were the dominant presence in Catholic colleges and universities, teaching was honored as a worthy way to spend one's time and energies? And can it be that with the diminished numbers of religious and the greater number of professors trained in the graduate schools of the great state universities, the values connected with the Christian sense of vocation have slipped into more secular ways of thinking?

There is an interesting, additional factor that is troubling us. In the wake of the Second Vatican Council, there has been tremendous enthusiasm for social transformation—direct social action. Highly qualified people have fled the classrooms to go into direct social action. In many ways, it was good, since we had not been present in those places. But in the process, we did forget that the best strategy, the best instrumentality for social transformation, is the way we teach younger people. One of the reasons that we forgot that has a lot to do with the last historical part of Father van Beeck's paper. One of the reasons we forgot the immense intrinsic value of teaching is that the understanding and practice of teaching and schooling had become so restricted.

There is a distinction to be made between teaching as a generic term and education in the full sense of the word. One can teach people to drive a car, to read a map, to operate a machine. Education, however, is the drawing forth of human potential in a far deeper sense, and Christian education is the drawing forth of the Christian potential that is in the baptized people, the children, the adolescents, the young adults, the mature adults whom we are educating in our colleges and universities. It is also true that education and schooling are not the same thing, that education happens in very many ways, beyond schooling. But at least we ought to be focusing the schools on really educating and not only teaching in some much more restricted sense. This, surely, is integral to the Christian vocation in our times when personal discernment and responsibility needs to be redeemed from mass culture and media domination, when the sense of human community needs to be redeemed from defensive factions and rampant competition for the world's wealth and power, and when human values need to be redeemed from the idolatry of the dollar sign.

At the conclusion of this response to Father van Beeck's paper, I offer words of wisdom from four key wisdom figures of our world. The first is Moses Maimonides, who said the following in answer to the question whether converts to Judaism were on the same footing with born and raised Jews: Of course, he said, when people convert to the Jewish tradition, we have to put them on a footing of equality with the rest of us. But they are really never on a footing of equality because those who have been born and raised in the devoutly observant Jewish community feel God like the ground under their feet. That is applicable to Catholic tradition also when it is fully lived, and it indicates what Catholic education has the potential to be.

The second word of wisdom is from philosopher Hans-Georg Gadamer, who said that the heart of the meaning of the dance is in the dancing of it. And only in some secondary sense, by bridges of imagination and empathy, does one enjoy the dancing of somebody else on the stage in a great ballet, because one can, so to speak, cross on a bridge of empathy from personal experience into the experience of the dancer. This suggests much about Catholic tradition, with its iconography, its literature, its saints, its festivals offering a basis for education and drawing forth from people both their human potential and their Christian potential.

A third word of wisdom is not by, but about the Baal Shem Tov, the founder of the Hassidic tradition of Judaism in Eastern

Europe. When he was alive, his way of teaching his disciples was to take them apart into a place in the forest. They would light a fire, they would initiate very slowly the wordless songs of the Hassidim, the meditative, mystical singing, and they would dance, slowly, solemnly, establishing a rhythm, establishing quiet and so on, and in the context of that, they would learn sublime mysteries. Unfortunately, the story says, when the Baal Shem Tov died, at first we went and built the fire and sang and danced. After a while we no longer danced, then again after a while we no longer sang, and presently we no long built the fire, and after that we forgot the place in the forest. I hope that in our schools, in our colleges, we are going to be working on real education and that we are not going to forget these things.

The fourth word of wisdom is from the Dalai Lama. It was relayed to me second hand, and perhaps it is not, therefore, exactly his vocabulary. Someone had asked him, what is the source of knowledge of the truth. And he said that the source is experience—honed, fully enhanced, and grasped experience. But he said, it is also logical deduction if it leads to such experience, and it is also authority if it leads to that kind of logical deduction which in turn leads to such experience.

CHAPTER FOURTEEN

The Vocation of Teaching

MILDRED HAIPT

I t is a great privilege for me to be part of this discussion of the vocation of teaching. I am awed and moved by the presentations at this conference that have preceded mine, and in some sense, I feel like the caboose on the train.

Since my preparation for this experience has been a salutary one, I want to thank especially President Cernera for his invitation. I first met Tony when he was with Bread for the World. He has spent the intervening years in higher education, where he has fed thousands of men and women with the intellectual and spiritual bread that so many yearn for today. In a very real sense, his life exemplifies an unswerving commitment to education and to the Catholic intellectual tradition.

The vocation of teaching is, first of all, a mystery. It is a little like falling in love, an attraction for something: in this case, a profession that one cannot fully understand and explain. I yielded to the attraction in the midst of my undergraduate years at Fordham University when I decided to prepare for teaching rather than social work. I would like to say that the decision occurred in a dramatic moment, but I cannot. Instead, I came to teaching through a gradual turning in the direction where my heart, and I dare say, God was leading me. That turning point took place many, many years ago. Since then, I have taught in a variety of settings and situations, which include religious instruction to children and adolescents, homebound instruction for the disabled, elementary and secondary school education, in-service workshops for teachers here and abroad, English as a second language in Mexico and Thailand, workshops for inmates in Sing Sing prison, and most important, higher education for over thirty years. The teaching profession has provided me with varied experiences, always new and challenging opportunities in which to stretch and to grow.

During my tenure in higher education, the vocation of teaching has been marked by profound changes. Many transformations in education reflect the changes from the modern to a postmodern world. When I first came to the College of New Rochelle in 1961, teaching was primarily a search for the truth, some of which I thought I possessed as a result of my many years of preparation and experience. My primary task was to impart knowledge, help students in their search for truth, and in particular, provide my teacher education students with the intellectual foundation and framework for their teaching careers. Now the experience of the students and the part they play in their own education have assumed greater importance in my teaching. Education for me has become much more student-centered. The focus is on the outcomes of teaching as much as on the content and delivery of instruction. What are the students learning in terms of knowledge, skills, and attitudes? And, how will the students demonstrate what they have learned? These are questions heard from many sides.

My Ursuline experience in the Catholic faith tradition stressed the education of the whole person, the dignity of each individual, knowledge enlightened by faith, and a social consciousness based on justice and peace. These realizations were and still are fundamental to my teaching practices, and they certainly were reinforced by the Catholic intellectual tradition that I found at the College of New Rochelle in the early 1960s. Today, my students are more diverse in nationality, race, academic preparation, and ethnic backgrounds. And the majority of students, faculty, and administrators are no longer Catholic.

A general acknowledgment of the importance of knowledge enlightened by faith on the part of the college community as a whole is at best elusive. The human landscape of the campus has undergone a radical change that is especially challenging to the Catholic intellectual tradition. Given these cultural and religious differences, the temptation is to suppress the Catholic intellectual tradition rather then to explore, with faculty and students, the richness of each tradition and to value and appreciate what each brings to the multicultural and ecumenical world in which we find ourselves. My colleagues and I encourage students to get in touch with their own traditions, to share them and learn about their neighbors' background. Through this educational process, they develop a sense of pride, discover commonalities, and gain an appreciation and openness towards others.

When asked to describe a multicultural experience that had prepared her to teach in a multicultural classroom, one of my African-American Hispanic students wrote that before coming to college, the only cultures she was exposed to were African-American and Hispanic. It was then that she wrote, and I quote, "I met many people who came from all across the country and even from different countries. At first, I was not open to meeting new people and learning new things. After freshman orientation week, I had already met three people whom I knew nothing about: one person from Michigan, one who was born in Lebanon, and one from Florida. Each person had a personality much like mine. This opened my mind to new people. Being a part of the College of New Rochelle community has opened my eyes and taught me things I never realized existed."

Our teacher education programs in particular emphasize community service. Students in the introductory courses are expected to perform service in an educational setting in or outside of a school. They are asked to reflect on their interactions with, and teaching of, children and adolescents, and to draw from the experiences implications for their future as classroom teachers. These assignments bring a sense of realism to the process of teacher education and enable the students to test their own interest and fitness for the teaching profession.

Moral education is a special topic in two of the education courses I teach. Students research the topic on the Internet, discuss case studies involving moral decision-making and write about the moral education they received at home, school, church, and community. It is a question that brings to the surface many strong opinions and ideals, that they hold for future generations. In the course of their professional preparation, education students develop and state their personal philosophy of education in terms of the goals of education, the roles of teacher and students, the teaching/learning process, and the learning environment. Some of their ideas are derived from the study of outstanding philosophers of education, but a good number of their ideas evolve from their personal history and practice in the classroom. Now, we might say that multicultural education, community service, moral education, and a personal philosophy of education are not particularly Catholic with a capital C, yet each is consistent with what is most basic to the tradition, especially as it evolved in the Twentieth Century.

The Vatican II *Declaration on Christian Education* of October 28, 1965, notes the following:

Among the various organs of education, the school is of outstanding importance. In nurturing the intellectual faculties, which is its special mission, it develops a capacity for sound judgment and introduces the students to the cultural heritage bequeathed to them by former generations. It fosters a sense of values and prepares them for professional life. By providing for friendly contact, between pupils of different characters and backgrounds, it encourages mutual understanding. Splendid therefore, and of the highest importance, is the vocation of those who help parents in carrying out their duties and act in the name of the community by undertaking a teaching career. This vocation requires special qualities of mind and heart and most careful preparation and a constant readiness to accept new ideas and to adapt the old.[1]

Influenced by the *Declaration on Christian Education*, events following the Second Vatican Council, and movements in the secular society, many Catholic educators have shifted their thinking about schools as institutions to schools as communities. By creating a sense of community in the classroom and school, we as teachers can provide a supportive and caring learning environment for students whose lives are often troubled by disruptive home conditions and societal pressures. The Church's document, *To Teach as Jesus Did*, issued in 1972, identified this community as one in which

> one person's problem is everyone's problem, and one person's victory is everyone's victory. . . . Community is at the heart of Christian education not simply as a concept to be taught but as a reality to be lived. Through education, men must be moved to build community in all areas of life; they can do it best if they have learned the meaning of community by experiencing it. Formed by this experience, they are better able to build community in their families, their places of work, their neighborhoods, their nation, their world.[2]

Since our global society is becoming more and more diverse in terms of nationality, race and educational background, customs, and religion, there is an ever-growing need to create learning environments that give students a feeling of self-worth and belonging. A caring school environment may be compared to that of a family, where each person is loved, nurtured, and given the freedom to be all that he or she is capable of becoming. The bonds that bind us together in a school community, as elsewhere, are a set of shared ideas and ideals. These are formed over time through relationships among those who make up the school. From time to time, these connections and relationships are ritualized and sanctified in practices rich in meaning and significance. Eventually, as Sergiovani points out, schools become "communities of relationship, of place, of mind and of memory."[3]

The vocation of teaching in the twenty-first century invites me to a life-long or a long-term energetic commitment to the human development of each college student, who at times can appear as a stranger, in her cool speech, manner, likes, appearance, and lifestyle. I am summoned to trust her desire and capacity to learn, even when she shows a lack of interest in her studies, absents herself from class, or is late in submitting assignments. My daily recommitment as a teacher calls for new enthusiasm, energy, and expressions of love for my subject and my students.

A second quality I need in living out the vocation of teaching is reflection on the students' experience and on my own. In retrospect, the roles and responsibilities of a teacher seemed much clearer and well-defined in the past than they do today. Students' lives and ours were more stable and predictable. The content of the curriculum changed, but not so rapidly as it does today. Each year, I ask a group of my students who have been out in the field to describe a metaphor for the school they have been visiting. This has proven to be an interesting and rewarding activity for them and it has also prompted me to think of a metaphor for teaching.

My current metaphor for the vocation of teaching is that of a postmodern circus with acrobats only. There are no animals, no safety nets. This high-tech circus from Montreal, Canada, is called the *Cirque du Soleil*. It made its first appearance in New York City in 1995. The performers are described as incredibly strong, graceful, and nimble. They tumble and fly in the air without nets or trapezes. The most frequently used prop is a thick rope that hangs from a moving track on the ceiling from which an acrobat swings, spins, and ties himself up in knots. The performances are daring and amazing at the same time. The vocation of teaching is somewhat like this, especially in the context of the Catholic intellectual tradition. Many of the familiar characters and acts are gone. The traditional props are removed, uncertainty is in the air. As the producer states in a program note, the *Cirque du Soleil* highlights our frailties and our anguish in the face of the new millennium.

Two months ago, university professors and administrators from around the world met in Rome, Italy, to explore the theme, "The University for a New Humanism." In the course of his remarks to the assembly, Pope John Paul II commended university professors for their reaffirmation of the need for a university culture which is genuinely humanistic. He went on to say, "The humanism which we desire advocates a vision of society centered on the human person and his inalienable rights, on the values of peace and justice, on a correct relationship between individuals, society, and the state, and on the logic of solidarity and subsidiarity. It is a humanism capable of giving a soul to economic progress itself so that it may be directed to the promotion of each individual and of the whole person."[4]

John Paul's challenge, I believe, is realistic and feasible. It is one that inspires me to renew my commitment to the vocation of teaching while discerning its potential to strengthen the relationship between knowledge and faith, the human and the divine, in a spirit of courage and hope.

Notes

1. In Austin Flannery, ed., *Vatican Council II: The Conciliar and Post-Conciliar Documents*, vol 1, rev. ed. (Northport, NY: Costello Publishing, 1988), 730.

2. "To Teach as Jesus Did," A Pastoral Message on Catholic Education, November 1972, National Conference of Catholic Bishops (Washington, D.C.: U.S. Catholic Conference, 1972), 7.

3. Thomas J. Sergiovanni, *The Principalship: A Reflective Practice Perspective*, 3rd ed. (Boston: Allyn and Bacon, 1995), 157.

4. "Address of John Paul II to University professors of All Nations," September 9, 2000, given in Rome on the occasion of the Jubilee of University Professors, unpublished ms., 3.

CHAPTER FIFTEEN

Teaching and Learning, Faith and Reason

GERALD A. MCCOOL

I n his wide-ranging and insightful survey of the Catholic
tradition of teaching and learning, Father van Beeck has given
us a lot to think about. Although I agree with a good deal of what
he has said, I would like to make a few additions to his
presentation focused more on faith and reason than on faith and
learning. Before doing that, however, it might be well to review
what I consider some of the main points in Father van Beeck's
remarkable presentation.

Through the first millennium of undivided Christianity, in the
works of a small band of believers, thoroughly at home in the
world in which they lived, a Catholic culture, universal in its
scope, religious and profane in its content, came into being. The
inspiration for that culture was the Christian conviction that the
Word of God had manifested himself to human reflection not
only as the redeeming source of supernatural grace but also as the
exemplary cause of the created natural world. Fallen reason was
not considered incapable of recognizing God's glory in his
creation as theologians in the tradition of the Reformation would
later claim. The Word of God, by his natural and supernatural
influence, was also believed to enlighten the thinking and the
believing mind. Christians therefore were able to feel at home
with the culture of their world. Creation's natural intelligibility
and the created wisdom of the world's inhabitants, coming as both

did from God himself, were able to bring into being a culture hospitable to the reflections of an inquiring faith. Furthermore, the tranquil, open, welcoming faith of its first centuries could draw upon the unified culture of a still undivided Church, and, for the early part of the first millennium at least, could draw on the wisdom of a still undivided Empire. Enduring classics on Christian education, inspired by that early comprehensive vision of an as yet undivided world of grace and nature, such as Augustine's *De Doctrina Christiana*, have come down to us from that time.

Unfortunately, as Father van Beeck and I both believe, in a later period of Christian history, due to the influence of medieval nominalism, that earlier all-embracing comprehensive vision of Christian truth (singular) was narrowed in its scope by an emphasis on clear definitions as the norm of truth (truths). When nominalism and Augustinianism came together, as they did in Luther, the Reformation exaltation of faith under grace and the distrust of fallen reason led to a separated world of faith from the world of natural reason. The unified culture of a unified Church was no longer possible, and the educational consequences of the consequent narrowing of Christian faith would make themselves evident in the history of modern Europe.

Once Western Christianity was divided by the Reformation controversial theology became the principal weapon employed in the acrimonious disputes between the divided churches. Clear propositional definition could then establish itself as the criterion of religious peace was finally established by the secular powers of Europe, the temporal princes of the continent replaced the Church as the authority which determined the religious faith of their subjects. The religious norm of Westphalia, *cujus regio ejus religio*, then added exterior social control to propositional definition as the communal guarantee of religious truth. The age of the state church had come. Controlled by the secular governments of Catholic and Protestant Europe the state church was the most powerful influence in religious life during the century and a half between the Treaty of Westphalia and the French Revolution. During the *ancien régime* of the seventeenth and eighteenth century absolute monarchs, the papacy progressively lost its power and influence. European governments rather than the Church appointed bishops, controlled the universities, and by an increasingly ruthless use of the royal *exsequatur*, made it extremely difficult for external definition of religious truth. The comprehensive universality of *truth*, characteristic of the early centuries of the Church, had been narrowed into propositional definition and into a restrictive multiplicity of confessional state approved *truths*. In the age of the absolute monarchies of the *ancien régime*, first the interior freedom of individual Catholic scholars, and, toward the end of the *ancien régime*, even of the pope and of religious orders, was hemmed in by exterior state control. Under these conditions it was hard for the older Catholic tradition of teaching and learning to survive.

More happily, with the Renaissance and the Reformation came a stress on the subject whose philosophical and religious value would later be recognized. Less happily for religion, Protestant distrust of human reason made the objective world of human experience an alien universe, a world no longer open to the subjective inner light of faith. It was easy for an alien universe like that to transform itself during the seventeenth century into a mechanical world of science and philosophy, a world whose only meaning was the meaning imposed on it by human manipulation. Such, for example, was the world of Francis Bacon. As we recall, the unified culture of the first millennium came from faith's reflection on the intrinsic intelligibility of God's created universe, a universe through which God revealed himself. In the early Christian centuries, that universe was understood through the Greek metaphysics of form and finality. The Reformer's distrust of reason, already nurtured by nominalism, built a wall between reflecting faith and the natural intelligibility of God's created universe. Post-Cartesian mathematical philosophy then rejected the metaphysics of form and finality on which the Church of the ancient world and the high Middle Ages had built both its theology and its spirituality. For radical empiricism in the tradition of Francis Bacon, as we know, human reason was no longer the discoverer of the world's intelligibility. Human reason was the creator of that intelligibility.

By the eighteenth century, faith and reason, subject and object could no longer cooperate, as once they had, in forming the unified vision of the world typical of classical Christian teaching and learning. The unified view of truth of classical Christian wisdom had dissolved into the distance and disconnected truths of religious and scientific knowledge. In the divided secular and religious intellectual world of modern Europe, propositional truth ruled supreme. Confessional religious truth had become propositional statements, whose content was determined all too often by the theologians and lawyers of the absolute monarchies. And, since science was propositional and deductive, scientific truth was propositional as well. The ideal of European rationalism in both its rationalist and empiricist forms was a deductive system, working down from a set of evident propositional first principles or propositionally describable facts. The unifying role of intuition in the older metaphysics, ethics, speculative, and spiritual theology had been forgotten, with consequences whose destructive nature are becoming evident today. In the Church of the first millennium reason was far from being the deductive propositional reason of seventeenth and eighteenth century science and philosophy. It was Aristotelian, Platonic, or Stoic reason, an intuitive reason, broader, more subtle, and much more capable of unifying the full extent of subjective and objective reality than the narrower, highly restrictive reason which we have inherited from seventeenth-century science and philosophy.

Fortunately for the Catholic tradition of teaching and learning, St. Ignatius of Loyola, whose influence on that tradition has been enormous, was able to avoid the narrowness of mind brought about by truth understood as propositional definition. Why was that so? Father van Beeck believes because the fundamental vision of reality—the one which gave determined the horizon of Ignatius' world view and, by doing so, gave meaning to the objects contained in it—came to him from his mystical experience at Manresa. That original vision, the result of prayer, rather than of the subsequent instruction received at the universities of Spain and Paris, defined his world. The intuitive unity of his primordial vision of reality helps to account for the Ignatius' extraordinary power of intellectual synthesis. In working out his own design for Jesuit education, Ignatius was able to combine the humanistic pedagogy of the Brothers of the Common

Life and the revived theology of St. Thomas, both of which he
encountered in Paris. Both were joined together in the unified
educational theory which we find in the Constitutions of his
Order. In the educational initiatives inspired by those
Constitutions the early Jesuits, directed by their founder, showed
the freedom of a small band of scholars thoroughly at home in the
richness and variety of the broad world in which they lived. To
that Jesuit freedom and to the synthesizing power of Ignatian
spirituality we owe the remarkable educational revolution brought
about by the Jesuit colleges in Europe and the spirit of innovative
flexibility with which Jesuit missionaries responded to the
radically different cultures of the Far East.

I must say that, by and large, I am quite impressed by Father
van Beeck's brilliant overview of the Catholic tradition of teaching
and learning. Nonetheless, I would like to make some additions to
it on my own responsibility in the hope that those additions may
prove helpful. I will make them under the following headings.

Faith and Reason

From the early days of her history the Church has been
forced to make use of propositional definitions to defend her
authentic faith against teaching which she felt obliged to reject as
erroneous. Propositional definitions of the Church's faith are
already found in her early condemnations of heresies, such as
Gnosticism. They are also found in the Church's early Baptismal
creeds and, at a later date, in her conciliar definitions. In order to
be faithful to her mission, the Church, when her faith is
challenged, cannot avoid using propositional statements to
distinguishing her authentic teaching from erroneous and heretical
beliefs. In every period of Christian history, therefore, definitions
have been judged necessary. Thus the unitary truth of the
Church's faith and discrete propositional truths formulating its
content are by no means mutually exclusive. Faith's need of
reason for its own defense by definitions is undeniable.
Nonetheless, propositional definitions, when called for, should be
accurate, appropriate, and not overly restrictive. Furthermore,
since propositional statements require the use of concepts, who

can deny the legitimate place for discursive reason in the formulation of the unitary Christian faith? Father van Beeck, I am sure, does not. But the point which I take it that he is making is that, although Christian reason makes use of restrictive propositions, Christian reason cannot be exclusively discursive reason, as reason was all too often taken to be in the climate of the seventeenth- and eighteenth-century rationalism. Discursive reason alone will not suffice. The use of intuitive reason is also required for an adequate grasp of reality. Aristotle, of course, was perfectly aware of that. For Aristotle, as we recall, concepts depend on the operation of intuitive *nous* for their original formation and for their subsequent application to reality in the judgment.

Furthermore, as we know, Aristotelian ethics makes use of intuitive reason's intellectual grasp of the singular and its grasp of the broader context of knowledge in making its moral judgments. Reason's restriction to conceptual judgments is a limitation characteristic of modern philosophy, a limitation which modern philosophy inherited from medieval nominalism and whose damaging influence on ethics and philosophy of religion is well known. The older, richer Greek philosophy used by the Christian thinkers in the Church's early centuries and in the high Middle Ages, was able to make use of Aristotelian intuition in order to control the meaning of its concepts and, through the use of that intuition, the same philosophy could acquire the broader synthetic view of reality required for the proper application of conceptual judgments. Because of that, the older intuitive reason showed an appreciation of analogy in speculative argument which modern philosophy does not possess and manifested a breadth and flexibility in its ethical reasoning which modern philosophy cannot achieve.

It is instructive in this respect to recall that the revival of Catholic speculative theology in the period after Council of Trent and the rebirth of Catholic moral teaching and flowering of the Church's social philosophy in the twentieth century were associated with the Catholic revival of the epistemology, metaphysics, and ethics of her earlier medieval philosophy. When, therefore, we are asked to discuss the relationship between faith and reason, truth and truths, several important questions must first be asked. What is the understanding of faith which is governing the discussion? Is it faith in the Catholic or the Reformed understanding of faith? What is the understanding of reason to which the faith under discussion is being opposed? Is that reason the modern discursive, conceptual reason of post-Cartesian philosophy, associated, as post-Cartesian reason all too often has been, with knowledge as a deductive enchainment of discrete objective truths? Or is it the older, richer, more inclusive, intuitive reason known to classical Greece and to the high Middle Ages, a reason open to both subject and object? Unless there is clarity on both those points at the outset, no subsequent discussion will be fruitful. But, if, on the other hand, our understanding of faith and reason is clear and accurate, fideism and rationalism can readily be avoided, and we will not be forced to choose between relativism on one hand and dependence on overly restrictive, uncritically accepted concepts on the other. There will be room for both the unity of truth and the plurality of defined truths in the Catholic tradition of teaching and learning.

The Dominant Role of the State

One of my colleagues at Fordham is accustomed to point out that we should no longer speak of Our Holy Mother, the Church. We are now in the age of our Omnipotent Mother, the State. His comment, I believe, is a remarkably accurate description of the domination by the state of larger areas of human activity which, before the age of absolute monarchies, were still under the control of subordinate civil societies or of the Church. Although the intrusion of the state into these areas of human life did not begin with the Treaty of Westphalia, that treaty, together with the weakening of the papacy and the effective destruction of the Holy Roman Empire which it deliberately brought about, marked the beginning of a new and increasingly secular era in the history of Europe. The Treaty of Westphalia, as we recall, together with its religious norm, *cujus regio ejus religio*, was imposed on a protesting Catholic Church by the secular rulers of Europe. Significantly, the treaty itself was no longer written, as earlier treaties had been, in Latin, the universal language of the Church and undivided

Christendom. It was written in French, the national language of Europe's dominant secular state. At Westphalia, Europe's secular monarchies took into their own hands the regulation of Europe's religious life. In increasing measure, from that time on the civil and canon lawyers of the monarchies, using modern philosophy to frame their legal systems, created, in the interest of those monarchies, a modern ecclesiology, very hostile to the ecclesiology of Vitoria, Bellarmine, and the great scholastic theologians of the post-Tridentine Catholic revival. Under the influence of powerful and ambitious statesmen, like Cardinal Richelieu, the French crown was unrelenting in its efforts to submit the Church, its institutions, and its religious orders to its own rigid control. In this effort, despite the often tense relations between them, the ministers of the crown were given strong theoretical support by the Jansenist and Gallican lawyers and theologians of France, whose hatred of the papacy and of the pope's supporters among the religious orders was fierce and unremitting.

During the eighteenth century, encouraged by the growth of Enlightenment thought within the Church, the ongoing campaign to make the Church completely subject to the state grew in intensity. Febronian ecclesiology and canon law, which had become dominant in Germany, provided the theoretical justification for the Prince Bishops and the secular rulers of Bavaria and Austria in their own campaign to reduce the Church and its institutions to the status of government departments. Under those conditions it became increasingly difficult for small bands of independent scholars to exercise their Christian apostolate of teaching and learning freely. Father van Beeck and I are both painfully aware of this fact, since this is the period of history in which the papal suppression of the Society of Jesus, to which we both belong, was forced by the pressure of the European monarchies. Absolute European monarchies would no longer tolerate the continuing existence of an international network of schools independent of their control. In the tradition of Catholic teaching and learning the greatest threat to freedom and independent initiative could no longer be claimed to come from the Church. It came instead from an increasingly intrusive and powerful state.

After the French Revolution, in continental Europe, anti-Catholic secular governments did more than attempt to control religion. They endeavored to drive religion from culture and education. Secular universities under rigid state control became the norm in Latin- and German-speaking Europe and, throughout the continent, the influence of governments hostile to the Church over all education notably increased.

In English-speaking countries much greater freedom was given to independent schools, and because of that freedom, particularly in the United States, religiously influenced schools, both Catholic and Protestant, flourished. In a legal and cultural climate strikingly different from the climate of continental Europe, small groups of teachers and scholars were allowed to go about their work without undue interference. The foundations of our system of Catholic education were laid. In the twentieth century, on the other hand, that generous educational freedom was progressively restricted. The increasing involvement of the state in all areas of human life, the dominant role assigned to accrediting agencies, professional associations, and teachers' unions in determining the content and method of education, together with the power of a court system increasingly hostile to religion over independent schools, has made it more and more difficult for religiously oriented educational institutions to maintain their basic identity. In the recent debate about *Ex Corde Ecclesiae*, for example, a recurrent objection raised against the practicality of that document was the anticipated refusal of the courts, the professional associations, and the teachers' unions to permit its implementation in Catholic education. Whatever one's opinion about *Ex Corde Ecclesiae* may be, one thing has clearly emerged from the discussions about it. The amount of liberty which our Omnipotent Mother the State and her secular institutions are prepared to concede today to independent bands of teachers in their work of education is very limited. Catholic scholars may be able to appeal to Church authorities with some hope of success. When their appeals are made to secular authorities, governmental and professional, on the other hand, they are much less likely to succeed. This is a reality which Catholic scholars will have to keep in mind. It will tax their ingenuity.

Postmodern Culture

The struggle which Catholic educators waged with the secular states of Europe in the nineteenth and earlier twentieth century was a struggle against a state bureaucracy which endeavored to exclude religious faith from the realm of education in the name of Enlightenment reason. This was the struggle which provoked Maurice Blondel to defend the legitimate place in liberal education in his masterpiece, *L'Action*. Supported by modern philosophy and the nineteenth-century prestige accorded to science, Enlightenment reason was absolutely sure of itself at that time and, even in the realm of philosophy, set itself up as the ruling norm of acceptable religious teaching.

That is why Vatican I was forced to defend the claims of Christian revelation against nineteenth-century reason's refusal to admit their validity. Today, however, even though the intrusion of the secular state into Catholic education is more pervasive than ever, Enlightenment reason has been largely discredited. The self-evident foundations on whose basis modern philosophy has justified its right to determine the universal norms of knowledge have been undermined by anti-foundational epistemology, and the universal rational grounding claimed for modern Western culture has been denied by the relativism of contemporary postmodern literary and historical theory. John Paul II has observed in *Fides et Ratio* that, unfortunately for Catholic educators, postmodern rejection of Enlightenment reason has not brought our society back to Christian faith. On the contrary, it has supported the popular conviction, more evident in Northern Europe than in America, that the meaning of the world lies beyond the reach of human reason, and that neither human reason nor Christian revelation can possibly provide any credible solutions to life's most urgent problems. The Catholic tradition of teaching and learning, as we have seen, was born of the endeavor of Christian scholars to find the meaning of God's created world and of human life through the unified reflection on both by faith and reason. Faith is no longer challenged, as it was in the nineteenth century, by confident rationalist hostility. It is dismissed out of hand, together with reason, by a pervasive indifference to both. In this changed cultural climate, the challenge to the Christian tradition of faith and reason has become formidable indeed.

Some Concluding Remarks

That formidable challenge to our tradition should not lead us to despair of its future. As Father van Beeck has shown, the Catholic tradition of teaching and learning has always been carried on by small bands of teachers and scholars. That was true in the patristic age. It was true in the Middle Ages when the Cathedral School and the University came into being. It was true during the Catholic renaissance of the fifteenth and sixteenth centuries, and at the time when Catholic education came back to life again during the nineteenth century. Some of that small band of Catholic pioneers, Ignatius of Loyola and John Henry Newman, for example, made their major contribution on the strategic level of educational strategy. Other pioneers, like Vincent de Paul and John Baptiste de la Salle, did their most creative work on the practical level of tactics by adapting the Catholic education of their time to the specific needs of groups of students which, up to that time, had not been met. Catholic scholars today will have to work hard and creatively on both the more general level of theory and the more concrete level of practical adaptation to changing needs in order to carry on the Catholic tradition of teaching and learning. That is the work which the group of scholars who have met here at Sacred Heart University have been considering at this conference. Small groups of pioneers, as history has shown us, have been able in the past to inspire great movements in Catholic education. Let us hope that our small group may able to be of help in doing something like that.

CHAPTER SIXTEEN

Learning in the
Catholic Intellectual Tradition

ANTHONY J. CERNERA AND OLIVER J. MORGAN

As we complete this second volume in the series, *Examining the Catholic Intellectual Tradition*, we would like to focus on a theme that has been only partially addressed thus far. The theme is "learning."

Learning is most often used as a noun, signifying a body of information or some form of content. What did I learn from that lecture, at that conference? What was the learning that emerged from that event in my life? We sometimes speak of another as a person "of real or solid learning." In this way "learning" is often used synonymously with scholarship, or erudition, or wisdom.

There is much to be learned from the chapters that grace this second volume, for example, and no one who reads the chapters by Frs. Himes or van Beeck would doubt that much learning went into their writing. Their content and style are examples of the kind of integrative learning that underlies the Catholic intellectual tradition at its best; the chapters attest to the value of that "marriage of literacy and faith" about which van Beeck speaks.[1] The holistic and challenging learning that emerges from many of the chapters in this and the first volume allows the attentive reader to experience that "integrative whole in knowledge" alluded to by Fr. McCool in this volume; that is, a dynamic interrelationship of the sacred and profane, of culture and faith.[2]

This kind of learning implies an appreciation for the treasury and library of authors, secular and religious, who comment on the human situation while maintaining a deep connection to God's commitment to and love for humanity. Such integrated, holistic learning is a goal of the Catholic intellectual tradition.

However, we would like to focus our reflections here on "learning" used as a verb, signifying a kind of process. Learning may be seen as an active word that suggests the process, energy, and strategies used to assimilate new information and integrate it into a coherent body of knowledge and sense of meaning. How does one learn, as that process is envisioned in the Catholic intellectual tradition? What is distinctive about learning in this tradition?[3] What does it mean to be a learner in this approach?

We would like to focus briefly on the process of learning as we understand it from the perspective of the Catholic intellectual tradition. More precisely, How are new learners and their development nurtured within the Catholic intellectual tradition? What are some implications for undergraduate and graduate education today? We will attempt to reflect on our own experiences of learning within this tradition and, from that experiential reflection, draw out some issues, or themes, or activities that we believe merit consideration.

A Reflection on Experience

We have alluded previously to our common schooling in the Catholic intellectual tradition as undergraduates at Fordham University in the late 1960s and early 1970s.[4] Reflecting back on those days and remembering our graduate studies as well, it is clear that, although the scope and disciplinary context of our studies were different (Tony was a History and Theology double-major; Ollie was an English and Philosophy double-major), there was a kind of "formation" we each encountered that facilitated the learning process. In some ways this formation had formal elements to it; there were clear academic expectations of learners. However, much of what we describe below was also informal; it was part of the intellectual air we breathed and was often transmitted in informal conversations with professors and others who had the responsibility to pass on an intellectual tradition that was distinctively Catholic.

Our hope is that, in describing our experience at one point in time and at one institution dedicated to transmitting the Catholic intellectual tradition, we will touch on some enduring elements that are common across such institutions. We do not believe that these reflections are simply a ride down memory lane. Rather, we believe that these thoughts may also help to bring to light and underline a topic that is critical for the future of this tradition, namely, How do those who bear the responsibility today nurture the handing on and development of the Catholic intellectual tradition for future generations? Perhaps some reflection on how the authors acquired and nurtured the tradition in our own lives and concrete situations (Tony is a Catholic university administrator; Ollie is a clinical counselor and tenured faculty member at a Catholic university) will yield some learning about how best to pass it on, both to students and to aspiring young scholars and contributors to the tradition.

One note of caution as we proceed: we will be reflecting on *our* experience of learning within the Catholic intellectual tradition. Clearly, however, not every student in classes with us learned in the same way or learned the same things. The fact that we have both given ourselves to Catholic higher education as professional educators, and are committed to the ongoing development of the Catholic intellectual tradition, is as much a result of temperament and opportunity as it is a testimony to some kind of conscious formation. As van Beeck reminds us all, and we openly confess, we were in that minority of students who "simply loved school."[5] However, this fact itself has some utility in our reflections. We hope to arrive at some suggestions about how to nurture the gift and hard work of learning in the Catholic intellectual tradition for the future. As the reader will see, this means—among other things—assisting those who "simply love school" to become Catholic intellectuals.

Six Common Characteristics

In our personal and shared reflections we have outlined six common characteristics that helped us in assimilating the Catholic intellectual tradition. We will take some time below to describe these characteristics. From these reflections we will attempt to draw some conclusions about the work of fostering this tradition in the future.

1. Formal learning (e.g., courses, classes, syllabi, instructors, requirements) with exemplary Catholic intellectuals, both clergy and lay

Our experience was similar to many others seeking an education at one of the many U.S. institutions of higher education during the 1960s and 1970s. Students registered for, or were assigned to, specific courses that were constructed to stimulate learning in an orderly fashion. Each course had a syllabus and instructor(s); class sessions were scheduled for specific times; a set of requirements and assignments governed the assessment of each student's progress. Students had to master the material from introductory courses before being able to benefit from more advanced work. These formal contacts occurred largely in classrooms, or seminar rooms, or in tutorials. There was nothing particularly novel about this.

One element, however, was important as an approach to the Catholic intellectual tradition. It was expected that the student-professor interaction in these formal settings was managed by someone who was an exemplary Catholic intellectual. Care was taken to see that, for the most part, a Catholic professor and scholar, either clergy or lay (or, if non-Catholic, then someone committed to the mission of the institution) was at the center of this educational interaction. At a place such as Fordham at that time, one could assume that at least one or two priests were teaching in most departments; there was also an unspoken assumption (more or less accurate) that the lay faculty were also committed to transmitting a "Catholic" education. In the disciplines we pursued these assumptions were largely true.

Our experience was that, in the context of this formal coursework across a variety of disciplines, faculty regularly made connections between the material being studied and its place within a larger context of intellectual history and religious traditions. This kind of "connected knowing," and the inherently holistic viewpoint it conveyed, was contagious. One had a sense of how ideas "hung together." The approach, woven into lectures and developed in response to students' questions, taught an integrated vision by example.

Towards the end of our undergraduate careers, we both attended a class in Metaphysics taught by Fr. Gerald McCool, S.J. One day, at about the middle of the semester, a student raised an elementary question about "being," indicating a sense of bewilderment with the course material. Fr. McCool took a step backward, and then for the next forty minutes spoke without notes about the essence of such a question throughout the history of the West, making connections with a variety of philosophers and pointing out how the question was a fundamental one for theological inquiry as well as philosophy. It was a breathtaking moment. Speaking about it afterwards, we both commented how Fr. McCool's performance, rooted in such a basic question and given essentially *ex tempore*, had enlightened us about the material and about the way Catholic intellectuals might approach such ideas.

This is but one example of the value of having exemplars of the Catholic intellectual tradition manage the formal educational process so that it nurtures the kind of learning that is needed.

2. Informal social and intellectual mingling with Catholic intellectuals

Of course, much learning occurs outside the formal classroom setting. Whether the learning continues in discussions, labs, office hours, additional readings, campus events—and now, in e-mail, chatrooms, and "threaded discussions"—the additional learning that comes from informal contact with professors and others can often be significant for conveying the value of an intellectual life and a passion for learning, as well as exemplifying the connections between learning and faith.

For example, many authors and institutions of higher learning are exploring the role of "mentoring" for students' academic and personal development.[6] As Catholic educators, we might benefit from sustained reflection about the potential role of mentoring within the Catholic intellectual tradition.

Both of us had opportunities to develop such relationships with several Catholic intellectuals during our time at Fordham. Fr. William Richardson, S.J., for example, a world-class scholar in the philosophy of Martin Heidegger, would regularly gather for coffee after his class in Phenomenology—at the invitation of a group of students—to engage in lively discussion of that day's topic. Often the conversation would range more widely, including his own commitment to teaching, scholarship, and an intellectual life as a Catholic and Jesuit. Conversations such as these conveyed a "felt sense" of the Catholic intellectual tradition that has remained with us.

Perhaps experiences such as this one were palpable because of the Jesuit commitment to the *cura personalis* (care of the person). We think, however, that care for the learner as well as care for what was being learned, are both sides of the coin of successful and dynamic learning that the broader Catholic intellectual tradition seeks to promote. Such a respect for the person and the process of learning provided an environment of healthy competition, challenge, humor, and support along the intellectual journey.

3. Reading and assimilation of representative authors and publications from within the Catholic intellectual tradition and outside of it

Many colleges and universities have struggled with issues around a "core" or "liberal arts" curriculum. As undergraduates, we knew that there were a number of basic courses in writing, English, math, history, social sciences, and physical sciences that were required. This was all part of being a "well-rounded, educated person." Again, nothing much new here; there was a basic core curriculum that established guidelines for course choices. And, of course, debates around these issues continue today in academe.

What differentiated our collegiate experience was the reality that the liberal arts core at Fordham was expanded to include philosophy and theology as central disciplines. We and our classmates were required to take courses in philosophy and theology, some of it historical, some of it more conceptual. In a Catholic institution this was seen as part of the intellectual formation of informed lay Catholic leaders. Students, parents, and faculty all understood that this was central to what Fordham and other institutions like it were all about.[7]

This set of expectations—about familiarity with a wide range of subjects and with the philosophical and theological roots of Catholic faith—was our first introduction into the breadth and depth of the Catholic intellectual tradition and its ongoing dialogue with other traditions and cultures. The history of ideas began to open up for us as we came to understand the questions, literature, and science of other times and places (e.g., sixteenth-century literature and science as well as their relation to philosophical and religious developments).

This "introduction" modeled for us a deeper expectation about the need to stay in touch with the thinking, questions, literature, science, media, theater, art, and history of our own culture, and the need to keep learning from a variety of cultural sources. In these ways we began to understand the need to understand Bach and Beethoven, Plato and Augustine, Bonaventure and Descartes, Ignatius and Benedict, Freud and Winnicott, Rahner and Tillich, Stravinsky and Eliot, Monet and O'Neill, Merton and Heschel, Hippocrates and Einstein, on their own terms and in relation to a developing sense of a human whole.

There were many ways in which such a "human whole" might be formed and integrated. For Ollie, the integrating hub became a theological anthropology, that is, how human beings and their relationship with God are examined within a wealth of cultural sources and are viewed in light of theology and spirituality; for Tony, the integrating point was a sense of history and development, and the relation of social, ecclesial, political action, and the notion of God's "incarnation" within that history. But always, the integration was a blending of cultural and religious resources, and the effort was to find points of contact between culture and faith, even when the two seemed at odds.

This ongoing dialogue or conversation between culture and faith was seen as central to the Catholic intellectual tradition and we were encouraged to participate actively in the conversation. Today the challenge to participate in this dialogue has received new impetus through the call of John Paul II in *Ex Corde Ecclesiae*:

A Catholic university . . . is a primary and privileged place for a fruitful dialogue between the Gospel and culture. . . . Through this dialogue a Catholic university assists the Church, enabling it to come to a better knowledge of diverse cultures, discern their positive and negative aspects, to receive their authentically human contributions and to develop a means by which it can make the faith better understood by the men and women of a particular culture.

A Catholic university must become more attentive to the cultures of the world of today and to the various cultural traditions existing within the church in a way that will promote a continuous and profitable dialogue between the Gospel and modern society.[8]

4. An environment that inculcates and models the skills and virtues necessary to an intellectual life that is at the same time spiritually rooted

In *To Know As We Are Known*, Parker J. Palmer explores the concept of "wholesight," a vision of education that unites head, heart, and spirituality.[9] He describes a quest "to find a common focus for my spirit-seeking heart and my knowledge-seeking mind that embraces reality in all its amazing dimensions" (xxiv). This quest is similar to the kind of holistic integrative instinct that is at the center of the Catholic intellectual tradition.

Throughout the book, but especially in a beautiful chapter at the end of the book entitled, "The Spiritual Formation of Teachers" (106-25), he outlines a number of virtues that are essential for, and are the deepening product of, education in wholeness. These are "classic spiritual virtues [that] are epistemological virtues as well" (108). He speaks of "humility" that allows us to "pay attention to the other" (108), that allows the "other" to reveal himself or herself on his or her own terms, that gives us an openness to experience as well as criticism, that creates a space of silent wonder in which we can "withhold the instant answer so the question can really be heard" (108-09). Clearly, deep research as well as spiritual maturity requires this virtue.

He describes the virtue of "reverence without idolatry," which respects the greater community of truth and its ultimate source and does not overly exalt or give ultimacy to one's own circle or experience. This virtue allows one to give reverence to the community of nature and humanity as well as to the full majesty of its transcendent source, not just to one conception of that source. Fr. Himes's essay earlier in the present volume contains a long meditation on this virtue when he discusses God's inexhaustible mystery.[10]

Palmer also speaks of "openness to grace" as a guiding virtue in both intellectual and spiritual development (112-15). This openness creates a space within which new and fresh ideas, bold questions, and a willingness to play with different and imaginative formulations all become part of the learning process. And he describes a "capacity for hospitality and empathy," which allows us to find ways "to re-search the world by occupying the other's viewpoint" (116), to study and learn from the inside, to learn that knowing and the research on which it is built is ultimately an act of relationship, of love. These virtues of hospitality and empathy also build toward another essential ingredient of learning and spirituality, namely "reliance on community." Fr. Himes speaks eloquently of the need for this in his essay.[11]

In this connection, Palmer also describes the virtue of "obedience to truth." In fact, woven throughout *To Know As We Are Known* is this central concept of obedience to truth. Here "obedience" signifies "to listen with a discerning ear and respond faithfully to the personal implications of what one has heard" (89). This demands real dialogue, community, collaboration, and friendship, inviting students and other learners into relationship with a given subject and with each other, not as competitors but as full partners (103-05).

At Fordham we were privileged to experience professors who often—not always and not always perfectly, but often—embodied these virtues. Whether in classrooms or in informal discussions, we were taught to approach our learning in these ways—humbly, reverently, collaboratively, with openness and a welcoming attitude toward new discoveries, and with discerning eyes and ears—and we saw our mentors and professors approach their subjects in these ways as well. Palmer's words toward the end of his fine chapter might well be said of those educators we encountered:

> The original and authentic meaning of the word "professor" is "one who professes a faith." The true professor is not one who *controls* facts and theories and techniques. The true professor is one who *affirms* a transcendent center of truth, a center that lies beyond our contriving, that enters history through the lives of those who profess it and brings us into community with each other and the world. If professors are to create a space in which obedience to truth is practiced, we must become "professors" again.[12]

5. Encouragement to develop and nurture a prayerful spiritual life, while also engaged in the building of an intellectual life

A number of the Jesuit faculty and administrators who guided our intellectual development were also available for spiritual conversation and direction, and we were encouraged to take advantage of this unique opportunity. Spiritual development here was understood to include a commitment to personal and communal prayer, liturgy, and spiritual reading. Reading the works of the great spiritual writers (e.g., Benedict, Ignatius, Bonaventure) was encouraged, along with the inclusion of more contemporary writers such as Merton and Leclerq.

Spiritual development was seen as an essential element in the formation of a truly Catholic perspective that would suffuse and orient our intellectual development.[13] The two were understood to complement one another in forming that holistic, integrative perspective that was the goal of learning in the Catholic intellectual tradition. In particular, prayer and Eucharist would facilitate and nourish the inclusion of a God-centered perspective into the developing worldview we were establishing. They would allow us to glimpse the inter-connectedness of things with their Source, and to understand the connectedness of persons with their Creator and Redeemer Lord. Palmer describes well this role for prayer, particularly as it accompanies intellectual development:

What do I mean by prayer? I mean the practice of relatedness. On one side, prayer is our capacity to enter into that vast community of life in which self and other, human and non-human, visible and invisible, are intricately intertwined. While my senses discriminate and my mind dissects, my prayer acknowledges and re-creates the unity of life. In prayer, I no longer set myself apart from others and the world, manipulating them to suit my needs. Instead, I reach for relationship, allow myself to feel the tuggings of mutuality and accountability, take my place in community by knowing the transcendent center that connects it all.

On the other side, prayer means opening myself to the fact that as I reach for that connecting center, the center is reaching for me. As I move toward the heart of reality, reality is moving toward my heart. As I recollect the unity of life, life is recollecting me in my original wholeness. In prayer, I not only address the love at the core of all things; I listen as that love addresses me, calling me out of isolation and self-centeredness into community and compassion. In prayer, I begin to realize that I not only know but am known.[14]

We have both come to understand how essential this kind of spiritual development is for the full development of the Catholic intellectual tradition. Fr. Himes's essay speaks eloquently about the need for deep reflection on the faith, hope, and love that both "ground" the Catholic intellectual tradition and uniquely challenge its development today and into the future. If these are the "three basic attitudes" establishing humanity in a right relationship with God, as Himes states, then they are also essential in rooting and orienting the development of the Catholic intellectual tradition. The nourishment of these "attitudes" can only happen in a life rooted in prayer and worship. Prayer at its depth reminds us that our primary commitment is not to a "tradition," or to a set of propositions, or even to a "holistic worldview" however well imagined, but ultimately to the One who upholds all. It is the ongoing relationship with God in prayer that assists the development of a fully Catholic intellectual tradition, at both the individual and institutional levels, and that enables one to face the contemporary challenges that Himes outlines.

6. *Encouragement to develop and nurture a lifestyle engaged with the challenges of the times, and the hope that both learning and prayer would be brought to bear in reflection on these engagements*

Over the last several years, Fr. Peter-Hans Kolvenbach, S.J., Superior General of the Society of Jesus, has enunciated several descriptions of the ideal graduate of Jesuit and Catholic education. In 1991 he spoke of Catholic and Jesuit education producing "leaders in service to others in building the Kingdom of God in the market place of business and ideas, of service, of law and justice, of economics, theology and all areas of human life . . . men and women of competence and conscience who generously give of themselves for others."[15] More recently, in an address entitled "The Service of Faith and the Promotion of Justice in American Jesuit Higher Education," he spoke about the significant contemporary challenge that faces the person of learning and prayer:

> For four hundred and fifty years, Jesuit education has sought to educate "the whole person" intellectually and professionally, psychologically, morally and spiritually. But in the emerging global reality, with its great possibilities and deep contradictions, the whole person is different from the whole person of the Counter-Reformation, the Industrial Revolution, or the Twentieth Century. Tomorrow's "whole person" cannot be whole without an educated awareness of society and culture with which to contribute socially, generously, in the real world. Tomorrow's whole person must have, in brief, *a well-educated solidarity.* We must therefore raise our Jesuit educational standard to *educate the whole person in solidarity for the real world.*[16]

In regard to educating and forming this person of solidarity, Fr. Kolvenbach makes the intriguing suggestion that "solidarity is learned through contact rather than through concepts," that is, through practical experience rather than simply through book learning.[17] While conceptual learning is clearly important in the mission of higher education and in the development of the Catholic intellectual tradition, what we as educators are being challenged to explore is the appropriate role of "learning through contact." There is a focus here on *praxis* and reflection that is related to the "connected knowing" espoused by Parker Palmer and others. As Fr. Kolvenbach further elaborates:

> When the heart is touched by direct experience, the mind may be challenged to change. Personal involvement with innocent suffering, with the injustice others suffer, is the catalyst for solidarity which then gives rise to intellectual inquiry and moral reflection.[18]

The educational and formation experiences we received at Fordham in the late 1960s and early 1970s included the kind of "learning through contact" which Fr. Kolvenbach promotes. We were both encouraged by our mentors, professors, and spiritual directors to become involved in the issues of justice that were endemic to those times. We each engaged in volunteer activities in soup kitchens and a home for the elderly, what would today be called "service-learning" opportunities; we both became involved in offering spiritual retreats for high school and college students during which the challenges of the day were spoken about within the language of faith; and, we both became involved in the anti-war activities of the Vietnam era as a faith response to a uniquely American struggle of conscience at that time. In each instance we were encouraged to bring the resources of the Catholic intellectual tradition and our ongoing intellectual and spiritual development to reflection on these engagements.

One of the most significant "mentors" in this regard for both of us was Fr. Daniel Berrigan, S.J., the noted poet-priest and anti-war activist, who had recently been released from prison and came to live on campus for a time. He was (and is) a person of deep prayer, scholarship, and imagination, and he was strongly engaged in the struggles of those times. We came to see first-hand how these threads of learning and faith, prayer, and action could be woven together into a life-commitment. We have each tried in our own way to emulate this kind of integrated and engaged commitment.

Related Suggestions for the Future

Fr. van Beeck speaks of the Catholic intellectual tradition as both a "cultivator" of basic attitudes (virtues) toward learning, God, humanity and the world, and as an active *habitus* for the marriage of literacy and faith, of learning and spirituality. As the reader can tell, this was the experience of the current authors, who matriculated at one institution where there was a conscious effort to transmit learning and an intellectual tradition that was distinctively Catholic. We have taken some time to reflect on our past experience so as to highlight several characteristics of the process of learning in the Catholic intellectual tradition as we came to know it.

What remains now is to offer some reflections that might tie together these characteristics from the past with a look forward. We acknowledge that many Catholic colleges and universities across the country are working hard to integrate their Catholic identity into the educational mission of the institutions. We acknowledge, too, the challenges and achievements of many institutions in trying to incorporate aspects of the Catholic intellectual tradition into the curriculum for undergraduate and graduate students. Indeed, Michele Dillon's research published in this volume highlights some of the successes and challenges faced by these institutions, and conveys a sense of optimism about the potential outcome. Finally, we acknowledge the good work of *Collegium*, the variety of Catholic Studies programs, and other efforts to further the growth of Catholic identity and intellectual activity.

Nevertheless, we want to suggest that one critically important way to foster the long-term development of the Catholic intellectual tradition is for Catholic intellectual and ecclesial leaders to be more intentional and proactive in selecting, mentoring, guiding, and supporting promising young Catholic educators and scholars. Our own experience in this regard prompts us to offer some ideas for further reflection. In this way we would like to suggest something akin to an "action agenda" for the continued nurturing and development of the Catholic intellectual tradition through attention to the development of young Catholic intellectuals. This agenda must not be left to chance: it must become a priority commitment of those dedicated to the Catholic intellectual tradition.

Fr. van Beeck's essay was intended to address teaching as vital to the Catholic intellectual tradition. He makes the point that teaching is best thought of as a "profession," more than a "vocation," and that teaching and learning are a matter of Catholic "mission." One way, then, to begin our reflections is to ask, How do we cultivate and support the professional development of teachers and scholars in the Catholic intellectual tradition?

In a few paragraphs below we will provide a brief imaginative sketch of how such a process might work. We invite the reader to consider an approach that could be called the Institute for the Development of Catholic Scholars, or IDCS.

Faculty, staff, and others at Catholic colleges and universities often become aware of undergraduate and graduate students who demonstrate an interest and willingness to develop as scholar-educators within their faith tradition. Perhaps a conversation between such a student and a faculty or staff mentor leads to encouragement to pursue further intellectual work and spiritual development. But practically, where and how might the student take a next step? What can the mentor offer?

We suggest that it is in the best interests of the Catholic community to create and support a process of "formation" for such women and men, who may be seen as the next generation of Catholic intellectuals. An Institute could be developed, not as a place or an institution (although elements of it would require a location), but as a process of intellectual formation and spiritual guidance. This process would reflect each of the six common characteristics mentioned above, as well as other elements that the community would decide upon. Scholarships would be provided for students participating in the IDCS.

A director as well as a team of faculty from various disciplines, staff mentors, and others would be selected and trained for the IDCS. Their preparation would occur both in small groups and with the support of the entire team. Criteria would be developed for admitting students and grouping them into cohort groups according to each student's interests and ability. The director and university team would facilitate the cohort selection process. Each individual would be assigned a mentor and spiritual advisor and would be encouraged to develop and nurture a prayerful spiritual life, while developing in his or her intellectual life. The mentors and advisors would meet regularly with students individually and as a group. After a year, students would choose their own mentors and advisors.

The IDCS process would be a gradual one where members within a cohort group would challenge each other to live a lifestyle that would inculcate and model the skills and virtues necessary to a Catholic intellectual and spiritually-rooted life. Formal learning with exemplary teachers through rigorous courses of study with specific requirements of representative authors and publications (from within and outside of the tradition) would be effectively organized to create a healthy environment for future Catholic intellectuals to be initiated into the tradition. Informal socializing and intellectual mingling with Catholic intellectuals would also be expected of the mentors and faculty involved with this process. Concurrently, the university community would provide the necessary resources, space, and time that such a process would require.

Every effort would be made to prevent the IDCS from becoming a closed or elitist group. To counteract such tendencies, members would be encouraged to offer their gifts and talents to the service of the larger University community and Church through service-learning. Examples could include: enhancing classroom experiences, sponsoring lectures, supporting social justice activities, facilitating retreats or days of reflection, or leading discussion groups where people would come together to reflect on a theme or activity connected with the Catholic intellectual tradition.

Each semester all of the cohorts and interested members of the University community would meet together for liturgy and a meal. Other rituals and celebrations would evolve naturally as the process became a permanent part of the University's life and mission. Assessment of the program as well as an individual's growth would take place each year. To allow for a normal process of discernment to occur with undergraduate students, an individual would choose to be part of the process on a yearly basis. Students engaged in graduate and doctoral work could be expected to make more substantial time commitments to the process.

After these students are graduated, they would be invited back to be an integral part of ongoing discussions with each other, experts in their fields of interest, as well be a resource and mentors to new students who are interested in pursuing a Catholic intellectual lifestyle. Their names and the names of those from other programs would be gathered and disseminated in a formal way to other institutions seeking to employ such individuals, as well as to institutions committed to furthering the education of these scholars in a critical and supportive environment.

Notes

1. See Frans Jozef van Beeck, "Teaching as Vocation: Faith and Literacy," in the present volume, 151-78.

2. Gerald A. McCool, "The Jesuit Ideal of a Teacher: A Complex and Developing Tradition," in the present volume, 131-50.

3. "Distinctive," as used here, is not meant to suggest "one of a kind," as though only the Catholic intellectual tradition has such characteristics or does this or that. Rather the term is meant to indicate "a special attention to" or "concern for" certain qualities or characteristics.

4. See the preface to *Examining the Catholic Intellectual Tradition*, volume 1, ed. Anthony J. Cernera and Oliver J. Morgan (Fairfield, CT: Sacred Heart University Press, 2000), vii-viii.

5. van Beeck, "Teaching as Vocation," in the present volume, 149.

6. Some representative titles include Sharon Parks, *Big Questions, Worthy Dreams: Mentoring Young Adults in Their Search for Meaning, Purpose, and Faith* (New York: Jossey-Bass, 2000); L.A. Daloz, *Mentor: Guiding the Journey of Adult Learners* (New York: Jossey-Bass, 1999); and "President's Review Council on Students' Lifestyles: Report Calls for Stronger Mentoring Community," *The Scranton Record* (University of Scranton), 4, available from President's Office, University of Scranton, Scranton, PA 18510.

7. It is an interesting question for discussion whether this kind of "consensus" about the role of Catholic higher education is shared by *any*

of the relevant constituencies, i.e., students, parents, or faculty. Michele Dillon's intriguing chapter in the present volume, "College Educators and the Maintenance of the Catholic Intellectual Tradition," 39-77, offers some food for thought, although it doesn't specifically address this important question.

8. John Paul II, *Ex Corde Ecclesiae* [The Apostolic Constitution on Catholic Universities], September 25, 1990; reprinted in *Origins*, 20 (17), 265-76.

9. Parker J. Palmer, *To Know As We Are Known: Education As a Spiritual Journey* (San Francisco, Harper and Row, 1993). References to this book are cited by page number in the text of our essay.

10. Michael Himes, "Major Challenges and Opportunities Facing the Catholic Intellectual Tradition," in the present volume, 81-104.

11. Himes, "Major Challenges and Opportunities Facing the Catholic Intellectual Tradition," esp. 93-102.

12. Palmer, *To Know As We Are Known*, 113 (emphasis added).

13. The essay by Dillon in the present volume suggests that indicators of religious commitment systematically differentiated faculty views regarding the Catholic tradition and its relation to the institution. It is important to note that, in her research, it is not Catholicism *per se*, but *commitment to a religious tradition* that is more salient in a positive disposition toward integration of Catholic institutional identity. An intentional focus on one's own spiritual development is such an indicator of religious commitment.

14. Palmer, *To Know As We Are Known*, 11.

15. Peter Hans Kolvenbach, "To Friends and Colleagues of the Society of Jesus." A letter on the anniversary of the papal approval of the Society of Jesus, September 27, 1991; in *Acta Romana Societatis Jesu*, XX (iv), 601-07.

16. Peter Hans Kolvenbach, "The Service of Faith and the Promotion of Justice in American Jesuit Higher Education," Santa Clara University, October 6, 2000, 7 (emphasis added).

17. Kolvenbach, "The Service of Faith and the Promotion of Justice in American Jesuit Higher Education," 7.

18. Kolvenbach, "The Service of Faith and the Promotion of Justice in American Jesuit Higher Education," 7.

NOTES ON CONTRIBUTORS

ANTHONY J. CERNERA, PH.D., President of Sacred Heart University since 1988, is a three-time graduate of Fordham University, where he earned his doctorate in systematic theology. He continues to teach undergraduate and graduate students in related disciplines. He is a vice-president of the International Federation of Catholic Universities and chairman of the Connecticut Conference of Independent Colleges. Dr. Cernera is the editor of *Toward Greater Understanding, Vatican II: The Continuing Agenda, Continuity and Plurality in Catholic Theology,* and, with Dr. Oliver J. Morgan, *Examining the Catholic Intellectual Tradition.*

FRANCIS X. CLOONEY, S.J., PH.D., is Professor of Comparative Theology at Boston College. He is a 1973 graduate, *summa cum laude*, of Fordham University and a member of the Society of Jesus. After college he taught high school in Nepal for two years, and then earned his master of divinity degree, with distinction, at the Weston School of Theology (1978), and his Ph.D. from the University of Chicago (1984), in the Department of South Asian Languages and Civilizations. He was the founding president of the International Society for Hindu-Christian Studies and is currently the coordinator for interreligious dialogue in Jesuit-related ministries in the United States. His works include *Hindu Wisdom for All God's Children* (Orbis, 1998) and *Hindu God, Christian God* (Oxford, 2001), dozens of articles and lectures, and more than 100 book reviews.

MICHELE DILLON, PH.D., is Associate Professor of Sociology at the University of New Hampshire. She is author of *Catholic Identity: Balancing Reason, Faith, and Power* (Cambridge University

Press, 1999), *Debating Divorce: Moral Conflict in Ireland* (University Press of Kentucky, 1993), and editor of *A Handbook for the Sociology of Religion* (Cambridge University Press, 2002).

LOUIS DUPRÉ, PH.D., has long held the T. Lawrason Riggs Chair of Philosophy and Religion at Yale University. A native of Belgium, he is a graduate of the University of Louvain, where his dissertation was on *The Starting Point of Marxist Philosophy*. He has published hundreds of articles in learned journals and collected works, concentrating on phenomenology and the philosophy of religion, early modern thought, and spiritual theology. The former president of the American Catholic Philosophical Association and of the Hegel Society of America, he has lectured extensively in the United States and in Europe. Numerous universities have honored Dr. Dupré, including Sacred Heart University, which bestowed on him an honorary doctorate in 1992.

MILDRED HAIPT, O.S.U., PH.D. is a member of the Order of St. Ursula. She received her bachelor's degree in social studies and secondary education and her master's in educational psychology and guidance, both from Fordham University, and she earned her doctorate in administration, supervision, and curriculum from the University of Maryland at College Park. Her sabbatical studies have included time spent at the Maryknoll College School of Theology, and six-months as a visiting scholar and professor at Assumption University in Bangkok, where she returned this past summer. She has been a member of the Education Department at the College of New Rochelle for twenty-eight years, and has written extensively about multicultural education and teacher preparation.

MONIKA K. HELLWIG, PH.D., has been executive director of the Association of Catholic Colleges and Universities since 1996. Before that she spent three decades teaching theology at Georgetown University. An alumna of the University of Liverpool, where she earned her LL.B. and her C.S.Sc., she received her master's degree in 1956 from the Catholic University of America, and her Ph.D., also from CUA, twelve years later. Summer teaching assignments have ranged from West Hartford, Connecticut, to San Francisco and further to Taiwan. A former president of the Catholic Theological Society of America, she has received honorary doctoral degrees from schools across the nation, including Sacred Heart University in 1998. Her books include *Understanding Catholicism, Jesus the Compassion of God, The Eucharist and the Hunger of the World,* and *Sign of Reconciliation and Conversion.* She is the mother of three now grown adopted children.

MICHAEL HIMES, PH.D., is a graduate of Cathedral College in Brooklyn, and earned his master of divinity degree from Immaculate Conception Seminary in Huntington, New York, and his doctorate in the history of Christianity from the University of Chicago. A priest of the Diocese of Brooklyn, he taught at Immaculate Conception Seminary for a decade and then at the University of Notre Dame. He has been a professor at Boston College since 1993. He is the author of three major books in the past six years, and his hundreds of articles include such titles as "Catholic Education and the Seduction of Success" and "Incarnational Spirituality and the Terror of Time." He was given a doctor of humane letters degree, *honoris causa,* by Sacred Heart University, in 1999.

ROBERT P. IMBELLI, PH.D., a priest of the Archdiocese of New York, studied in Rome during the years of the Second Vatican Council and was ordained there in 1965. He obtained his Ph.D. in Systematic Theology from Yale University. As an Associate Professor of Theology at Boston College, he directed its Institute of Religious Education and Pastoral Ministry from 1986 to 1993. He is a member of the Steering Committee of the Catholic Common Ground Initiative and a member of the official Anglican Roman Catholic Dialogue in the United States. He has published in such journals as *Theological Studies, Communio, Commonweal,* and *Priests & People* in the areas of Christology, Trinitarian theology, and spirituality.

DR. URSULA KING, PH.D., is the director of the Centre for Comparative Studies in Religion and Gender and, from 1989-2001, she was a professor in the Department of Theology and Religious Studies, both at the University of Bristol in England. She earned her licentiate in sacred theology at the Institut Catholique in Paris, her master of arts degree in philosophy from the University of Delhi, and her doctorate from the Department of History and Philosophy of Religion at King's College, University of London. She also holds honorary doctorates in theology from the universities of Edinburgh and Oslo. She has lectured in many countries and is a visiting professor in feminist theology at the University of Oslo. An editor or author of eighteen books and hundreds of articles and reviews, she is an authority on the life and work of Pierre Teilhard de Chardin. Her current research deals with religion and gender, especially with reference to spirituality. Her latest book is *Christian Mystics: Their Lives and Legacies throughout the Ages* (Paulist Press, 2001).

KATHLEEN MAHONEY, PH.D., has taught in Catholic high schools and several universities, most recently at Boston College, where she was an assistant professor in the Lynch School of Education. An alumna of St. Michael's College at the University of Toronto, she holds a master's degree in theology from the University of Notre Dame and a doctorate in education from the University of Rochester. Her publications include the forthcoming *Catholic Higher Education in Protestant America: The Jesuits and Harvard in the Age of the University, 1893-1910*. In 1998 she received a major grant from the Lilly Endowment to conduct an evaluation of its work in the field of religion and higher education. She is currently executive vice-president of the Humanitas Foundation.

GERALD A. MCCOOL, S.J., Professor Emeritus at Fordham University in New York, is a preeminent scholar of Thomistic thought. His many published works include influential studies of the roots of contemporary Catholic thought, such as *Catholic Theology in the Nineteenth Century* (Seabury, 1977), and his history of Thomism, *From Unity to Pluralism: The Internal Evolution of Thomism* (Fordham University Press, 1989). The collection of essays *Continuity and Plurality in Catholic Theology*, published in 1998 by the Sacred Heart University Press, honors and further elaborates on Father McCool's many contributions to examining the Catholic intellectual tradition.

OLIVER J. MORGAN, PH.D., NCC, is Associate Professor and Chair of the Department of Counseling and Human Services at the University of Scranton. A 1973 graduate of Fordham University, he earned his master's of divinity from the Weston Jesuit School of Theology and his master's in family therapy from the Hahnemann Medical University and Hospital in Philadelphia. A nationally certified counselor, he received his Ph.D. in pastoral psychology from Boston University in 1992. His special interests include marital and family therapy, pastoral psychology, and issues related to addiction and spirituality. With Dr. Anthony J. Cernera, he edited *Examining the Catholic Intellectual Tradition* (Sacred Heart University Press, 2000).

DAVID O'BRIEN, PH.D., is a graduate of the University of Notre Dame, and earned his Ph.D. at the University of Rochester in 1964. He taught for five years at Loyola College in Montreal prior to joining the faculty of the College of the Holy Cross in 1969, where he is currently a professor of history, Loyola Professor of Roman Catholic Studies, and director of the Center for Religion, Ethics and Culture. His most recent book is *From the Heart of the American Church: Catholic Higher Education and American Culture.* He is active in a number of national organizations, including the American Catholic Historical Society, where he was president from 1998-99, and the Catholic Commission on Intellectual and Cultural Affairs, where he chairs the executive committee.

MARGARET O'BRIEN STEINFELS has been editor of *Commonweal* magazine for the past dozen years. An honors graduate of Loyola University in Chicago, she earned her master's in history at New York University, complemented by studies in film at Columbia University and French at the Sorbonne. Concern for family issues dominates her major published works, and her reviews and articles have appeared in such journals as *National Catholic Reporter, New York Times, Times Book Review, Psychology Today,* and *New Republic.*

BRIAN STILTNER, PH.D., majored in religious studies and Latin to earn his bachelor's degree from John Carroll University. He is a three-time graduate of Yale, where he received his M.A.R., *magna cum laude*, from Yale Divinity School and his master's in philosophy and doctorate from Yale University, the latter in religious ethics. An assistant professor of religious studies at Sacred Heart University, he is director of the University's Hersher Institute for Applied Ethics. He is the author of *Religion and the Common Good: Catholic Contributions to Building Community in a Liberal Society*. In June, 2000, he presented a paper to the Catholic Theological Society of America, "Will Eschatology Be Relevant to Social Action in the Third Christian Millennium?"

FRANS JOZEF VAN BEECK, S.J., PH.D., is the John Cardinal Cody Professor of Sacred Theology at Loyola University in Chicago. He is a native of the Netherlands, where he entered the Society of Jesus in 1948. He earned licentiates in philosophy and theology there and received his doctorate in 1961 from the University of Amsterdam after studies in English literature and Italian language and literature. He has taught in Holland, the United States, Indonesia, Canada, England, and Italy. A former professor of theology at Boston College, he has been at Loyola since 1985. He is the author of a dozen books and scores of articles in scholarly journals.

INDEX